Collaborative Programs in Indigenous Communities

I am grateful to Harry F. Wolcott for his editorial and personal support for many years and particularly acknowledge his assistance in the development of this book. I offer many thanks to Jennifer Collier and Alan Dick for encouragement and critical reviews. I am grateful for the hospitality and continuing friendship of the people of the indigenous communities where I have lived and worked. They made this book possible.

Collaborative Programs in Indigenous Communities

From Fieldwork to Practice

Barbara Harrison

ALTAMIRA
PRESS

A Division of
ROWMAN & LITTLEFIELD PUBLISHERS, INC.
Walnut Creek • Lanham • New York • Oxford

ALTAMIRA PRESS

A Division of Rowman & Littlefield Publishers, Inc.
1630 North Main Street, #367
Walnut Creek, CA 94596
www.altamirapress.com

Rowman & Littlefield Publishers, Inc.
4720 Boston Way
Lanham, MD 20706

12 Hid's Copse Road
Cumnor Hill, Oxford OX2 9JJ, England

British Library Cataloguing-in-Publication Information Available

Library of Congress Cataloging-in-Publication Data

Harrison, Barbara, 1940–
    Collaborative programs in indigenous communities : from fieldwork to practice /
    Barbara Harrison.
        p. cm.
    Includes bibliographical references and index.
    ISBN 0-7591-0060-8 (cloth : alk. paper)—ISBN 0-7591-0061-6 (pbk. : alk. paper)
        1. Indigenous peoples—Services for. 2. Indigenous peoples—Education. 3. Social
    service—Field work. 4. Social service—Citizen participation. 5. Community development.
    I. Title.

HV3176.H38 2001
362.84—dc21   2001033584

Printed in the United States of America

∞™ The paper used in this publication meets the minimum requirements of American
National Standard for Information Sciences—Permanence of Paper for Printed Library
Materials, ANSI/NISO Z.39.48-1992.

Contents

Part 1 Surviving and Succeeding in Collaborative Programs   1

  1 European and Indigenous Contact History:
     The United States, Canada, Australia, and New Zealand   5

  2 The Evolution of Collaborative Programs   31

  3 Collaborative Fieldworkers   47

  4 Designing Collaborative Programs   79

Part 2 Lessons Learned   103

  5 The Small High Schools Project, 1977–78   107

  6 College Pilot Projects, 1978–81   133

  7 Manokotak School, 1983–85   161

  8 Rakaumanga School, 1986–87   169

  9 The Community Training Centre, 1986–90   189

  10 Maori Community Projects, 1990–96   211

  11 Collaborative Programs in Indigenous Communities   225

Appendix: Draft Declaration on the Rights of Indigenous Peoples   239

References   251

Author Index   257

Subject Index   261

About the Author   265

Part One

SURVIVING AND SUCCEEDING IN COLLABORATIVE PROGRAMS

In 1977, I entered a master's degree program in cross-cultural education at the University of Alaska Fairbanks. At the same time, I was employed as a graduate assistant to collect information for a research project. I spent the academic year in a rural village in Alaska where I was expected to integrate my studies and research tasks with tutoring responsibilities in an undergraduate program in that village.

Like most novice researchers of the day, my training for this situation was virtually nonexistent. A group of two faculty and nine graduate assistants met on campus in Fairbanks for one week of orientation at the beginning of the project. Then, each of the nine graduate assistants made a short visit to the field site where that particular assistant would work and study for the 1977–78 academic year. The group met again for a second week of orientation before the assistants left for the villages where they would live for the year. It was more or less a "sink or swim" approach. I jumped in headfirst. Although I felt as though I was drowning many times during that year, I lived to tell the tale.

In the more than twenty years since then, I have been involved in a number of projects in different indigenous communities where I have been asked to collaborate in the development of new programs at the community level. Most of these programs have been in education, and most have incorporated some aspects of formal research in the program plan. Some of these programs can be considered to have "worked"; some did not. On reflection, it seems apparent that some programs were destined from the beginning to stumble along ineffectually or to fail entirely because they were lacking in one or several essential components. The cases in this book illustrate that life can be truly miserable for participants who are trying desperately to get unworkable programs

1

to work. Clearly, it is better to design programs that are most likely to succeed rather than designing programs that have little chance of success. For individual fieldworkers, it is usually preferable to participate in programs that include all the essential components as opposed to participating in programs in which some essential elements are missing.

Based on my experience in collaborative programs, I have proposed in part 1 of the book guidelines for program design for fieldworkers and indigenous communities to consider before embarking on new collaborative programs. In part 2, I have illustrated the way these guidelines might be used to identify potential or actual problems in real life situations.

PERSONAL NARRATIVES

I have presented the examples in part 2 as personal narratives. In most of the programs, the object of study was something other than the program itself. Research reports on the particular objects of study have already been published elsewhere. In 1977–78, for example, I was part of a team studying small high schools in rural Alaska. The research report *Small High School Programs for Rural Alaska* was published in 1979. As a graduate assistant, I was not expected to study the structure and design of the research program itself except to the extent of acquiring the information I needed so that I could play an appropriate part in it. In order to play that part, I necessarily collected information on the program history, structure, and operation. My field notes and journals for those years contain the documentation that became the basis for reflection about the program several years later.

Similar situations existed in each of the other settings. Because the programs themselves were not the objects of intentional study, I can only present descriptions of them from my own standpoint as one participant. I did not systematically collect data on the perceptions of other participants at the time. However, drafts of each of the cases were sent for comment to people who were key participants in each program. This review process served two purposes. First, it provided indigenous participants with the opportunity to agree to the publication of a chapter about a program in their communities. Second, it provided an opportunity for other participants to critique my perceptions of the situation.

THIS BOOK IS INTENDED FOR . . .

Donald Schön has described the way that reflective narratives can contribute to the accumulation of knowledge useful to professionals: "Description and analysis of images, category schemes, cases, precedents, and exemplars can help to build the repertoires which practitioners bring to unique situations" (1983: 309). I started writing narratives after nearly twenty years of work in collaborative programs in Alaska and New Zealand intending to use the writing to enhance my own understanding of what had taken place in the various programs. I had been working diligently (and sometimes frantically), but I had never taken the time to try to "make sense" of what seemed to be a long series of discrete and unrelated experiences. Some things seemed to have worked, and some things had not—but I was not sure of the reasons for success or failure. As I worked my way through the narratives, I realized that guidelines could be developed that might help fieldworkers, program designers, and indigenous communities to avoid many of the pitfalls that I had encountered over my twenty-year experience.

Initially, I intended the guidelines—and the book—to be for researchers in collaborative research programs, but, as I reviewed field notes and published literature, I realized that, by the end of the twentieth century, very few professionals were going to work in indigenous communities for the primary purpose of conducting research. Sometimes outside "experts" tied research goals into their collaborative efforts, but research was not usually the primary purpose. Indigenous peoples appreciated outsiders who were willing to collaborate in programs for education, health, economic development, social welfare, and other purposes, but they were suspicious of research. Schön has pointed out, however, that "practitioners may *become* reflective researchers in situations of uncertainty, instability, uniqueness, and conflict" (1983: 308). Therefore, I have written about collaboration between indigenous groups and outside experts (including researchers) in a range of different types of programs. The book is intended for readers who are or are preparing to become program designers, researchers, or fieldworkers in other capacities. Although most of the examples in the book are drawn from education or vocational training, the book is intended for readers who have stakes in different kinds of programs, including economic development, social services, and health. It is also intended for indigenous communities that may be planning an innovative program in collaboration with outside experts.

The book is intended for people planning collaborative programs with specifically defined research outcomes as well as innovative programs—pilot projects, for example—for which a publishable research report may not be required. The processes of program design, data collection, analysis, and interpretation may be quite similar in pilot projects to the processes employed in more formal research. This book should be useful in planning either type of program.

INDIGENOUS COMMUNITIES IN THE UNITED STATES, CANADA, NEW ZEALAND, AND AUSTRALIA

Narratives of programs in Alaska Native communities and in New Zealand Maori communities have been used to illustrate the way that programs were developed in indigenous communities in the closing decades of the twentieth century. The commonalities between the communities and programs in Alaska and New Zealand may not be immediately apparent to readers unfamiliar with the history of contact in English-speaking countries. The opening chapter provides brief summaries of the history of contact and the history of relevant policy development in four countries: the United States, Canada, New Zealand, and Australia. The emphasis is on the United States and New Zealand because my program experiences have been in these countries. However, the similarities in contemporary circumstances in Canada and Australia have warranted mention. The histories are followed by a review of the major issues that indigenous peoples in the four countries are facing as they enter the twenty-first century. As the result of similar histories, indigenous peoples are facing similar situations in each of these countries, and they are demanding authority to develop programs within their own communities to address the circumstances, as they perceive them.

FIELDWORKERS AND PROGRAMS

A discussion of the literature relating to collaborative programs in indigenous communities is given in chapter 2. Then, in chapter 3, the individual fieldworker is considered. Virtually everyone who has worked in or written about collaborative programs in indigenous communities has agreed that the attitudes and actions of the fieldworker are critical components in determining the success of the collaboration. Individuals who are preparing for their first fieldwork experience should carefully consider their ability to adapt to new, collaborative relationships and settings.

Chapter 4 is intended to assist in planning programs that will work. For many decades, program planners of European descent developed programs for the indigenous peoples in English-speaking countries, and the results were often·disastrous. There have also been instances in which indigenous communities have been able to institute social change programs, but the programs have not succeeded. Hopefully, the discussion of program design in chapter 4 will be useful to outside experts as well as indigenous communities that are planning new programs.

Chapter One

European and
Indigenous Contact History

The United States,
Canada, Australia, and New Zealand

COMPARATIVE STUDIES

An international political movement developed in the early years of the twentieth century as the demands of colonized people for independence gained momentum. Gandhi's leadership in India led to one of the most famous movements, but people in the Middle East, Asia, Africa, the Pacific, and Central and South America also demanded independence. Slowly, European colonizers responded to revolutions and political pressure by granting independence. A second and related international movement developed at about the same time—a movement among indigenous peoples seeking self-determination and recognition of land and other resource claims from governments with political authority over them.

There are many definitions of the term *indigenous*. According to one dictionary, it means "native or belonging naturally," so plants and animals that have existed in a particular environment for long periods of time are called indigenous. Julian Burger has noted that "taken in its literal sense, most people are indigenous to their country" (1987: 6). In recent decades, however, the term has come to have special significance for people whose ancestors were the inhabitants of any given region before the region was colonized. In many instances, the countries have gained independence, but the descendants of the colonizers have become the dominant group within the country, leaving the descendants of the original inhabitants powerless and in subordinate positions. These descendants of the original inhabitants are referred to as indigenous peoples.

Burger (1987: 5–13) discusses some of the questions associated with definitions. The United Nations Working Group on Indigenous Populations, the International Labour Organisation, the World Bank, the World Council of Indigenous

5

Peoples, and national governments have developed differing definitions. In addition, indigenous peoples believe that they have the right to choose who is a member of their communities and who is not. After reviewing the various definitions, Burger presents six elements that could be used as criteria:

> An indigenous people may contain all of the following elements or just some. Indigenous peoples:
>
> 1. are the descendants of the original inhabitants of a territory which has been overcome by conquest;
> 2. are nomadic and semi-nomadic peoples . . . ;
> 3. do not have centralized political institutions and organize at the level of the community and make decisions on a consensus basis;
> 4. have all the characteristics of a national minority: they share a common language, religion, culture and other identifying characteristics and a relationship to a particular territory, but are subjugated by a dominant culture and society;
> 5. have a different world-view, consisting of a custodial and non-materialist attitude to land and natural resources, and want to pursue a separate development to that proffered by the dominant society;
> 6. consist of individuals who subjectively consider themselves to be indigenous, and are accepted by the group as such. (1987: 9)

More recently, Working Group on Indigenous Populations Rapporteur Erica Irene Daes's report defines indigenous people in terms of the following criteria:

> * priority in time
> * voluntary perpetuation of their cultural distinctiveness
> * self-identification as indigenous
> * experience of subjugation, marginalization, dispossession, exclusion, and discrimination by the dominant society. (Havemann 1999: 21)

As these criteria demonstrate, there is great diversity among the peoples who are called indigenous. According to Linda Smith, "The term 'indigenous' is problematic in that it appears to collectivize many distinct populations whose experiences under imperialism have been vastly different" (1999: 6).

However, the term is important because it indicates that people affiliated by the term have characteristics in common as well as many differences. There are several good reasons for comparing the situations of indigenous peoples in similar social, political, and economic settings. Paul Havemann has listed seven justifications for comparative research, but one is of particular importance here: it helps to "provide some perspective on one's own context from the knowledge of what occurs elsewhere and so avoid ethnocentrism" (1999: 2). Fieldworkers in indigenous communities should be aware of the history of contact between Europeans and the people of the particular community where they work, and they should be aware of similar histories of other indigenous groups. Hopefully, the introduction to the histories given here will stimulate the prospective fieldworker to search out more specific information about the given setting where she or he will work or about specific comparisons with other groups.

Several different authors have compared the circumstances of indigenous peoples, but each has taken a different perspective. John Ogbu's 1978 comparison of the context and effects of schooling for American minorities—including Native Americans—and for Maori in New Zealand first attracted rny attention shortly after it was published. It seemed amazing to me that there could be so many similarities in histories and circumstances for indigenous peoples on opposite sides of the world. Ogbu's comparisons eventually led me from my work in Alaska to work in New Zealand. As a result, programs in indigenous communities in Alaska and in New Zealand are described in the second section of the book.

Other authors have chosen to emphasize other dimensions and similarities. Burger includes the indigenous peoples of Australia, New Zealand, the United States, and Canada along with the Ainu of Japan, the Sami of Scandinavia, the Inuit of the Arctic, and other colonized peoples of the Pacific in a chapter entitled "Indigenous Peoples in Rich Countries" (1987: 177–220). Augie Fleras and Jean Elliott (1992) look at aboriginal–state relations in Canada, the United States, and New Zealand. Kayleen M. Hazlehurst (1995) finds significant similarities in contemporary indigenous justice systems in Canada, the United States, Australia, and New Zealand and includes case studies from these countries in her book. Elspeth Young (1995) looks at colonial policy, parallels, and common traits in Outback Australia and Canada. Richard J. Perry (1996) sees similarities in the circumstances for indigenous peoples and state systems in Mexico, the United States, Canada, and Australia, as well as other states and indigenous peoples. Terrence Loomis (1999) looks at the history of colonial exploitation of indigenous labor and the current economic position of indigenous peoples, while Havemann (1999) has collected and edited papers on indigenous peoples' rights in Australia, Canada, and New Zealand.

The countries chosen for comparison by each author have depended to a certain extent, at least, on the interests, perspectives, and circumstances of the particular author. However, there are clearly several specific and significant commonalities linking the indigenous peoples in the United States, Canada, Australia, and New Zealand:

- Europeans invaded these countries, and the indigenous inhabitants suffered from violence and the loss of their land, other resources, and political autonomy.
- Diseases introduced by the Europeans decimated the populations of the indigenous inhabitants.

- Indigenous beliefs, families, and social structures came under attack from Western religious, educational, and political systems.
- English became the language shared by the indigenous peoples in these countries and the nonindigenous researchers and developers.
- The national governments in the four countries have shared common origins and beliefs over extended periods of time.
- Indigenous peoples in all four countries are at the bottom of the socioeconomic scale, but they have nevertheless experienced a resurgence of population and cultural revitalization in the twentieth century.

Indigenous peoples in the four countries have also shared beliefs about the land. To Europeans, land is a commodity to be bought and sold, but indigenous peoples have viewed the land very differently. The commentaries of indigenous authors about their traditions and cultures consistently include statements about the spiritual relationships of their peoples to the land. The following comment by a renowned Maori historian illustrates this point, but indigenous writers from the other three countries have noted similar beliefs:

> Maori attachment to land is rooted in mythology, tradition and the long history of tribal wars. Mythology conceived the earth as Papatuanuku, the earth mother, from whose bosom sprang plants, birds, animals and fish for human sustenance. Therefore the earth was loved as a mother is loved. The eternal nature of the earth in relation to man's brief life span is encapsulated in the aphorism "man perishes but land remains." When man dies, he is thought of as returning to the bosom of the earth mother, where he is met by his ancestor Hinenuitepo. (Walker 1990: 70)

It is important to recognize the diversity as well as the similarities among the indigenous peoples in these countries. Before European contact, hundreds of different languages were spoken, and there were hundreds of different ways in which the peoples had adapted to physical environments ranging from deserts to rain forests, mountains, plains, and tundra. Much of that diversity still exists today, but indigenous peoples in these countries share the common experience of colonization.

Historically, different terms have been used to identify indigenous people in each of the four countries, and terms have changed over time. In Canada, the terms *First Nations* and *Aboriginal* have referred to the groups of people whose ancestors inhabited the country at the time of colonization by Europeans. In the United States, the terms *Native American*, *American Indian*, and *Alaska Native* have been used. In Australia, the term *Aborigines* has been used to identify the indigenous peoples. In New Zealand, the term has been *Maori* or *tangata whenua*. Of course, indigenous peoples can choose appropriate terms that may be different from the ones given here, and their choices should be respected.

The assumptions supporting government policies with respect to the indigenous peoples in each of the countries had similar origins in European policy and law. Although conflicting viewpoints were presented by policy makers at various stages of colonization, one European viewpoint effectively dominated policy in each country: European civilization was believed to be superior to all other ways of life, and that superiority carried with it the inherent right to take and develop the land and resources in each territory. Thomas R. Berger made the following statement with respect to European viewpoints in the Americas, but the statement can apply equally well to Australia and New Zealand: "Ideology has blinkered us. . . . The measures we have taken since 1492 have been designed to ensure that Indian land passed into European ownership, whether that of individuals or of the state. The colonies of Europeans established throughout North and South America—and the nation-states that succeeded them—adopted legal regimes to achieve this" (1991: 109).

HISTORY OF EUROPEAN CONTACT

Indigenous peoples have come to be in similar positions in North America, Australia, and New Zealand in part because of the similarities in the history of European invasion and conquest in each country: "Imperialism frames the indigenous experience. It is part of our story, our version of modernity" (Smith 1999: 19). It is essential for outside experts who are working in indigenous communities to have a general understanding of the history of European contact because that history influences the contemporary lives of indigenous people and their relationships with people of European descent. In many situations, ancestors of indigenous peoples have passed from generation to generation their versions of what happened when Europeans arrived in their lands. In other instances, older generations have taught the younger not to speak of the pain of the past, but the consequences of the historical tragedies are still felt (Napoleon 1991). The events of the past live on in the material circumstances and in the viewpoints of contemporary peoples. The legacies of the past are joined to their own individual memories of removal to boarding schools or foster homes, punishment for use of their home languages, and other painful instances of discrimination. They look at the wealth of the mainstream populations and realize that it was derived from resources that once belonged to their own communities.

Fieldworkers are likely to be confronted with some of the grief and anger over losses and injustices of the past. They will be better able to deal with these confrontations if they have gained some insight into the events that caused the pain. There may be occasions when fieldworkers find that stereotypes of Europeans

or European behavior exist in indigenous communities as the result of historical circumstances, but these stereotypes can usually be overcome with time
and effort. Fieldworkers also need to realize that the attitudes and policies of
contemporary mainstream institutions have their origins in the history of contact, too. Sometimes, policies, government regulations, or laws seem totally
baffling until the historical origins are revealed.

The histories given here are brief and are intended only as introductions to
the issues that influence relationships among indigenous peoples, European
settlers, and their descendents. The historical overview should help fieldworkers to understand that the communities they are working with are immersed in
larger networks of history, law, and policy. The problems and opportunities in
one community, indigenous group, or national setting are linked to the past as
well as to the problems and opportunities in other groups and communities.

The particular versions of each history were chosen because of the emphasis on the indigenous perspective. In the case of the history of North America, Berger's 1991 history was selected because of its comparative approach
as well as its emphasis on the indigenous perspective. Although the author is
of European descent, he worked for many years in legal action and research
relating to indigenous claims in Canada and Alaska. Ranginui Walker has had
a distinguished career as a professor of Maori studies, and his history (1990)
was selected because it is the most recent comprehensive history of New
Zealand written by a Maori. Eleanor and Colin Bourke, from whose 1994 collection (with Bill Edwards) the brief history of Australia was taken, are Aboriginal academics in Australia.

Berger (1991) prepared a commentary on the history of European and
American beliefs that formed the basis for government policies and actions
relating to indigenous peoples in North and South America. Other accounts
indicate that similar beliefs influenced government policies and actions relating to indigenous people in New Zealand and Australia. Policy makers and
intellectuals communicated with each other, so ideas about appropriate policies have circulated from one country to another.

The general outline of events is similar in each of the four countries. Havemann has summarized several reports and analyses of the similarities among
policy development in Australia, Canada, and New Zealand and has provided
a detailed comparison (1999: 22–64). Indigenous peoples in each of the four
countries suffered through periods of wars when they tried to defend their territories against European invaders. Many died as the result of newly introduced diseases. Europeans and their descendants instituted policies of extermination or removal against them. In the mid– to late nineteenth century,
when war, disease, and removal from ancestral lands had decimated indigenous populations, policies aimed at "protecting" and then assimilating in-

digenous peoples into the dominant populations became prevalent. Missionary education aimed at assimilation through separate systems of schooling for indigenous children and emphasized vocational education. The dominant views of educators were that indigenous peoples were not capable of academic or intellectual study.

However, the indigenous peoples of North America, Australia, and New Zealand did not die out. Some were assimilated, but many were not. Their populations began to increase in the early years of the twentieth century, and cultural and political revitalization movements have followed. The period of assimilation policies lasted well into the twentieth century. It was only in the 1960s and 1970s, with the development of civil rights movements around the world, that public attention was drawn to the rights of indigenous peoples to self-determination.

A BRIEF CONTACT HISTORY: THE UNITED STATES AND CANADA

In looking more specifically at the history of relationships between indigenous peoples and Europeans in the four countries, we can begin with the United States because European contact came earliest to North America and because the basic outline of European–indigenous contact will be familiar to most readers. Most American schoolchildren have learned that America was "discovered" by an Italian, Christopher Columbus, sailing on behalf of Spain in 1492. Native Americans, however, view this event as the beginning of the European invasion. In the early years of the sixteenth century, other Spaniards—Coronado, Cortes, and Pizzaro—made their way to the "New World," leading expeditions of conquest. Among their stated purposes was the Christianization of the indigenous peoples, but the primary purpose was the acquisition of wealth and territory on behalf of the Spanish Crown. The methods of the *conquistadores* were violent and brutal, although the diseases they inadvertently carried with them and passed on to the indigenous peoples may have played as great a part in their victories as their military skill.

During this period, one man led a crusade to draw attention to the rights of the indigenous peoples of the Americas. Berger has provided an enlightening account of the arguments put forward by Bartolomé de Las Casas, "father of human rights in the New World, God's angry man of the sixteenth century" (1991: 5). Las Casas traveled to Hispaniola and acquired land granted in the name of the Crown along with Indians to work the land. He became a priest, and in 1514 he gave up his lands and his Indians. He gave a sermon condemning his countrymen for the means they had used to acquire their fortunes.

For the next thirty years Las Casas brought petitions to Ferdinand and his successor, Charles V, who in 1520 was crowned Holy Roman Emperor. Las Casas was eventually successful in convincing King Charles that changes should be made. Charles decreed that no further land would be granted and that the Indians would eventually be released. These were the New Laws, designed to protect the Indians. The settlers refused to submit, and Charles could not risk rebellion. He could not enforce the changes.

Berger describes similar instances that occurred later in the history of the United States. In 1763, the British Crown issued a Royal Proclamation that would have protected Indian land. The first principle of the proclamation was that Indian land could not be sold except to the Crown. The land beyond the established colonies was to be closed to European expansion. The British Crown was not able to enforce this proclamation, and the "British policy exemplified by the Proclamation was one of the 'Intolerable Acts' used to justify the American War of Independence." However, the proclamation was "instrumental in the recognition by the courts of both countries of the distinctive political status and aboriginal rights of the Indians" (Berger 1991: 62).

There were other prominent occasions in U.S. history when a voice of authority spoke on behalf of the indigenous peoples but the decision could not be enforced. The Indian Non-Intercourse Act, passed by Congress in 1790, provided that the consent of the federal government was needed for anyone to enter into agreements with the Indians. On 7 August 1790, President Washington, other government officials, and Creek leaders signed a treaty, but the State of Georgia refused to abide by the terms. Washington took no action— "a pattern had emerged: encroachment by White settlers on Indian lands, failed attempts by the federal government to impose order, further concessions by the Indians, guarantees for the Indians, and then the repetition of the whole process" (Berger 1991: 71).

John Marshall was chief justice of the United States from 1801 to 1835. He was influential in establishing policies recognizing Native American sovereignty that eventually became important throughout the English-speaking world. In a series of judgments he described the relationship between American sovereignty and Indian self-government. He took the Royal Proclamation of 1763 as his starting point; "he accepted the legitimacy of Native sovereignty, Native institutions and Native title to the land and wove them into the American system" (Berger 1991: 73).

However, Marshall could not enforce the policies that he helped to develop. President Jackson rejected the Supreme Court's decision and allowed the State of Georgia to assume jurisdiction over Cherokee lands. The forced removal (the Trail of Tears) of the Cherokees and other tribes of the eastern United States followed Jackson's decision: "By 1840, nearly all the Indians east of the Mississippi had been removed west of that great river" (Berger 1991: 84). All of the removals were tragic. One result of Marshall's work, however, was that aboriginal title became a legal concept that has been recognized internationally and has gained special significance to the indigenous peoples in the four countries under discussion.

Berger summarizes the events that led to the U.S. Indian wars: the annexation of Texas in 1845, the Oregon Treaty in 1846, the Mexican War in 1846–48, the discovery of gold in California in 1849, the Homestead Act of 1862, the establishment of Indian reservations, and the Civil War. Then, he notes, "for the next twenty-five years the United States made war against the Indians, in a series of campaigns of virtual extermination, that lasted from the close of the Civil War until 1890" (1991: 88).

The next phase in government policy toward indigenous peoples began with the General Allotment Act of 1887, known as the Dawes Act. The act authorized the division of reservations into individual allotments for each Indian family. Congress rejected tribal ownership of land. The Indians were to become farmers and citizens of the United States if they severed their links with the tribe. The effects of the Dawes Act were disastrous for the Native Americans: "Two-thirds of all reservation lands were deeded to individual Indians. Nearly all of this land passed to non-Indian owners, often through state property tax foreclosures" (Berger 1991: 103).

In both the United States and Canada, boarding schools were established so that the process of assimilating Indian children into mainstream society could be undertaken. The schools removed children from the influence of their families and tribes, sometimes for years at a time. Indian languages, clothing, and religious practices were banned in the schools so that whole generations of people were cut off from their cultural origins.

These policies remained in place until the election of Franklin D. Roosevelt as president. The loss of tribal lands came to an end with the Indian Reorganization Act in 1934, but in 1953 Congress adopted a policy of "terminating" Indian tribal status. Indian reservations were once again broken up and sold. Eventually, after John F. Kennedy became president, further attempts to implement the policy were abandoned. From the 1960s onward, legislation and decisions of the Supreme Court have affirmed the exercise of tribal government on reservations. Another major shift in policy occurred in 1971, when Congress passed the Alaska Native Claims Settlement Act. This time the Native Americans were to become businesspeople:

> It set up a complicated scheme under which Native land—Indian, Eskimo and Aleut—would be held by Native corporations, in which the Natives would be shareholders. . . .

> In Alaska today, two decades after the enactment of the settlement, the net worth of the Native corporations is less than it was when they were established. They have not brought prosperity except to a few Natives and a very few communities. . . . Among Alaska Natives there has been a resurgence of support for tribal government. (Berger 1991: 105)

Berger compares the history of European contact in Canada with the history in the United States. Canada's policies went through cycles similar to those in the United States with only feeble attempts by the Canadian government to protect the Indians. The British established a policy of treating with the Indians in Canada for their lands, and this policy was manifested in the Royal Proclamation of 1763. Treaties were negotiated through the nineteenth century as settlement proceeded westward and the Canadian Pacific Railway opened the country to settlement. Later treaties in 1899 and 1921 allowed for development of oil on the frontier.

The arrival of the British Navy in the person of Captain Cook on Vancouver Island in 1778 is of interest because it was Cook's exploration of the coasts of both New Zealand (1769) and Australia (1770) that opened these regions to continuing European contact and trade. However, settlement of Vancouver Island began only after 1849 when it was made a Crown colony (Berger 1991: 143).

Encroachment on Indian reserves began after the turn of the century, and the government did everything possible to prevent Indians from pursuing land claims, including adopting legislation in 1927 making it punishable by law to raise funds for that purpose. But the Indian people continued to pursue their claims. In 1967, the Nisga'a Indians filed a lawsuit claiming that Indian title had never been extinguished in British Columbia. The Nisga'a case was considered in various Canadian courts for about three decades and forced the Canadian government to attend to the land claims of indigenous peoples around the country. In 1973, the intention to settle all native land claims was announced. The 1982 Constitution contains a guarantee of native rights: "'The existing aboriginal rights and treaty rights of the aboriginal peoples of Canada are hereby recognized and affirmed.' These words are binding not only on the federal government but also on the provinces. They give the Native people the means to enforce their right to a distinct place in the life of the nation" (Berger 1991: 154).

By the end of the twentieth century, several major settlements had been negotiated—including a settlement that recognized the Nisga'a Nation within British Columbia—but there were many questions relating to sovereignty, self-determination, land claims, and the roles of the indigenous peoples in the life of the country still to be resolved. The lives of most First Nations people in Canada were still affected by the Indian Act:

The Indian Act still controls every facet of our lives. It allows a certain amount of local self-government, but there is not a single thing on which we can make a law that does not have to go to a department official. . . .

Today, every time we see a movement beginning among indigenous people somewhere in this country, the Department of Indian Affairs finds some way to divide those people—discredit their organization, discredit their leadership, create an opposition group, fund an opposition group. (Erasmus and Sanders 1992: 8–9)

A BRIEF CONTACT HISTORY: NEW ZEALAND

Walker's detailed work, published in 1990, describes the history of contact with Europeans in New Zealand from the perspective of the indigenous Maori tribes. The first European ship arrived under Abel Tasman in 1642. A century passed before another European, James Cook, arrived in 1769. Maori welcomed seal hunters, timber traders, and whaling ships from several nations after that, but contagious diseases—measles, rubella, chicken pox, influenza, scarlet fever, venereal disease—came with contact. By 1840, the Maori population had been reduced by 40 percent, and it fell to 45,000 by the turn of the century (Walker 1990: 80–81).

The first missionary arrived in 1814. Trade in muskets was common, and in 1821 the musket wars began, "taking tribal warfare to an unprecedented level in the history of New Zealand" (Walker 1990: 82). By the 1830s, however, the missionaries became economically independent and influential. Whole tribes began converting to Christianity (Walker 1990: 86). Missionaries helped to arrange the circumstances leading to the signing by thirty-four North Island Maori chiefs of the Declaration of Independence in 1835. A copy of the declaration was sent to the king of England.

In January 1840, New Zealand was annexed as a colony of New South Wales. Captain Hobson arrived in the Bay of Islands with instructions to treat for sovereignty over the whole or part of the islands. He was instructed to issue a proclamation that all land titles would emanate from Crown grants but that acquisition of land should come only from districts that Maori could alienate without distress to themselves. On the basis of these instructions, the Treaty of Waitangi was signed on 6 February 1840.

There were several drafts of the Treaty of Waitangi in English and a missionary translation into Maori. The outcome was four English versions and one in Maori. The British Crown claimed sovereignty on the basis of the English versions, but these were not the versions signed by the chiefs. According to Walker (1990: 93), the chiefs believed that they had confirmed their own sovereignty, but, in fact, they had ceded the right to establish a governor to the British Crown.

A Royal Charter for the colony was issued later in 1840: "The charter gave the Governor power to survey the whole of New Zealand and divide it up into districts, counties, towns, townships, and parishes" (Walker 1990: 98). In the years immediately following the signing of the treaty, Maori prospered:

> Within fifteen years of having signed the Treaty of Waitangi, the tribes had success- fully developed their own economic infrastructure. They were the primary produc- ers of agricultural produce, the millers of flour and the transporters of their own products to the markets. Their dream of achieving progress through sharing their country with the Pakeha [people of European descent] under the Treaty was appar- ently coming to fruition. (Walker 1990: 101)

However, conflicts erupted between Maori and Europeans. The first of the New Zealand wars was fought in the north. "The war with Heke [one of the northern chiefs] was brought to a quick end at the Battle of Ruapekapeka in 1846" (Walker 1990: 103), but there was large-scale land buying over the whole of the South Island and much of the North Island. The tribes that agreed to the sales of nearly the whole South Island did so with the understanding that one-tenth of all lands purchased would be reserved for them, but Governor Grey instructed his commissioners to alter the tenths to four hectares a head.

In the North Island, the chiefs were at first willing sellers of land. However, in 1852 the country became self-governing under the New Zealand Constitu- tion Act. A property qualification effectively disenfranchised most Maori peo- ple "whose land was still in customary tribal title. The Pakeha population at the time was 30,000, approximately half that of the Maori. When the General Assembly met in 1854, a white minority government was effectively installed in power" (Walker 1990: 111).

Tribal representatives met in several locations to discuss unification. These meetings led to the idea of "withholding land from sale as a means of con- trolling and slowing down settlement" (Walker 1990: 111). The movement to- ward unification of the tribes eventually led to the installation of Te Wherowhero as the Maori king in April 1858, and he adopted the title Potatau I (Walker 1990: 112).

Questions of land acquisitions by settlers created a series of conflicts in the Taranaki region on the southwestern coast of the North Island. A temporary truce was agreed on, but in March 1863 Governor Grey sent troops, and the truce ended on "4 May with a skirmish in which nine soldiers were killed" (Walker 1990: 119). About two months later, on 12 July 1863, General Cameron's forces invaded the Waikato region in the central North Island (Walker 1990: 120). The Suppression of Rebellion Act was legislated to jus- tify Grey's plan, and the New Zealand Settlements Act of 1863 gave the gov- ernment power to confiscate any district where natives "were believed to be in rebellion" (Walker 1990: 122).

Battles between General Cameron's troops and Waikato Maori took place at several sites along the Waikato River as Maori retreated to the south. At Rangiaowhia, a massacre occurred: "On Sunday morning, 21 February 1864, while the people of the village were at church . . . rifle fire pinned down the congregation inside and the house was set alight. All inside perished" (Walker 1990: 124).

One more battle took place in the region before the Maori king and his Waikato people crossed into the mountainous territory of their relatives to the south, and a truce was declared in that region. Then, Cameron's troops moved to the east, where battles over land continued. The wars ended within a few years, but the struggles of the Maori tribes to regain their mana and their land did not. Prophets and freedom fighters led a series of movements in different regions of the North Island lasting well into the twentieth century.

War was not the only means used by the settler government to acquire Maori land. The Native Land Act of 1862 abolished the Crown right of preemption and established the Native Land Court to decide ownership of Maori lands. The Native Land Court was successful in making land available for European settlement. Within thirty years, four million hectares had been acquired, and the settler population increased from 100,000 to 600,000 between 1861 and 1881 (Walker 1990: 136). From the last decades of the nineteenth century through the first half of the twentieth century, a series of acts passed that effectively transferred land from Maori to Europeans and their descendants.

An official policy of assimilating Maori through schooling was implemented beginning in the mid–nineteenth century:

> Initially the mission schools did their teaching in the Maori language. But when Governor Grey arrived, he diverted them from that sound pedagogical practice with his 1847 Education Ordinance subsidising the mission schools, and insisting that instruction be conducted in English. It was also his expressed hope that the schools would take the children away from the "demoralising influences of their village," thereby "speedily assimilating the Maori to the habits and usages of the European." (Walker 1990: 146)

The struggle for Maori autonomy and the return of land continued through the remainder of the nineteenth century and through all of the twentieth. A nineteenth-century movement of passive resistance led by the prophet Te Whiti was overcome by the violence of the settler army. Deputations of Maori chiefs went to England hoping to meet with the British Crown, but all were unsuccessful. Various attempts were made to unify the tribes, but none of these was successful either. Twentieth-century prophets Rua Kenana and Wiremu Ratana began religious movements that became important politically as well as spiritually. Cultural revitalization movements accompanied political action, and the Maori population expanded from less than 50,000 at the beginning of the twentieth century to more than ten times that number, over half a million, by century's end.

Various movements—for land claims settlements, for Maori-language education programs, for increased political representation—came to fruition in the final decade of the twentieth century. The Waikato–Tainui tribe of the central North Island and the Ngai Tahu of the South Island achieved major settlements of land claims. Maori communities established early childhood and primary school Maori-language immersion programs at various locations around the country. After almost 130 years, the Maori Representation Act of 1867, which provided that four members of Parliament would be Maori, each from a different region of the country, was changed. In 1996, legislation came into effect basing the number of Maori seats in Parliament on the number of people on the Maori electoral roll, just as the number of general seats was based on the number on the general roll. Walker describes each of these developments as steps forward in the Maori struggle against an unjust social order.

A BRIEF CONTACT HISTORY: AUSTRALIA

James Cook, who surveyed much of the Pacific on behalf of the British Navy, is given credit for initial British contact with Australia in 1770. For Aborigines, 1788—the year when Governor Phillip assumed British sovereignty over Australia—represents the beginning of the European invasion of their land (Hemming 1994: 17). There is continuing speculation about the numbers of Aboriginal people in Australia when Cook arrived; estimates range from 300,000 to over a million. There may have been as many as 250 languages and 600 dialects. Territories were clearly defined by language, geography, beliefs, and descent. In spite of the diversity among the various groups of Aboriginal people, Bourke has noted that geography and climate influenced a characteristic, common framework among the various dialect groups (1994: 35–36).

Bourke's examination of the records indicates that the British government intended to deal fairly with the Aboriginal people, but despite Aboriginal resistance, England declared itself the ruler of Australia. The laws of England were imported. Australia was considered to be *terra nullius*, an empty land, uninhabited or occupied by people without settled laws or customs. The Aboriginal peoples' legal systems were not seen as organized and so were not recognized. The settlers recognized that Aboriginal people were present in Australia, but

resistance, massacres and genocide were also ignored in the application of the doctrine of *terra nullius*, which justified the acquisition of land. Aboriginal resistance was far from insignificant, as many documented examples show. . . . In 1828 the Governor of Tasmania (Arthur) proclaimed martial law, which was tantamount to a declaration of war against Aborigines. During the three years in which martial law remained in force, the military were entitled to shoot on sight any Aboriginal person in the settled districts. (Bourke and Cox 1994: 53)

The nineteenth-century practice of missionary schooling in Australia was similar to that in North America and New Zealand. Schooling was intended as a means of assimilation of the indigenous peoples. Schools for Aborigines operated in the 1830s and 1840s near all of the coastal settlements that are now the major cities of Australia. The central focus was the need to civilize and Christianize "the children of a people who were regarded as living in total degradation. . . . Aborigines failed to see why they should surrender their children to be inducted into alien ways" (Groome 1994: 142). For over 100 years, churches and welfare groups operated schools along with missions and reserves throughout rural Australia.

Protection legislation was introduced in all states of Australia during the nineteenth century. The explicit intention was to "protect" Aboriginal people, but

> in reality, such legislation supported a thoroughgoing program of assimilation through institutionalisation.
>
> The various state acts gave the Protectors of Aborigines total power over Aboriginal people, and the authority to remove their children. . . . The Acts reinforced the already common practice of forcibly removing Aboriginal children. . . . This practice continued in some states until the 1970s. (Groome 1994: 146)

Historians and legal analysts of the late twentieth century believe that basic human rights of the Aboriginal peoples of Australia were denied through the legal system. Under the protection legislation, children were removed from their parents, and Aboriginal marriage, movement, and employment were regulated. Aborigines were compelled to live on reserves and missions. The first Aborigines Protection Act was legislated in 1869 in Victoria. Acts such as this were based on the belief in the racial superiority of the British and were intended to exclude Aboriginal people from modern Australian life (Bourke 1994: 37). The acts defined who would and would not be considered Aboriginal and thereby reinforced divisions among people.

The legislation justified discrimination: "The *South Australian Aborigines Act* 1911 emphasised control and expanded segregation. The *South Australian Aborigines Amendment Act* 1939 changed the definition of 'Aboriginal' to include all people of Aboriginal descent. However, it introduced the 'dog tag' or the exemption certificate" (Bourke 1994: 38). The exemption certificate made it possible to exempt Aborigines who, "by reason of their character, standard of intelligence, and development are considered to be capable of living in the general community without supervision" (Bourke 1994:38). Exemption was also used to force Aboriginal people out of institutions and reserves as a means of punishment. Various acts defined who would and would not be considered to be full blood, half caste, and so on. The protection legislation facilitated the takeover of land because many people were sent to areas away from their own country and their families. Other legislation also had the effect of excluding Aboriginal people from employment because of their race. They were excluded under acts intended to control the employment of foreigners (Bourke 1994: 39).

Just before World War II, the Aborigines Progressive Association published a document called "Aborigines Demand Citizenship Rights" (1938), but it was not until the 1950s that the number of enforced separations was reduced. Finally, in the 1960s, major changes in the status of Aboriginal people were legislated:

> Aboriginal people did not have the right to vote in federal elections until 1962. The movement for full citizenship rights gathered momentum, and in 1967, 90 per cent of Australians voted "yes" to a referendum removing the constitutional provision excluding "Aboriginal natives" from being counted in the national census . . . and giving the commonwealth government . . . power to legislate in relation to Aboriginal Affairs. (ALRC Report 31:22, quoted in Bourke and Cox 1994: 55)

These changes were only the beginning of the many changes needed to remove the injustices inherent in Australia's legal system. South Australia passed the first Australian land rights legislation in 1966, but the fight for recognition of land claims had only just begun. Aborigines, Torres Strait Islanders, and their supporters fought for legislative reform. An Aboriginal Tent Embassy was set up at Parliament House in 1972, and numerous land rights marches were held in the years following (Bourke and Cox 1994: 57).

A case that became known as the "Mabo" case drew attention to issues surrounding native title and the original doctrine of terra nullius. In May 1982, Eddie Mabo and others from the Murray Islands in the Torres Strait sought legal recognition of common law title in the land. The case was in court for ten years before the Australian High Court gave its decision in June 1992: "The High Court stated that, at the time of occupation, Australia was *not terra nullius* and rejected the application of this doctrine and its consequences for native title" (Bourke and Cox 1994: 58).

The High Court decision in the Mabo case had reverberations throughout Australia. The decision opened the question of ownership of land by Aborigines everywhere in the country, but it did not immediately resolve the issues involved: "Native title is easily extinguished. . . . If the people have left the land either voluntarily or forcibly and lost connection with their land, then the title is lost. If the government has dealt with the land in a way that is inconsistent with traditional native title, then that title is extinguished. Once the title is extinguished in any way, it cannot be revived" (Bourke and Cox 1994: 59).

The Mabo case raised the priority of Aboriginal and Islander self-determination on the political agenda. The land rights issues have been associated with other issues of self-determination and have led politicians and the public to reflect on questions of justice for Aborigines. In the final decade of the twentieth century, the Aboriginal and Torres Strait Islander Commission was established to provide people with greater self-determination, and a Royal Commission into Aboriginal Deaths in Custody examined Australian history from an Aboriginal perspective (Hemming 1994: 31).

Bourke (1994: 43) describes the Aboriginal feelings of resentment because of non-Aboriginal attempts to define and categorize them and their desire for recognition: "Aboriginal people do feel compelled to gain the acknowledgement of their prior ownership, their sovereignty and the recognition of a continuous adapting Aboriginal identity" (1994: 44). Bourke and Edwards further note the continuing impact of European contact on Aboriginal family life:

> Aboriginal family life has been irreversibly changed in most of Australia. Many of the changes have come about merely by the presence of Europeans in this country; many others are attributable to the direct actions of the colonisers, actions which were deliberately aimed at destroying family as it existed in Aboriginal society. . . .
>
> Nearly all Aboriginal families know of relatives who were removed as children and put into European custody. Aboriginal people refer to them as "taken" or "stolen." (1994: 85)

These authors provide references indicating that, in the closing years of the twentieth century, there may have been 100,000 people of Aboriginal descent who did not know their families or their communities of origin:

> These people have been institutionalised, fostered or adopted, loved, hated or ignored. They all share the mental torment of not belonging in the society into which European Australia had decided they belonged. Australian society accepted the young Aboriginal children into its institutions, but rejected them when they became adults.
>
> Many of these adults have sought, and some are still seeking, to find their families. (Bourke and Edwards 1994: 87)

SOCIOECONOMIC POSITION OF INDIGENOUS PEOPLES

The United States, Canada, Australia, and New Zealand have been among the richest countries in the world, but in the twentieth century indigenous peoples have ranked at the lowest level of the socioeconomic scale in each (Burger 1987: 177–220). This has been the direct result of a colonization process whereby land, other environmental resources, and independence were taken

from the indigenous peoples and whereby the indigenous peoples are still denied the right to self-determination in many aspects of life. Indigenous educational levels have been low, and in each country the rates of indigenous ill
health, unemployment, and imprisonment have been higher than the average
for the country. The indigenous peoples have been discriminated against and
marginalized. In many instances, they have been viewed as "just another minority": "They are more likely to be unemployed than the major population,
they will probably receive less remuneration than comparable workers and
will almost certainly be concentrated, when they do find work, in the more
menial and poorly paid occupations" (Burger 1987: 17).

In the 1980s Burger reported that, in all four of the wealthy countries considered here, the economic position of the indigenous people was far below
that of other groups:

> In the United States of America the average per capita income for Indians is less than
> that for blacks, and half that of the white population. On the reservations average in-
> comes are lower still because of unemployment. . . .
>   In Australia the Aboriginal unemployment rate is estimated at five or six times the
> rate of the country as a whole; in Canada, unemployment rates on reserves reach
> nearly 50 per cent and on certain of these less than five per cent of the workforce had
> jobs; in New Zealand one in seven Maoris is unemployed against one in 30 whites.
> (1987: 22)

Indigenous peoples have also suffered from less opportunity for schooling
and from poor health. They have had less access to medical care and other
services. When they have moved to urban areas, they have occupied ghettos
with substandard facilities and housing (Burger 1987: 17). Burger reports that
rates of malnutrition, tuberculosis, and dysentery were higher among Indians
than in any other group in the United States, and infant mortality was two
times higher among Indians than among other Canadians. In Australia, the
death rate from infectious diseases was nine times higher on the reserves than
in the rest of the nation (Burger 1987: 23). Health problems were related to
economic status: "In the United States the low incomes of the Indian peoples
mean they cannot afford medical insurance and must depend upon public
health care which is deemed substandard" (Burger 1987: 24). In Canada,
where there is a national health system, "only officially recognized Indians are
entitled to comprehensive health benefits while the majority of non-federally
recognized Indians are dependent on inadequate state services" (Burger 1987:
24). Burger concludes that "poor health among indigenous communities is
due to many factors beyond the scope of doctors or health administrators:
poverty, unemployment, bad housing and so on. Indeed, poor health is really
an indicator of the social position of these communities" (1987: 25).

Yet, in spite of the appalling historical and contemporary conditions described above, the twentieth century saw populations of indigenous peoples in the United States, Canada, New Zealand, and Australia increasing and communities maintaining their cohesiveness and identity. Indigenous political movements have influenced government policies and legislation in all four countries. Language and culture revitalization movements have expanded. Increasing numbers of indigenous young people have completed secondary school and higher education, gaining mainstream qualifications in education, health, management, and other vitally important areas of study. These trends have continued into the twenty-first century.

THE TWENTY-FIRST CENTURY: SELF-DETERMINATION

The First Nations peoples of Canada, Native Americans and Alaska Natives in the United States, Aborigines in Australia, and Maori in New Zealand have established regular means of communicating about the things that they now have in common. Some argue that recognition of sovereignty should be the goal—recognition by national governments and international organizations of their peoples' status as sovereign or independent nations. Political movements aimed at achieving recognition of sovereignty of indigenous groups have developed among the indigenous peoples in all four countries (Deloria and Lytle 1984; Engelstad and Bird 1992; Havemann 1999).

However, the concept of sovereignty has a long history in European, colonial, and postcolonial law (Havemann 1999: 13–17). Fleras and Elliott note that an indigenous people's commitment to recognition of sovereignty "carries with it a dual objective to restructure their relational status in society and to secure the entitlements that derive from formal recognition of this restored status" (1992: 220). These are difficult objectives to achieve, and there are some who believe that, even if the governments of the four countries were to recognize the sovereignty of indigenous peoples, it would not solve all the problems. Canada's Royal Commission on Aboriginal Peoples identified three basic, necessary elements of good or effective government: one is power, the second is legitimacy, and the third element is resources (Chartrand 1999: 95). The low socioeconomic status of indigenous people in all four countries is described in an earlier section. Paul Chartrand has argued that redistributive justice is needed to correct the imbalances, but "we know from the history of peoples everywhere that those who have power and those who have resources do not give them up easily; they need good reasons to do so" (1999: 96). Without a major redistribution of resources, the lack of resources hampers the ability of indigenous peoples to establish effective self-government or sovereignty: "So when you look at the circumstances of indigenous people in Canada and ask how happy are the prospects for getting effective Aboriginal self-government, that answer has to be given in the context of realisation that right now they do not have the power and the resources, and in order to have effective self-government we need that big shift in distribution. It's a big challenge" (Chartrand 1999: 96).

Because the literature, discourse, questions, and issues surrounding sovereignty are so complex, there are those who believe that membership in existing states is fait accompli but that their peoples should have greater participation and authority to determine what takes place in their own communities. One 1999 Canadian settlement resulted in the establishment of the new political entity Nunavut, a territory that "returned to Inuit control over their own affairs" according to the territory's website. The 1999 settlement recognizing the Nisga'a Nation within British Columbia provides another model of an indigenous political structure within provincial and national structures. Both settlements are examples of the way in which indigenous political structures and territories can be incorporated as part of a federal system. Whether one argues for sovereignty or for the more general empowerment within existing political structures, there is widespread agreement that indigenous peoples should be able to empower their communities and to increase self-determination. The term *self-determination* is important because it links into the universal guarantees of the United Nations.

DRAFT DECLARATION ON THE RIGHTS OF INDIGENOUS PEOPLES

The indigenous peoples of the United States, Canada, New Zealand, and Australia are not alone in their shared perceptions of their common situation and ideas about ways to overcome contemporary problems. Indigenous peoples around the world share their common concerns through visits and exchanges, conferences, international organizations, publications, and electronic communication: "Thus the world's indigenous populations belong to a network of peoples. They share experiences as peoples who have been subjected to the colonization of their lands and cultures, and the denial of their sovereignty, by a colonizing society that has come to dominate and determine the shape and quality of their lives, even after it has formally pulled out" (Smith 1999: 7).

Internationally, indigenous peoples are concerned about a range of issues relating to their rights. The United Nations recognized and publicized the concept of human rights by adopting the Universal Declaration of Human

Rights in 1948. This declaration endorses very basic principles of the rights of human beings to life, liberty, security, nondiscrimination, equal protection under the law, marriage and family, religion, free expression, work, education, and political and cultural life. Unfortunately, more than fifty years after the adoption of this declaration, international human rights organizations continue to draw public attention to human rights abuses in countries on every continent of the world. However, recognition of the concept of universal human rights marks an important step toward ensuring that those rights are guaranteed for everyone.

Indigenous peoples note, however, that although the Universal Declaration of Human Rights acknowledges the rights of individuals, the rights of indigenous peoples are not made explicit. They have expressed the desire for the rights of indigenous peoples to be specifically acknowledged, and that desire is reflected in the Draft Declaration on the Rights of Indigenous Peoples. The Draft Declaration was developed by the United Nations Working Group on Indigenous Populations (made up of five independent experts) and has been widely circulated for discussion. It provides a clear statement of the rights that indigenous peoples believe should be recognized internationally. The Draft Declaration also includes statements about the requirements for states to protect those rights. Although this declaration has been circulated for comment, the final text had not been agreed on at the time of this writing. Nevertheless, the rights described and the obligations of states to protect those rights serve as useful descriptions of the viewpoints held in common by indigenous peoples as they entered the twenty-first century.

A copy of the complete Draft Declaration (as of May 2001) is included in the appendix. The main points include the acknowledgment that other covenants of the United Nations—the U.N. Charter, the International Covenant on Economic, Social, and Cultural Rights, and the International Covenant on Civil and Political Rights—affirm the fundamental importance of the right of self-determination of all peoples. Indigenous peoples have the collective and individual right not to be subjected to ethnocide and cultural genocide, including prevention and redress for any action depriving them of their integrity or dispossessing them of their lands (Article 7). Indigenous peoples shall not be forcibly removed from their lands or territories (Article 10). Indigenous peoples have the right to practice and revitalize their cultural traditions and customs (Article 12). They have the right to manifest, practice, develop, and teach their spiritual and religious traditions (Article 13). They have the right to revitalize, use, develop, and transmit to future generations their histories, languages, oral traditions, philosophies, writing systems, and literatures and to designate and retain their own names for communities, places, and persons (Article 14).

Indigenous children have the right to all levels and forms of education of the state. All indigenous peoples also have the right to establish and control their educational systems and institutions providing education in their own languages, in a manner appropriate to their cultural methods of teaching and learning (Article 15). They have the right to maintain and develop their political, economic, and social systems; to be secure in the enjoyment of their own means of subsistence and development; and to engage freely in all their traditional and other economic activities (Article 21). Indigenous peoples have the right to own, develop, control, and use their lands and territories (Article 26). They have the right to the restitution of the lands, territories, and resources that they have traditionally owned (Article 27).

Indigenous peoples are entitled to recognition of the full ownership, control, and protection of their cultural and intellectual property (Article 29). They have the right to autonomy or self-government in matters relating to their internal and local affairs (Article 31). And further, indigenous peoples have the right to the recognition, observance, and enforcement of treaties (Article 36).

CHALLENGES

The indigenous peoples in the four countries share major challenges for the future. The Draft Declaration on the Rights of Indigenous Peoples outlines the range of issues that they are dealing with. Increased self-determination is the issue of highest priority, partially because it influences access to all other rights. Three closely related issues are land claims, governance structures, and economic development. Indigenous peoples in the four countries will continue to bring land and other resource claims to the public and press, to courts, and to legislators. They will continue to adapt and develop governance structures for the new conditions in their communities. And they will continue to seek workable economic improvement for their peoples as part of a holistic approach to development that includes cultural and social development as well as economics.

Land Claims

People in all four countries have gained some government recognition of their land claims, but only a few claims have been settled to the satisfaction of the indigenous people, and negotiations continue on other claims. Berger notes the essential nature of the claims in the following comments with respect to North and South America, but this statement could apply to New Zealand and Australia as well:

Land claims are being advanced by Native peoples all over North and South America. The defence of Native land rights is the issue upon which Native peoples base claims to their identity, culture and political autonomy, and ultimately to their survival. Throughout the New World Native people understand that without a secure land base they will cease to exist as distinct peoples; their fate will be assimilation.

These claims can only be achieved, however, where Native collective identity is acknowledged and their claim to land itself entrenched in the law. Where these are disputed, conflict rages. It is so throughout the New World. (1991: 141)

Governance Structures

Indigenous peoples in the four countries are also confronting challenges because of the transformation of the governance structures in their own communities. In the twentieth century, national governments put in place legislation requiring particular forms of governance for bands, tribes, and other local indigenous communities. If local communities wanted the benefits offered by the national governments, they had to organize the governance of their local communities to conform to the legislation. Traditional governance structures gave way to band councils, tribal councils, tribal trust boards, chapters, regional councils, and other organizations. In many situations, the transformations were accomplished with remarkable ease, but in others the coerced changes have led to major problems in governance. Burger makes the following comments with respect to the United States, but similar problems exist in other settings as well:

> It needs to be noted that the tribal councils, together with the Bureau of Indian Affairs, are the main employers on the reservation and provide nearly all the welfare benefits. They are able to exert considerable influence on the community and the bribery of local representatives and other forms of coercion are known to occur. In the past, ambitious chairmen of the tribal councils have made virtual fiefdoms of their office and a generally demoralized indigenous community has done little in practice to prevent them. In recent years the America Indian movement has begun to challenge these unrepresentative councils. (1987: 200–01)

Vine Deloria Jr. and Clifford Lytle have examined the laws in the United States that led to the tribal governance structures of the late twentieth century and conclude that reform should be a major priority: "As tribes increasingly call themselves nations, partially in response to traditional arguments and partially as a means of emphasizing sovereignty against state and federal government, some form of national government must be devised" (1984: 246). Indigenous groups could not simply return to traditional methods of governance because populations had grown too large, social change and economic development were too important, and national governments continued to dictate the structures that should be used. New structures were needed, but there were "no good guidelines for either policy or programs in this new area of activity" (Deloria and Lytle 1984: 264).

Economic Development

Economic development has been another major issue for indigenous peoples in all four countries. There were few, if any, situations in which the indigenous peoples were able to maintain their traditional economic systems because they lost their traditional territories and, with the territories, the economic resources necessary for survival. Although they were left with insufficient resources, many groups have instituted new programs aimed at developing the resources they have. Most people want to improve the economic positions of their communities, but, in addition to availability of resources, other factors must be considered because there have been instances in which developments have been destructive for indigenous communities. When outside companies or agencies have had profit motives and have not considered the welfare of the indigenous communities, the impact on the people has been disastrous. Mining and timber companies, for example, have gained international reputations for harm inflicted on indigenous peoples. Also, even when new programs are begun with the best intentions for the people, they can have unforeseen consequences on traditional relationships within the community, on traditional cultures and languages, or on the environment. Those who speak for indigenous communities consistently emphasize the point that development must occur holistically, with all dimensions of cultural and social life changing in harmony. Potential impact must be assessed, and new programs should be rejected if the impact will be damaging.

Economic development programs may require particular education or training that is lacking in the community, thereby increasing dependency on outsiders who may not have the best interests of the community at heart. Commercial developments may bring large numbers of outsiders into indigenous communities, and the impact of the outsiders must be considered. There have been instances in which large proportions of the proceeds of land claims settlements or resource royalties have been paid to outside consultants, leaving the indigenous people little better off than they were before the settlement.

In the United States, gambling casinos on reservations have led some members of the general public to conclude that Indian economic problems have been solved, but the casino movement provides an excellent example of the difficulties that indigenous communities face when considering new investments. Katherine A. Spilde has found that only one-half of the federally recognized tribes offer some form of gaming and that twenty facilities accounted for 50 percent of the total income:

Since the early 1980s, 188 tribes have established 285 casinos in 28 states. . . . In 1997, Indian gaming generated revenues of $6.68 billion. These profits are having a profound impact on the lives of many Native Americans. Tribal governments are re-vitalizing their communities by investing in housing, health care, education pro-grams, language and cultural revitalization programs, and numerous other commu-nity projects. Tribal casinos provide jobs and hope for tribal members at a time when Federal support for Native programs is at an all-time low.

Not all tribes benefit from Indian gaming. While 188 federally recognized tribes do offer some form of gaming, 368 do not. Of tribal governments that do have casi-nos, financial success is not evenly distributed. In 1997, 20 tribal gaming facilities account for 50 percent of the total Indian gaming revenues. (1999: 11)

Many reservations are located in areas of low population density where casinos could not attract sufficient clientele to be profitable. In other situa-tions, people feared gambling addiction or had moral reservations about prof-iting from gambling. Casinos have provided economic development for some but could not be considered an overall solution to issues of indigenous poverty and economic development.

SOCIAL CHANGE PROGRAMS

The brief histories have indicated that, for more than 150 years, governments, private organizations, and indigenous groups in the four countries have worked to establish programs aimed at improving health, social services, ed-ucation, vocational training, and the economic status of indigenous commu-nities. Although the rhetoric of self-determination has been an integral part of these programs since the 1970s, there has been a long history of external domination of the ideologies, policies, and legislation governing these pro-grams. Sometimes, the programs have been associated with formally stated research goals, but other programs have been termed pilots, trials, or demon-stration projects. Some have been collaborative programs undertaken with the participation of outside experts as well as members of local communities. Some programs have been successful; many have not. It is not surprising that indigenous people are skeptical about the promises for improvement that ac-company new program proposals or that they insist on the right to determine what programs will meet their needs. This chapter has presented an overview of the historical and political context for such programs. The chapters that fol-low describe the evolution of collaborative programs and workable ap-proaches to program design.

Chapter Two

The Evolution
of Collaborative Programs

INDIGENOUS SELF-DETERMINATION
AND SOCIAL SCIENCE RESEARCH

For most of the twentieth century, social science researchers tried to emulate the research methods of the natural sciences. Researchers who were immersed in the belief systems of their times tried to be objective recording instruments in the study of human "subjects." A renowned anthropologist offered the following description of the intentions of anthropologists during the early years of the twentieth century:

> The central scientific ethic of cultural or social anthropology . . . was to preserve a record of the precious and vanishing fabric of ancient customary behavior in whatever ways were open to us. This responsibility carried with it a respect for the dignity of the contemporary members of a culture; we valued every manifestation in folklore and myth, in the distinctiveness of the language spoken, in art and ritual, kinship and political organization, and the technologies of making a living. (Mead 1978: 426)

In the second half of the century, however, there was growing awareness of the subjectivity of researchers, the importance of the individual researcher's values in determining outcomes of research, the interpretive nature of research, and criticism of the links between Western science and colonialism. People in a variety of settings read the publications written about their communities and came to believe that the research served the interests of the researchers and their societies rather than the interests of the people studied.

European and indigenous critical theorists developed an extensive discourse on the underlying assumptions of Western science and the relationship of those assumptions to research in indigenous communities. A Maori educator

31

and researcher reviewed this discourse and concluded that there has been an "underlying connection between such things as: the nature of imperial social relations; the activities of Western science; the establishment of trade; the appropriation of sovereignty; the establishment of law" (Smith 1999: 27). The experience of indigenous peoples with "white research," "academic research," or "outsider research" has been an experience of "unrelenting research of a profoundly exploitative nature" (Smith 1999: 42).

In the late nineteenth and early twentieth centuries, there were numerous scientific publications that supported the belief in the superior position, culture, and society of Europeans. Early anthropologists developed theories of racial differences; they categorized societies as "primitive" or "civilized" and constructed hierarchies of societies with European civilization placed above all others. Even at mid–twentieth century there were anthropological accounts clearly perpetuating colonial stereotypes. One example comes from Elenore Smith Bowen, the pen name used by Laura Bohannan when she published an "anthropological novel" (1964) including descriptions of the servants—called "boys"—and the cook who made her fieldwork in Africa considerably more comfortable than it might otherwise have been. She thought of her own society as "civilized" and the other as "savage" and was not afraid to say so in her novel.

Medical, biological, and pharmaceutical researchers have taken indigenous intellectual property without permission and without compensation to the owners of the property (Greaves 1994). Indigenous researchers have drawn connections among the work of social scientists in their communities, the work of biological and pharmaceutical researchers, and colonialism: "Research within late-modern and late-colonial conditions continues relentlessly and brings with it a new wave of exploration, discovery, exploitation and appropriation. Researchers enter communities armed with goodwill in their front pockets and patents in their back pockets, they bring medicine into villages and extract blood for genetic analysis" (Smith 1999: 24).

Given the background and history of social science research in indigenous communities, it is hardly surprising that ethnic minorities and indigenous groups have questioned the value of research that does not take their perspectives and viewpoints into consideration. They believe that research should have positive outcomes for the people or programs being studied and that "subjects" are entitled to active roles in formulating the goals, managing the programs, and interpreting the outcomes of research. Indigenous people are developing their own approaches and methods for research, but there are still those among them who believe that they can take advantage of the viewpoints of researchers with cultural backgrounds other than their own. Some want research to be conducted only by people from their own group, but there are others who believe that collaboration with researchers from outside the community has certain advantages. These advantages can include drawing on expertise that is not available in the community and utilizing outsider perspectives as well as insider perspectives to interpret the research. Indigenous people may refuse permission for researchers to study them but can be willing and enthusiastic participants in research that recognizes their goals, their right to make decisions about the research, their intellectual property rights, their own methods of research, and their roles as authors of research. They are especially interested in research that will contribute to the development of their own successful programs in education, health, social welfare, and other aspects of community life.

Even if a researcher is given entrée to an indigenous community to carry out theoretical work, members of the community are quite likely to insist that the researcher contribute to the development of practical programs in the community at the same time. Efrat and Mitchell worked in Indian communities on the Pacific Northwest coast of North America and have concluded, "Not only will we be required to sign legal or quasi-legal agreements written by the Indian people . . . but also we must be prepared to carry out Indian-designed research activities that we had not intended" (1974: 407).

Contemporary researchers in indigenous communities are often called on to be program developers regardless of their original intent. The same is true for schoolteachers, administrators, health professionals, social workers, and others who are in regular contact with indigenous communities.

Indigenous people in the United States, Canada, Australia, and New Zealand are among those who have come to believe that much of the research that has been conducted in the past has contributed to negative stereotypes of their communities. Some believe that the primary beneficiaries have been the researchers, with little in the way of benefit accruing to the people who agreed to be the subjects of the research. As a result, many are skeptical of new research proposals and insist that new research show some benefits for their communities.

Government agencies and the public in the four countries have shown increased awareness of the rights of indigenous peoples to make decisions regarding education, health, and economic and social service programs in their own communities. Government and other funding agencies have continued to formulate policies but have acknowledged that, if programs are to be effective, indigenous groups must be involved in developing and implementing those policies. However, funding agencies have expected that staff members in the programs will, on the whole, have completed formal educational programs related to their work. Because there have been insufficient numbers of indigenous students completing the relevant programs, staff members in many programs are from the mainstream and are of European descent. Mainstream staff members are often expected to work collaboratively with indigenous representatives locally, regionally, or nationally, but they are not necessarily trained in how to go about it.

Collaborative programs can provide avenues for indigenous people who know the local community to work with outside experts with specialized Western knowledge. Collaborative programs also have the advantage that they can sometimes be designed in ways that will provide research training for people at the community level. Jean and Stephen Schensul (1992: 177–79) have established formal programs so that individuals from urban communities can gain research skills, and they have provided guidelines regarding instruction in particular skills for community researchers (1992: 188–89). Research training programs are feasible for indigenous communities, too. Many people who have not been trained as researchers have begun to see ways in which they can use training in research methods to evaluate and improve programs in their own communities and to collect information and prepare their own reports for their own purposes. Guyette's 1983 publication, *Community-Based Research: A Handbook for Native Americans*, is an excellent reference including a chapter on recommendations for successful cooperation with outside researchers (1983: 267–84).

The present work is about collaboration between indigenous groups and outside experts in programs for indigenous communities. It is intended for readers who are or are preparing to become fieldworkers. Wolcott has used the term *fieldworker* to refer to qualitatively oriented researchers in many fields who conduct field-based studies (1995: 17). I would like to extend his definition to include professionals who live and work in indigenous communities in order to participate in collaborative programs. According to this broader definition, the term includes researchers, but it also includes teachers; program developers; people in volunteer programs, the health field, and social service; and agricultural and economic development workers.

Anyone going into a new setting is likely to be collecting, analyzing, and interpreting information about the new community. People in any of the fieldworker roles mentioned above are likely to have been educated in a discipline based on social science research and, hopefully, will have acquired some familiarity with the research tradition of the discipline. When they enter new communities, they will focus on collecting, analyzing, and interpreting information even if they do not have an obligation to prepare a research report. They will necessarily collaborate with individuals in the community in order to complete the tasks associated with their roles.

Anyone in a fieldworker role in an indigenous community should consider recording and reporting, in collaboration with people from the local community, what they learn. In the past, people have learned a great deal about the factors that have affected the programs they have worked in, but they have not necessarily reported what they learned to anyone else. As a result, history has continually repeated itself as new people try new programs in new settings without the advantage of knowing what happened in similar situations in the past. Goodenough pointed out more than three decades ago that development workers could contribute far more to the body of knowledge if they documented and reported their activities: "He must make his own operations as development agent an object of study. By making predictions and checking their outcome, by keeping a careful record of his experience and subjecting it to periodic analysis, and by explicitly formulating his conclusions and communicating them to others, he will contribute to the knowledge and understanding on which the practice of his profession must rest" (1963: 45).

This book is also intended for indigenous communities that may be planning an innovative program in collaboration with outside experts. Indigenous people may be able to use the guidelines here in selecting outside experts who can make the best contributions to their programs and in working out guidelines and the implementation of their own programs.

There are many different ways for professionals to collaborate with members of local communities in social change or research programs. Some programs have collaborative aspects but are not wholly collaborative in the sharing of responsibility and authority for the project. The programs described in this book cover several different sets of arrangements for collaboration, but other sets of arrangements are also possible.

A BRIEF HISTORY OF COLLABORATIVE PROGRAMS IN INDIGENOUS COMMUNITIES

> We cannot judge what it is right to do now without knowing what has gone before.
>
> —Berger 1991: xiii

The term *collaboration* can have different meanings. For example, research in any field can be called collaborative when researchers form teams to collaborate among themselves on particular projects. Collaboration of this kind often occurs in natural science and health research. Then again, all research involving human subjects is collaborative, at least to the extent that individuals who are subjects must give consent to participate. By the closing years of the twentieth century, the term *collaborative research* had become quite popular in academic discourse and was used to describe mainstream programs in several different disciplines including education, management, law, women's studies, and community psychology. Terms such as *action research*, *partnership research*, and *participatory research* were sometimes used to describe programs with goals and relationships between participants that were similar to those in collaborative research (see, for example, Borman 1979; Chrisman et al. 1999; Craig and Mayo 1995; Nelson and Wright 1995; Rahman 1995; Schlesier 1974; Torres 1995). Stephen and Jean Schensul have published extensively on advocacy anthropology and collaborative research in urban health and education programs (see, for example, Schensul and Schensul 1992; Schensul and Schensul 1978). LeCompte and associates (1999: 85–164) provide an introduction to research partnerships focused specifically on ethnographic research goals. Bartunek and Louis (1996) analyze approaches to insider/outsider teams in other types of research including research in fields as diverse as community psychology and ethnomusicology.

The purpose of the present book, however, is to examine a different dimension of collaboration, specifically in programs in which an outside expert and members of an indigenous community intend to collaborate by sharing responsibility and authority. A community in a collaborative program may be a village, a neighborhood, a school, a tribe, a formal organization, or any other group of indigenous people who consider that they are related as a community. Collaborative programs can be linked to research when the program includes formally stated research outcomes among its goals. Certain types of programs do not include formal research goals but are called trials, pilots, or demonstration projects. These programs are closely related to formal research programs because they include the collection, analysis, and interpretation of information about the program. Alternatively, programs with the major emphasis on research outcomes can be collaborative, and they can be related to community development when practical outcomes for the community are among the intended outcomes of the research.

Collaborative programs have emerged in their diverse forms only after several decades of evolution. The following description of that evolution emphasizes collaborative research in indigenous communities because researchers have published about the collaborative programs where they have worked. There have been many fieldworkers—educators, health specialists, program designers, and others—who have worked collaboratively with indigenous people, but they did not publish reports that could be used in describing the evolution of programs. For a similar reason, the emphasis here is on the evolution of collaborative programs in the United States. Although I am quite certain that there have been collaborative programs in Canada, Australia, and New Zealand, I could find only a few publications describing such programs in New Zealand (including Barnes 2000 and Bishop 1996).

More than one discipline has claimed credit for originating the notion of collaborative research. Beginning in the 1940s, the term *action research* was used to describe research whereby outside experts worked with members of local communities to develop and implement programs for change. James A. Banks (1998:15) believes that the idea of having outside researchers and people within the community working together originated with Myrdal, the Swedish economist, who involved a number of African American researchers in his study *An American Dilemma*, published in 1944. Joe Kincheloe, however, credits Kurt Lewin for originating action research in social psychology:

> As early as the 1940s Kurt Lewin called for action research in social psychology. Taking their cue from Lewin, leaders in spheres as disparate as industry and American Indian affairs advocated action research. During the post–World War II era Stephen Corey at Teacher's College led the action-research movement in education. Corey argued that action research could help reform curriculum practice, as teachers applied the results of their own inquiry. There was considerable enthusiasm for the movement in the post-war period, but by the late 1950s action research became the target of serious criticism and started to decline. (1995: 71–72)

Anthropologists give credit to Sol Tax for introducing the term *action anthropology* through his program with the Fox Indians in Iowa, which began in the summer of 1948. According to Tax, the term was introduced at the 1951 meeting of the American Anthropological Association: "We knew no precedent for what we were trying to do in combining research and action. . . . So . . . we coined a new term" (1958: 17).

By the 1950s, major collaborative efforts were beginning. One became rather famous as the Cornell University Vicos Project in Peru: "From 1952 to 1966, Cornell University, in collaboration with the Peruvian government and the Quechua Indian community of Vicos, conducted a program in the Andean highlands. . . . Designed to create a viable community freed of serfdom and ultimately in possession of the estate, this was the first formal attempt at holistic rural development and agrarian reform in Peru" (Doughty 1987: 129). Paul L. Doughty has summarized the history of the project, one in which Holmberg and his colleagues intended that profits from the work of the hacienda would be invested in the people's interest in housing, schools, recreation, sanitary facilities, and agriculture. The major goal, however, was for the Quechua-speaking Indians to be able to purchase the hacienda and its lands. In 1962 the Vicos hacienda was sold to its peasant community. The outside researchers retired from Vicos by 1966. The community continued to expand economically and politically for the next two decades (Doughty 1987).

Applied social scientists from Cornell University were also active in the United States in the 1950s. The Cornell summer seminar in cross-cultural relations provided training for administrators and technicians from Asia, Africa, Europe, Australia, New Zealand, and North and South America. A number of noted anthropologists were involved during the summers of 1949–52. Instruction was based in Navajo, Papago, and Spanish American communities. Bureau of Indian Affairs staff and technical staff from other agencies participated. Although a certain amount of collaboration is implicit in the description by Robert Bunker and John Adair (1959), the authors provide no details on the collaborative arrangements, and they leave no doubt that the university anthropologists were the authorities and directors of the program.

The impact of the publication by Brazilian educator Paolo Freire of *Pedagogy of the Oppressed* in 1970 cannot be underestimated. Freire asserts that adult education programs in Latin America should be aimed at social transformation and empowerment of the people in the lowest socioeconomic positions. Carlos Torres has summarized the influence of Freire in Latin America:

> For Freire, the principal concerns of adult education are not pedagogical or methodological in the strictest sense, but are related to its political application as a form of advocacy for oppressed social groups. Adult education programs in Latin America are designed explicitly as mechanisms or instruments for pedagogical and political involvement with the socially subordinated sectors of the population. Following Freire, adult education constitutes a pedagogy for social transformation. (1995: 237)

Freire's books changed the perception of the purposes of education and research in the minds of many theorists. European and American educational and social science theorists expanded Freire's critical approaches and developed a body of literature that has become known as critical theory (McLaren and Giarelli 1995). For Third World and indigenous communities, Freire's framework supported the concept of empowerment and resulted in a restructuring of the roles of fieldworkers in many settings. There have been problems in defining and applying the term *empowerment*, but the basic notion has nevertheless become integral to collaborative programs. Even when *empowerment* is not explicitly defined or included in statements of program goals, increased authority of indigenous peoples to make decisions is implicit in the idea of collaboration. There can be no collaboration unless power to make decisions for the programs is shared.

In the 1970s, there were several reports by applied anthropologists on collaborative efforts with Native Americans. Efrat and Mitchell (1974) reported on written agreements with Pacific Northwest coast tribes that governed their relationships with the tribes while they conducted research. In the same year, Schlesier (1974) described the extensive process of initiation he underwent in order to become a collaborator and nondirective consultant on behalf of the

Southern Cheyenne. Parades (1976) became a publicist for the Eastern Creek as the result of his collaborative efforts, and Willard (1977) reported on a collaborative program funded by the Office of Economic Opportunity in a Sage Indian community.

The Hualapai Bilingual/Bicultural Education Program was initiated in 1975 as a collaboration between a linguist/anthropologist and a native Hualapai speaker: "During a decade of association and a number of projects, this relationship has developed into a full collaborative effort in which university-based linguists and native professionals work together on all aspects of program development, curriculum, and evaluation" (Watahomigie and Yamamoto 1987: 78). Lucille Watahomigie and Akira Yamamoto make several important points about successful collaboration in "action linguistics": "First, the Hualapai research was not his (the linguist's) dissertation; thus, he was not subject to the theoretical and temporal pressures that generally attend such research. Second, he was an educator with research interests, not a researcher with an interest in education" (1987: 85). Yamamoto received grants from the American Philosophical Society Phillips Fund and the National Endowment for the Humanities and thus could provide modest financial support for the team. The authors note that, in applied collaborative projects, publication of research results is sometimes delayed for several years while work proceeds toward the applied goals of the programs.

By the 1980s, experts in fields including development, community organizing, and education were advocating for the participation of local people in decision making for projects and programs within indigenous, ethnic minority, and Third World communities. There was increasing recognition of the importance of participatory or collaborative research in empowerment and social change: "Research continues to be an indispensable and powerful tool for social change. Organizers should pay special attention to the use of participatory approaches in which both researchers and community members are involved as equal participants in securing knowledge to empower the community" (Rivera and Erlich 1998: 17).

In the 1980s, indigenous communities in the United States were showing the effects of the withdrawal of federal funding from programs established in the 1970s. Donald D. Stull, Jerry A. Schultz, and Ken Cadue Sr. describe the "ever-shifting and often tumultuous landscape of federal policy" (1987: 34) and the impact of changing policies and funding on the development and eventual demise of the Kansas Kickapoo Technical Assistance Project (KKTAP), a collaborative project between the tribe and anthropologists at the University of Kansas. The goal of the collaboration was the development of a self-sustaining tribal economy. A number of films and applied publications were produced, but reductions in federal funding created pressure on the community and on the anthropologists: "There is no doubt that KKTAP was ultimately done in by forces over which neither the anthropologists nor the Kickapoo had any control—changes in federal Indian policy and funding" (Stull, Schultz, and Cadue 1987: 52).

Although collaborative programs are affected by changing policies and funding limitations and academic researchers must sometimes delay research publication, collaboration continues to provide the best approach to certain types of research. Noel Chrisman and associates describe the benefits of a partnership among university researchers, practitioners, tribal members, and officials in designing programs to increase women's use of Pap smears and the tribe's capacity to manage future projects. The authors conclude that participatory action research is a "valuable design for community capacity building research" (1999: 134).

COLLABORATIVE RESEARCH
IN CROSS-CULTURAL EDUCATION

Researchers in several academic disciplines have used the term *collaborative research*, but it appears most often in the literature on education. It can describe activities as diverse as collaboration between feminist academics, collaboration between teachers and students, or collaboration between school districts. The literature on collaborative research in cross-cultural educational settings can be instructive when we consider the best ways to approach collaborative programs in indigenous communities.

Margaret Gibson (1985) organized a collaborative research project in a California school district that included a large Punjabi Indian group. Although this program was in an immigrant community rather than an indigenous community, Gibson's publication of the problems encountered in the collaborative process should be required reading for every prospective fieldworker. She describes the goals of the program as follows: "The study was not formulated as a change effort. It may be characterized more appropriately as a basic research project designed to generate locally useful information while addressing issues of wider concern" (1985: 128). Research objectives were broadened after the initial interviews with mainstream teachers and parents in order to accommodate their concerns. The commitment "to full collaboration consumed valuable hours subtracted from fieldwork" (Gibson 1985: 135). They found that, even with the best intentions, not all collaborators could share equal power or control. The administration of the research grant was placed with a community organization away from the research site, but the budget did not include funding to compensate this organization for undertaking the administration, and members of the organization wanted the grant to further their own purposes. Conflict within the minority community led to a lawsuit and seriously threatened the program. Gibson shared responsibility with a co-researcher from the minority community, but the two researchers could not agree on their approach to the final report. Two reports were written, but the funding agency wanted only one.

There were a number of positive outcomes for the program and the proposed goals were achieved, but much learning about the nature of collaboration in diverse communities took place along the way. Gibson concludes that there should be three types of collaboration between anthropologists and host communities: "First, collaboration in the *development* of change strategies; second, collaboration with community institutions for the *administration* of research funds; and third, collaboration in the *research* itself" (1985: 142).

Concha Delgado-Gaitan's (1990) collaborative program in a California school district with a Spanish-speaking minority has many characteristics in common with Gibson's program, but it did not encounter the same problems. The research was initiated as a mutual agreement between a school district special projects director and the researcher, but the study was extended as the research progressed. Delgado-Gaitan sought the involvement of all participants in the research and regularly shared her data with the administration, families, and teachers to obtain accuracy checks. As the result of that sharing, Spanish-speaking parents suggested that a parent group be organized. Delgado-Gaitan encouraged parents and took the role of facilitator of the parent group. She made an important point regarding her intervention: she was only able to assume an active role in the change effort because, through research, she had gained the necessary background knowledge about the community to allow her to intervene appropriately. She had not originally intended that the program serve the function of empowering participants, but improved communication between parents and school resulting from the program empowered all the participants by facilitating mutual cooperation.

Margaret D. LeCompte describes a range of programs, some of them cross-cultural, in which she has been a participant and comments on the essential characteristics of collaborative research centered on critical theory: "By contrast, critical collaborative research de-centers the researcher, making him or her a participant in and subject of the investigative process, rather than simply the disembodied Other who directs and documents. Critical collaborative research thus rejects as arrogance what Mishler (1986) has called the inherent asymmetry of relationships between the researcher and the researched" (1995: 99). LeCompte expresses concerns about several educational research projects in which the researcher who published the report considered that the projects had been collaborative: "Each was generated by the researcher, not initiated by the participants. They reflected the needs of researchers and tended not to incorporate the feelings, wants, and desires of research participants. Several of the researchers seemed to be unaware of many structural constraints and realities operating in their participants' lives" (1995: 104).

LeCompte concludes her chapter by presenting her critical collaborative approach to a long-term program with a school district in the Navajo Nation. She was invited by the district to participate and was attempting to maintain her relationship with the district as "one among equals." The district identified problems that LeCompte sometimes reframed in scholarly terms. She hoped to set aside her own agendas from time to time to adopt the frameworks of the district participants, to integrate her version of the story with theirs, and to give the district people as much public opportunity to tell that story as she had (1995: 107).

LONG-TERM PROGRAMS IN ALASKA

Chapters 5 to 10 of this book describe my role in a series of programs in indigenous communities. In most of these cases, the programs were designed for short-term collaboration through the start-up phase of innovative programs, with the intention that indigenous groups could eventually operate the programs with occasional consultation from outside experts. In other words, my intention was to "work myself out of a job" in these cases. However, Alaska Natives and University of Alaska faculty have developed policies and have published accounts of longer-term programs, and there are good reasons to review and to note the success of these programs. Examples of the most notable of these programs are described below.

The Ciulistet Group

A program including Jerry Lipka, Gerald Mohatt, and the Ciulistet Group evolved into a collaborative project. The Ciulistet Group, a group of Yup'ik teachers in southwestern Alaska, was originally formed in 1987 by John Antonnen, the district superintendent, to advise the school board on education policy—"but we didn't have the models or knowledge to re[-]create schooling" (Ilutsik 1998: 14). Lipka, a staff member from the University of Alaska Fairbanks, had been working as an instructor for several members of the group in a field-based teacher training program: "With the assistance of Lipka, Nelson-Barber (Stanford University), and Mohatt (University of Alaska Fairbanks and former dean of the College of Rural Alaska), we obtained resources to conduct research" (Ilutsik 1998: 14). Initially, the group examined the way

Yup'ik teachers organize their classrooms, how they relate to their students, and how they integrate Yup'ik cultural values into their lessons. . . .

We, the group and Lipka, collaborated in obtaining funding from the University of Alaska Fairbanks, from the Eisenhower Math and Science program, and from the National Science Foundation. These funds supported our investigation into how Yup'ik culture, language, and everyday practice contain science and math concepts. As Yup'ik teachers, we continue to strengthen ourselves and our identity, and we hope that we can pass these values on to our students. After all, with a strong self-identity and language, we can do anything. (Ilutsik 1998: 14)

For more than a decade, the group's research has focused on the expression of Yup'ik culture in classrooms in southwestern Alaska and the training of Yup'ik teachers. The group has produced a number of papers for professional meetings, journal publications, and a book (Lipka, with Mohatt and the Ciulistet Group 1998).

Alaska Rural Systemic Initiative

In the mid-1990s, the Alaska Federation of Natives, in cooperation with the University of Alaska, received funding from the National Science Foundation and the Annenberg Rural Challenge to develop and implement the Alaska Rural Systemic Initiative (AKRSI). An extensive catalog of information on this program has been published on the World Wide Web at http://www.ankn .uaf.edu. The purpose of the program is described as follows:

Native Pathways to Education . . .

The purpose of the AKRSI is to bring people together from throughout the state to implement a five-year series of initiatives to systematically document the indigenous knowledge systems of Alaska Native people and develop educational policies and practices that effectively integrate indigenous and Western knowledge through a renewed educational system.

The program's emphasis is on "renewing Native pathways to education, so that traditional knowledge systems, ways of knowing and world views can be more effectively utilized as a foundation for learning all subject matter." Elders' Councils and the Alaska Native/Rural Education Consortium, made up of representatives of the partner organizations from throughout the state, provided overall guidance for the AKRSI.

Rural Human Services Certificate Program

Bryan MacLean (1998) describes the formation of this collaborative program beginning with the establishment of the Rural Human Services System Project as a product of a partnership initiative between the Alaska Native community, the State of Alaska, and the University of Alaska. The certificate program, a one-year program to train village-based "human service providers," was the University of Alaska component of the project:

> The Certificate Program was at the leading edge of innovative programme delivery to Alaska Natives. It represented an important step towards biculturalism. The hallmark of the Certificate Program was its unique curriculum and delivery format and process. The curriculum was characterised by the strong emphasis placed on:
> - use of Alaska Native values and principles;
> - validation of Alaska Native knowledge and ways of knowing;
> - use of Alaska Native facilitators and resource elders; and
> - personal growth as well as professional development. (MacLean 1998: 58)

The program operated from the Interior Campus of the University of Alaska Fairbanks, but a Coordinating Council of Alaska Native representatives and representatives of other branches of the University of Alaska collaborated in the governance of the program. MacLean served as a staff member of the program from 1991 to 1993 and based his doctoral dissertation on his observations, but the program continued to operate through the 1990s.

Alaska Native Science Commission

In the mid-1990s, the Alaska Native Science Commission (ANSC) was established to provide a forum for cooperation and collaboration between Alaska Natives and scientists. The Alaska Federation of Natives and the National Science Foundation provided initial sponsorship. The ANSC and the Institute of Social and Economic Research at the University of Alaska Anchorage, received a three-year grant from the Environmental Protection Agency for a project: "Alaska Natives have many concerns about radionuclides and other types of contamination. They are constantly reminded about the close proximity of the former Soviet Union and the potential for trans-boundary migration of radionuclides from this area" (Arctic Research Consortium of the United States 1998: 20).

The project aimed to use traditional practices to gather traditional knowledge about radionuclide concerns. Regional meetings were planned for the first year to document observations of changes in the environment as well as concerns, understandings, and questions. The second year would continue the series of regional meetings and would include a synthesis. Native elders, hunters, gatherers, scientists, and resource managers met to discuss and map observations of changes in their environment and document other issues of concern to their communities (Arctic Research Consortium of the United States 1998).

SUMMARY

Although there are many ways to define *collaboration*, for our purposes collaborative programs are programs in which an outside expert and members of an indigenous community collaborate by sharing responsibility and authority. Collaborative programs can emphasize research or development goals but are usually based on the intention to bring about empowerment, change, or innovation. Existing programs in education, health, social services, or economic development, administered under the sole authority of government agencies in the past, can become collaborative when the opportunity is provided for participants to share responsibility and authority.

The days are probably over—at least in North America, Australia, and New Zealand—when researchers could prepare proposals, obtain funding, and arrive in indigenous communities to study for their own reasons. Indigenous people have developed their own approaches to research, and most of them expect that proposals for programs will be developed in consultation with representatives of the communities. Collaborative programs have the underlying assumption that indigenous people will be empowered through their participation in the programs.

Publications describing collaborative programs have identified some of the many problems and pitfalls that can beset such programs. Watahomigie and Yamamoto (1987) note that researchers sometimes have to delay publication of research findings for substantial periods of time in order to achieve the applied goals of collaborative programs. Stull, Schultz, and Cadue (1987) note the difficulties that arise because of shifting government policies and funding as well as the problems that conflicts between factions in indigenous communities can create. Gibson's (1985) experience demonstrates that, unless a program has a very small number of participants, it simply is not feasible for all participants to share equally in decision making. Administration of funding can create problems, too. Delgado-Gaitan (1990) did not encounter the same problems that Gibson did, in part because she did not try to share decision-making authority with all participants. She tried to actively involve all the participants in the research process, but that was not the same as sharing decision-making authority. Although she does not say so explicitly, apparently her university administered the funding associated with the program.

LeCompte's (1995: 107) statement of her personal position as a collaborative researcher (to be one among equals, to set aside her own agenda, to give other participants the opportunity to tell the story) has implications for other fieldworkers to consider as well. One might wonder whether LeCompte's position would be appropriate for all collaborative fieldworkers in indigenous communities.

The foregoing review suggests that guidelines might be postulated regarding the individual positions of fieldworkers and the design of collaborative programs in indigenous communities. Tentative guidelines might begin thus:

- Fieldworkers need to be flexible because program goals may change as programs develop.
- Fieldworkers must be willing to collaborate by sharing authority, responsibility, and credit for success.
- A successful program must have sources of adequate and dependable funding.
- A successful program must have adequate support from the local community.
- A successful program is based on a plan including statements of roles and responsibilities, with special attention to the administration of funding.

In the next two chapters, we continue to examine issues regarding individual fieldworkers and the design of programs while considering whether it is useful to build on the notion of guidelines.

Chapter Three

Collaborative Fieldworkers

Every view is a way of seeing, not *the* way.

—Harry F. Wolcott

Harry F. Wolcott describes the development of the perceived dichotomy between the "insider's" view and the "outsider's" view in anthropology (1999: 136–56). In portrayals of indigenous peoples, anthropologists have traditionally presented the indigenous story in terms of the perspective of the outside observer. Some, however, have made deliberate efforts to "convey how things look to those 'inside'" (Wolcott 1999: 137). In other words, they have attempted to present the story of a native people from the native standpoint.

Researchers in other disciplines have used the terms *insider* and *outsider* to mean researchers who have come from a particular community as opposed to those who have come from outside the community. (These latter definitions of *insider* and *outsider* are probably the ones used most often by indigenous peoples.) In his presidential address to the American Educational Research Association in 1998, James A. Banks, an African American, offered his observations about the various contributions that have been made by researchers from inside minority communities and by those from outside minority communities (1998). Banks refers to "indigenous" researchers, but he intends this term to apply to researchers working in the communities where they were raised and where they acquired their first cultural orientation. So when Banks refers to "indigenous researchers," researchers who are indigenous people would be included in his definition, but his definition would also include researchers from other groups who are working in their home communities. His examples include Kenneth B. Clark and John Hope Franklin, African Americans whose life work concentrated on African American history and community in the United States.

Banks's opinion is that the insider–outsider dichotomy is not an accurate representation of types of researchers. He builds on the insider–outsider classification proposed by Robert K. Merton (1972) to develop a set of four ideal types of researchers. These types are the indigenous insider, the indigenous outsider, the external insider, and the external outsider. He notes that most researchers will fit into more than one of these types over the duration of their careers. The types he proposes are described in table 3.1.

Banks points out that very few researchers can expect to focus entire careers of twenty or thirty years on one community and that, for those who do, the community is likely to change during that time: "Depending on the situations and contexts, we are all both insiders and outsiders (Merton, 1972). Also, a researcher's insider-outsider status may change over the course of a lifetime, either because the institutionalized knowledge and paradigms within

Table 3.1. A Typology of Cross-Cultural Researchers

Type of Research	Description
The indigenous insider	This individual endorses the unique values, perspectives, behaviors, beliefs, and knowledge of his or her indigenous community and culture and is perceived by people within the community as a legitimate community member who can speak with authority about it.
The indigenous outsider	This individual was socialized within his or her indigenous community but has experienced high levels of cultural assimilation into an outsider or oppositional culture. The values, beliefs, perspectives, and knowledge of this individual are identical to those of the outside community. The indigenous outsider is perceived by indigenous people in the community as an outsider.
The external insider	This individual was socialized within another culture and acquired its beliefs, values, behaviors, attitudes, and knowledge. However, because of his or her unique experiences, the individual rejects many of the values, beliefs, and knowledge claims within his or her indigenous community and endorses those of the studied community. The external insider is viewed by the new community as an "adopted" insider.
The external outsider	The external outsider is socialized within a community different from the one in which he or she is doing research. The external outsider has a partial understanding of and little appreciation for the values, perspectives, and knowledge of the community he or she is studying and consequently often misunderstands and misinterprets the behaviors within the studied community.

Source: Banks 1998: 8.

the studied community change or because the researcher's value commitments are significantly modified" (1998: 7). Banks believes that each researcher will, at one time or another, fit into each of the categories he developed: "Each social science and educational researcher is, depending on the context and situation, likely to function at some point as an indigenous-insider, an indigenous-outsider, an external-insider, and an external-outsider" (1998: 15).

INDIGENOUS RESEARCH

There are now many representatives of indigenous groups who are acquiring research skills and qualifications and are conducting research in indigenous communities. Most researchers work in several communities during their careers, and indigenous researchers can be expected to follow that pattern as well. Indigenous North American educators and academics have made regular visits to New Zealand and Australia, while their Maori and Aboriginal counterparts have often visited North America. The University of Waikato in New Zealand, the University of South Australia, and Northern Arizona University in the United States have conducted exchanges of indigenous teaching staff. Indigenous university staff in these countries and Canada have conducted overseas research while on sabbatical leave and have presented research papers at international conferences in countries other than their own.

Members of indigenous groups can be effective researchers in communities outside their home communities, and they can be considered outsiders in these new situations. Beatrice Medicine, for example, provides the following anecdote to illustrate her status as an outsider in a Pueblo community, even though she is from another Native American tribe: "An elder of the sacred and secret realm always spoke to me in his native language, as he held my hand and put a turquoise ring on my finger during each visit to his home. Later, I saw him in his trader role in the southwestern city and heard him converse in excellent English. I rushed home to tell my son's father, 'Mr. Z speaks English!' Little did I realize that I was being tested. Was I native or white-oriented? Was I informer or friend?" (1978: 185). Linda Mead describes her feelings of being both insider and outsider in her research with Maori women that she knew. She set out to interview a group of Maori women whose children attended the same Maori-language immersion preschool attended by her daughter. The academic literature did not prepare her for the issues she confronted because she was not working cross-culturally. However, she discovered that she "was, at three levels at least, an 'insider,' as a *Maori*, as a woman and as a mother, and at another set of levels, an 'outsider,' as a postgraduate

student, as someone from a different tribe, as an older mother and as someone who actually had a partner" (1996: 197–98). In a later publication (Smith
1999: 137–38),[1] she describes the way the women she interviewed used signs
and comments to acknowledge her "outsider" status as a researcher even
though she had been well known to them before the research began.

Indigenous researchers bring unique strengths, perspectives, and philosophies to research among their own people. For many generations, most published research on indigenous communities was limited to viewpoints and
perspectives of nonindigenous researchers, but the perspectives of the indigenous people themselves can provide new insights and dimensions. Let
me illustrate with some examples. Karen Swisher (1986), by her own account
"an enrolled tribal member," describes the authenticity that she, as an indigenous researcher, brought to work on her own reservation. Oscar Kawagley,
who is Yupiaq, has conducted research in Alaskan communities in the same
region where he grew up: "It has been my intent to participate in and observe
life in a Yupiaq Eskimo community and fish camp to identify the varied ways
in which people incorporate traditional and Western knowledge in their daily
lives and determine how they have been able to reconcile the seemingly anti-
thetical values reflected in each" (1995: 142).

Kawagley has found that he needs both Yupiaq and Western modes of inquiry to understand the situation he was studying:

> The Yupiaq word *tangruarluku*, which means "to see with the mind's eye," tran-
> scends that which we can perceive with our endosomatic sense makers and illustrates
> how a Native perspective may provide a way of bridging the so-called mythical sub-
> jective world and the objective scientific world. To give credence to the range of
> phenomena that will need to be addressed from both the Yupiaq and Western per-
> spectives, it is necessary, therefore, that both modes of inquiry and sense making be
> incorporated. (1995: 145)

Kawagley has also found that he relies on the styles of inquiry among his people in his study: "In retrospect, I see that I relied heavily on the traditional Yupiaq method of research—that is, patient observation through participation
over a long period of time, reflection on things that I saw and heard, and, un-
obtrusively, informally checking out my tentative conclusions with villagers"
(1995: 156–57).

In New Zealand, Maori researchers have published a portion of the discourse that has taken place within their research community about the development of "*kaupapa* Maori" research. The term *kaupapa* can have several
meanings including philosophy, perspective, plan, and agenda. The simplest
definition for *kaupapa Maori* is something—an educational program or project, for example—based on a Maori belief system and principles of Maori social organization. However, Maori researchers have linked the term *kaupapa*

Maori to international literature on critical theory, and their discussions have expanded the meaning well beyond the simple definition given above.

Russell Bishop describes some of the elements that define kaupapa Maori: "Kaupapa Maori presupposes positions that are committed to a critical analysis of the existing unequal power relations within our society. These include rejection of hegemonic belittling 'Maori can't cope' stances, simplification and commodification of Maori intellectual property and the development of a social pathology analysis of Maori under-achievement" (1996: 12–13). Kaupapa Maori is, according to Bishop, "a discourse that has emerged and is legitimated from within the Maori community because it is based on historical precedence of culturally constituted validation processes" (1996: 13).

Bishop is among many who believe that kaupapa Maori research must be conducted in culturally appropriate ways and that it must advance Maori self-determination. However, he believes that non-Maori researchers have obligations to support kaupapa Maori research: "The call for self-determination is often misunderstood by non-Maori people. It is not a call for separatism, nor is it a call for non-Maori people to stand back and leave Maori alone. It is a call for Maori and non-Maori alike, to reposition themselves in relation to the aspirations of Maori people for an autonomous voice" (1996: 16). Power and control, however, must rest within Maori cultural understandings and practices:

> Non-Maori people should be involved in Maori research for two reasons. The first reason is that there is a cohort of highly-skilled, professionally-trained non-Maori who are becoming bicultural and are willing to work within Maori-controlled contexts. . . .
>
> The second reason why non-Maori should be involved in this area of research is simply that for Pakeha researchers to leave it all to Maori people is to abrogate their responsibilities as Treaty partners. (Bishop 1996: 17–18)

Bishop summarizes his discussion on kaupapa Maori research as follows:

> Therefore, Kaupapa Maori challenges the dominance of traditional, individualistic research which primarily, at least in its present form, benefits the researchers and their kaupapa. In contrast, Kaupapa Maori research is collectivistic and is oriented toward benefiting all the research participants and their collectively determined agendas—defining and acknowledging Maori aspirations for research, whilst developing and implementing Maori theoretical and methodological preferences and practices for research. (1996: 19)

Bishop also argues that collaborative research is particularly well suited to research among Maori. One could translate the term *whakawhanaungatanga*, which is included in the title of his 1996 book, to mean "making or building family-like relationships." One of the main points of his work is that Maori researchers will begin their research with others by establishing family-like relationships with participants. Non-Maori who want to be effective researchers working with Maori would do well to follow that example by establishing family-like relationships at the beginning of their research.

Linda Mead, in her chapter on kaupapa Maori research, summarizes the writings of other Maori researchers on the topic, including Irwin, Pihama, Bishop, and Smith: "From these comments it is clear that under the rubric of *Kaupapa Maori* research, there are different sets of ideas and issues being claimed as important. . . . Some of these features are framed as assumptions, some as practices and methods, and some are related to *Maori* conceptions of knowledge" (1996: 200). She noted that Maori have been linking their research to the international discourse on critical theory:

> Most discussion about *Kaupapa Maori* is also located in relation to critical theory, in particular to the notions of critique, resistance, struggle and emancipation. . . .
>
> The notion of strategic positioning as a deliberate practice is partially an attempt to contain the unevenness and unpredictability, under stress, of people engaged in emancipatory struggles. The broader *kaupapa* of *Kaupapa Maori* embraces that sense of strategic positioning, of being able to plan, predict and contain, across a number of sites, the engagement in struggle. (1996: 201–02)

She summarized her conclusions by saying: "In other words, there is more to *Kaupapa Maori* than our history under colonialism or our desires to restore *rangatiratanga*. We have a different epistemological tradition which frames the way we see the world, the way we organise ourselves in it, the questions we ask and the solutions which we seek. It is larger than the individuals in it and the specific 'moment' in which we are currently living" (1996: 204).

Linda Mead accepted that there may be circumstances where non-Maori researchers have appropriate places in kaupapa Maori research:

> *Kaupapa Maori* research, as currently framed, would argue that being *Maori* is an essential criteria for carrying out Kaupapa Maori research. At the same time, however, some writers suggest that we exercise restraint in becoming too involved in identity politics because of the potential these politics have for paralysing development. This position is based on the specificities of our history and our politics. However, this does not preclude those who are not *Maori* from participating in research which has a *Kaupapa Maori* orientation. (1996: 202–03)

However, in her later publication, she notes that there are more radical interpretations that might define kaupapa Maori research as exclusively Maori (Smith 1999: 184).

Although Banks does not use the term *collaborative research*, he recognizes the need for cooperation between outside researchers and people from local ethnic minority communities: "External researchers need to be keenly sensitive to their research status within the studied community and to work with people indigenous to the community who can provide them with an accurate knowledge of the perspectives, values, and beliefs within the community and who can help them to acquire insider status. One way to do this is to involve indigenous community members in the study as researchers" (1998: 15). Banks noted that new challenges arise when indigenous researchers do research in their home communities:

> Researchers indigenous to a marginalized community also face important challenges. When they become professionally trained at research universities, they are likely to experience at least two important risks: (a) They may become distanced from their communities during their professional training and thus become indigenous-outsiders, or (b) They may be perceived by many members of their indigenous communities as having "sold out" to the mainstream community and thus can no longer speak for the community or have an authentic voice. (1998: 15)

Fieldworkers who are members of indigenous communities sometimes face more pressures and problems than those faced by outsiders. It may be more difficult for indigenous insiders to remain neutral in factional disputes because of lifelong links to one faction or another. Or they may have relatives and close friends in the studied community who put pressure on the fieldworker to report particular outcomes against the fieldworker's better judgment. There have been instances where indigenous graduate students have withdrawn from community-based research because of pressures such as these.

BECOMING A FIELDWORKER
IN A COLLABORATIVE PROGRAM

How do fieldworkers find places in collaborative programs in indigenous communities? In general, they are invited to participate. One way that invitations are issued is through job advertisements. Indigenous communities and funding agencies advertise through mainstream channels for people to work in the programs they sponsor. Invitations to work in collaborative programs can also be issued through personal networks. Sometimes these networks involve staff in institutions of higher education, so that students have made contacts in indigenous communities through their faculty advisers. Conferences or other events involving indigenous people can also provide a basis for developing networks, and electronic resources—e-mail lists, document banks, websites of tribal authorities and other indigenous organizations—can provide instant contact.

Fieldworkers who are particularly interested in formal research can sometimes obtain permission to develop their own research goals in collaboration with a program that will employ them. There have been occasions when re-searchers have received permission to conduct research in conjunction with employment in community-based programs. The research goals have been in-tegrated with, or added to, the program goals. One possibility for fieldworkers—particularly doctoral students—who want to conduct research in collaborative programs is to apply for jobs in collaborative programs with the stipulation that their own research goals be integrated into the work role. In this situa-tion, it is essential for the researcher to gain permission for the research from the indigenous program participants. Issues relating to the ethics of "informed consent" are considered in greater depth later in this chapter.

It is nearly impossible to design and establish collaborative programs with-out knowing the community well. Collaborative programs must be based on locally perceived needs. An agency or individual fieldworker with a new the-oretical framework should proceed with caution insofar as attempting to ap-ply that framework in a wide range of unknown settings. Success is far more likely when the rationale for a program is developed in collaboration with lo-cal communities.

THE INDIVIDUAL FIELDWORKER

LeCompte and associates (1999: 26–44) have analyzed situations in which gender, age, physical characteristics, and dress have influenced community reaction to ethnographers. Several other authors have commented generally on the importance of the attitudes and actions of the individual fieldworker, but they have also noted the difficulties in defining the specific attributes that lead to success. In an e-mail list exchange, for example, several anthropolo-gists discussed the success or lack of success of volunteers in Pacific Island communities. One pointed out that it is hard to know who will do well, and another noted that success was unrelated to the intentions of the individual: "Just because folks wanted to help did not mean that they could do so."

More than thirty years ago, Ward Goodenough stated that there was wide-spread agreement that "supervised practical experience with underdeveloped communities" should be a requirement for training development workers (1963: 28). Some programs for volunteers such as the Peace Corps have pro-vided this type of supervision, but there have been many instances in which fieldworkers have entered culturally different communities without appropri-ate training or supervision. Students, teachers, health workers, program de-velopers, people in volunteer programs, and novice researchers all enter in-digenous communities to work, and they should have training for their specific situations. At the same time, there is agreement in the literature that fieldworkers need certain attributes that cannot necessarily be taught in short-term training or orientation programs. Goodenough believed that five attributes were worthy of mention:

1. *Technical Skill.* The expert has to be more flexible and creative in the application of his skills in development work overseas than in their routine application at home.
2. *Belief in Mission.* The development worker overseas has to have enough commitment and enthusiasm to work effectively without close supervision from above and in the face of manifold social pressures to slacken his efforts.
3. *Cultural Empathy.* The development worker must have the capacity to look at different cultures with interest, and respect is obviously essential.
4. *A Sense of Politics.* The development worker must be sensitive to the local political climate and be able to discover and reckon with political currents and cross-currents.
5. *Organization Ability.* The technical expert's job is less one of directly practicing his skill in building bridges, growing crops, healing the sick than it is one of developing local organizations that can do these things effectively; and this requires the capacity to develop viable organizations within the framework of the local social system. (Cleveland, Mangone, and Adams 1960: 123ff., quoted in Goodenough 1963: 377)

Goodenough has also offered his own opinion about the attitude that is necessary for workers in cross-cultural situations: "Basically, the attitude of mind we speak of is an agent's willingness to accept other people generally as fellow human beings, as entitled to the same respect for their wants, beliefs, felt needs, customs, values, and sense of personal worth, as he expects for his" (1963: 378). Meanwhile, Allan Kaplan's opinion of the individual characteristics necessary for development workers is somewhat different: "The art of facilitation demands acute powers of observation and the ability to self-reflect honestly on interventions. . . . Ultimately, practitioners' primary resources are their own inner resourcefulness and personal integrity" (1996: 120).

Rivera and Erlich have provided guidelines for community organizing, one type of collaborative endeavor whereby outside experts and local communities work together. They have provided an "organizer's profile," a summary of qualities that they believe are important for the success of organizers. They explain that it would be unrealistic to expect any individual to demonstrate all the desirable qualities in the profile:

Realistically, it is more a set of goals to be used by organizers and communities together to help achieve desired changes. . . .

1. Similar cultural and racial identification.
2. Familiarity with customs and traditions, social networks, and values.

   3. An intimate knowledge of language and subgroup slang.
   4. Leadership styles and development.
   5. A conceptual framework for political and economic analysis.
   6. Knowledge of past organizing strategies, their strengths and limitations.
   7. Skills in conscientization and empowerment.
   8. Skills in assessing community psychology.
   9. Knowledge of organizational behavior and decision making.
   10. Skills in evaluative and participatory research. One of the reasons that communities of color have lost some of their political, economic, and legal battles is the increasing vacuum created by the lack of supportive information. . . .
   11. Skills in program planning and development and administration management.
   12. An awareness of self and of personal strengths and limitations. (Rivera and Erlich 1998: 11–17)

Finally, Wolcott has observed that areas of social behavior may be important for successful fieldworkers:

> How researchers move their bodies around is not what makes art out of fieldwork. Nevertheless, one can offer suggestions as to how to move about with sufficient grace as to be perceived graciously by those with whom we hope to interact. . . . I regard them collectively as no more than the demonstration of everyday courtesy and common sense.
>
> 1. *Gaining entree and maintaining rapport*. . . . Maintaining rapport presents a continuing challenge through the very presence of an intrusive and inquiring observer forever wanting to know more and to understand better. . . .
> 2. *Reciprocity*. . . . On the other hand, a request for food, money, medical assistance, or a job can put a resident fieldworker in an awkward bind, damned if you do, damned if you don't. In the abstract, a firm policy seems advisable ("Sorry, I just don't loan money—to anyone."), but in the world of diplomacy, everything remains negotiable, and fieldwork requires the art of diplomacy. One seeks knowledge in the professional role of researcher but prays for wisdom in the personal roles that make it possible.
> 3. *A tolerance for ambiguity*. Another admonition that becomes trite in the saying but essential in the doing is the need to remain as adaptable as one is humanly capable of being, to exhibit a "tolerance for ambiguity. . . ."
> 4. *Personal determination coupled with faith in oneself*. Self-doubt must be held in check so that you can go about your business of conducting research, even when you may not always be sure what that entails. (1995: 90–95)

CHARACTERISTICS OF EFFECTIVE FIELDWORKERS

Good intentions are not enough to guarantee success. There have been many situations in which well-intentioned outside experts have failed by performing ineffectually or by leaving the community before completing the project. In the worst-case scenario, the outside expert's actions have resulted in turmoil or conflict that has been detrimental to the project or community.

The experts who have identified characteristics for success have described attributes that are difficult to define, assess, or measure in any objective way. Most of them refer to attributes covered by terms such as *flexibility*, *adaptability*, *resourcefulness*, or *tolerance for ambiguity*. Because attributes that can be grouped under the term *flexibility* are mentioned so often in the literature, the first of four guidelines that I believe are essential for the success of individual fieldworkers is based on this attribute. I developed these four guidelines from the literature and from my personal experiences in field settings over a twenty-year period. The topics are intended primarily for discussion among potential fieldworkers, teachers of fieldworkers, and indigenous communities. Novice fieldworkers may want to consider these guidelines in terms of self-assessment, considering each of the questions in terms of their abilities. Indigenous communities may be able to use these guidelines as they interview or select fieldworkers who will work in their communities. There are no objective ways to forecast the way that fieldworkers will actually behave in terms of any of the guidelines, but the guidelines themselves can serve as useful points for discussion in the selection process. The guidelines for fieldworkers are the following:

1. Be flexible but recognize that everyone has limits.
2. Be willing to collaborate by sharing authority, responsibility, and credit for success.
3. Give thoughtful attention to the ethical implications of your actions.
4. Apply the concept of culture in everyday working relationships.

Although these guidelines may seem straightforward, their apparent simplicity can be misleading. Living in accordance with these guidelines can be more complicated than might be imagined at first glance.

Be Flexible but Recognize That Everyone Has Limits

Although it may seem obvious that fieldworkers need to adapt to indigenous settings, this point has not always been obvious to everyone. In the process of colonization, Europeans and their descendants often tried to re-create European social settings and environments in the colonies. Plants, animals, and birds were transported to the colonies along with furniture, clothing, tools, artwork, and other European accoutrements of life. Schools, churches, and political systems were established based on European models, and European languages came to dominate.

In the closing years of the twentieth century, there was still a tendency for the descendants of European colonists to see their way of life as superior to the ways of those of indigenous peoples. Mainstream professionals often entered indigenous communities with ideas about the best ways to live in any environment and about what they and their programs should accomplish. The programs described in this book illustrate that fieldworkers in indigenous communities may have to adapt to different styles of housing, food, clothing, transportation, communication (including differences in English dialect), modern conveniences, entertainment, jokes, protocol, alcohol use, spirituality, and relationships between genders and between old and young. Sometimes the seemingly trivial things are the hardest to change, even when one has the best intentions. James Michener's *Hawaii* includes an excellent example of the unwillingness of nineteenth-century missionaries to adapt to new settings. In spite of the warm temperatures in the new climate, the missionaries continued to wear the woolen clothes they brought with them from New England (Michener 1960: 288).

In most instances, adapting to a new setting means depending on local people for knowledge about how to adapt. Fieldworkers in new settings often feel like they are asking constant questions about the society, culture, and environment just so they can manage the day-to-day aspects of life in the new community. Sometimes, too, one has to ask for something material from local people. Without local help, fieldworkers may find it impossible to live in the new setting. In the early stages, a professional person can feel helpless, dependent, and childlike (see Bowen 1964, for example). These are difficult emotions for people with university degrees who are used to feeling that they are in control of their environment. The best approach, however, is to recognize and acknowledge one's dependence on local people for assistance and to keep asking for assistance when it is needed.

Changes in the policies of institutions and in the expectations of local people also require flexibility from fieldworkers. Funding agencies are likely to make frequent changes in their policies because they operate in changing political contexts and because of politics internal to their organizations. Local people are also likely to change their expectations because of changing political contexts and because of internal politics. Professionals whose success depends on the policies of funding agencies and on the expectations of local communities can find frequent changes frustrating. However, the best approach is to accept the changes as they occur and to adapt as quickly and calmly as possible.

A third aspect of adaptation has been termed a "tolerance for ambiguity." Ray Barnhardt was among the first to write about the need for fieldworkers to develop this attribute. He explains the concept as follows:

> We also have learned that the single most important characteristic that program personnel must possess, if such an approach is to succeed, is a high tolerance for ambiguity. Many persons find it difficult to cope with uncertainty and to proceed with little more than intuition and instinct as guides. They seek structure or closure on a matter prematurely, thus reducing the opportunity for flexibility and adaptability. Under contemporary pressures for accountability and related demands for the delineation of specific objectives and the development of flow charts in pursuit of explicit end products, it is indeed difficult to survive on a creed that declares, "We will know where we are going when we get there." (1977: 94–95)

Steve Grubis, a faculty member at the University of Alaska Fairbanks, made the phrase a slogan among rural Alaskan teachers in the 1980s. Later, Wolcott (1995: 92–94) introduced the idea to a broader audience of fieldworkers. Wolcott defines it as "the need to remain as adaptable as one is humanly capable of being" (1995: 92). "Fieldworkers," he says, "would hardly go wrong to take 'tolerance for ambiguity' as their professional mantra if it is not by nature a personal one" (1995: 92).

In his novel *Walden Two*, B. F. Skinner describes another individual characteristic that should interest fieldworkers. Skinner describes this characteristic as a desirable one—something that children should be taught so that they will be successful as adults. He advocates fortifying individuals against discouragement by building perseverance (1948: 124). Fieldworkers can find it useful to remember that failures and discouragement are inevitable and that, therefore, a tolerance for discouragement is a quality to be highly desired, particularly in a field setting.

Someone who is working in a community different from his or her own is likely to feel a sense of frustration when things do not go according to plan. In my own case, I have experienced recurrent frustrations over differences in interpretations about time and punctuality. I know that there are differences in the way different groups of people conceptualize time, but I have never been able to adjust my behavior accordingly. I am compulsively punctual—and therefore I often find myself waiting impatiently and with frustration for others. However, that has not kept me from making appointments or agreeing to meet with community people at particular times and in particular places. My punctuality has become something of a joke in the Maori community where I have been working for the past decade, but everyone has graciously recognized my limitations.

Flexibility is an ideal attribute, but no one is totally flexible. By the time one is an adult, one has acquired certain characteristics that are extremely difficult, and perhaps impossible, to change. Food preferences are an example. One anthropologist described in an e-mail discussion what happened when he was served food he was not accustomed to:

Date: Wed, 7 Apr 1999
Sender: Oceanic Anthropology Discussion Group
From: Robert Levy
Subject: On the unique bond between humans and animals In Polynesia dogs were traditionally food animals. In my day in a Tahitian village they still were. (And I suspect they still are in more remote islands.) One evening the family I lived with served up one of the familiar household dogs for supper. They offered to serve me fish as "Europeans" (popa'a) don't eat dog. "I can eat whatever you can" I bragged. In fact—to my surprise—I couldn't physically swallow my portion much to their amusement. It literally stuck in my throat—my unique bond and theirs were rather different. Bob Levy

Once again, the best approach is to recognize one's limitations with respect to flexibility and adaptation. Most people will understand one's inability to adapt to certain aspects of life in their communities if one has demonstrated a sincere interest in adapting whenever one can. Note the willingness of the host family in the example above to accommodate the limitations of the anthropologist by serving fish to him.

The next step is to consider the specific group or community in which the program is to take place. It is much easier to begin in a compatible setting rather than struggling to adapt oneself to an incompatible setting or trying to change the setting to suit the individual. This is especially true if the fieldworker plans to work in a collaborative program because collaboration means working with the people of the local community to accomplish commonly agreed on goals. If the fieldworker does not have a sense of values shared with the community, it will be difficult to make a commitment to program goals, and collaborative work will be almost impossible to sustain for any length of time.

Fieldworkers also need to consider the physical setting, finding it at least tolerable if they are to live there. How are the climate and living facilities? How much difference does it make to the individual to have access to running water and bathing facilities, for example? Does the environment demand any special state of health, physical strength, or ability? If the fieldworker has a special health problem, are resources to deal with that problem available? What about food preferences? Are favorite foods available? If canned foods will necessarily form the basis of the fieldworker's diet, is that important? What about access to and communication with friends and family outside the community? What kind of assistance is needed in order to thrive in the environment, and who will provide it?

Hopefully, anyone considering work in an indigenous community will begin with a sense of respect for the values of other people. However, even the fieldworker with the best intentions may eventually find that his or her personal values are in conflict with those of the community. In one example, anthropologist Jean Briggs (1970) has described her life with an Eskimo family in Canada. She maintained satisfactory relationships with the group for many months, but when she let out an angry outburst intended to defend the group against outsiders, relationships disintegrated and so did her fieldwork. Expressions of anger were not acceptable to the members of this indigenous group under any circumstances.

No adult can set aside entirely his or her personal values, and if those values are in conflict with the dominant values of the community where he or she lives and works, unhappiness is certain to result. Two dimensions of community attitudes and values can be used as examples of the kinds of difficulties that have arisen on many occasions in the past. The first is the community's attitude toward sex outside of marriage. The second is the community's attitude toward alcoholic beverages.

In urban areas, it is possible for individuals to maintain private lives that are quite separate from their work lives. People feel they are entitled to privacy, and they can easily maintain anonymity in many dimensions of life. Many feel that their sex lives are their own business and should not be the concern of anyone in their places of work. In small communities, things may be quite different. There may be little privacy and no anonymity. And there may be ways in which people who deviate from dominant attitudes and values in the community are either brought into line or expelled.

If the dominant attitude in the community is one of disapproval of sex outside of marriage, outsiders can easily find themselves in deep trouble if they disregard the dominant attitude. Fieldworkers may be expected to be faithfully married or celibate for the extent of their residence in an indigenous community. All sorts of turmoil can result if an outsider is unwilling to adhere to the community norm. For example, there have been situations in which a local school board insisted that a teacher leave the job and the village because the teacher did not conform to local norms with respect to sex outside of marriage. Any single fieldworker who is not comfortable with celibacy in a community where celibacy is expected is better off finding work elsewhere.

People from the mainstream can also find themselves in communities where it appears that there is a much higher tolerance of sex outside of marriage than in mainstream society. Again, problems can result when the new resident enters into relationships without understanding all the implications of such relationships in that particular community (Goodenough 1963: 468–71). Turmoil and a sudden termination of work in the community can be the result.

Other examples of common problems come from differences in attitudes toward alcohol. Many of Alaska's villages are "dry"—no alcohol is permitted. There have been instances in which village officials searched people disembarking from airplanes to be certain that they carried no alcohol. Sometimes, nonnatives visiting these villages have strenuously objected to this process, seeing it as an infringement of individual rights. There have been other occasions when people from a local community as well as visitors have been asked to leave villages when the local rules for alcohol use have been broken. Someone who insists on drinking, or who cannot conform to local rules in this situation, should look for work in a setting where the use of alcohol is acceptable. On the other hand, there have been instances where the norm for alcohol consumption has been so high that professional visitors have had difficulty coping.

Another area of potential conflict between fieldworkers and local indigenous communities is in the values that each group holds regarding gender roles. My attention was first drawn to this issue in the late 1970s when I was a doctoral student. There were feminists at the university who insisted that male dominance was universal. They believed that, in every society, men held greater power and authority than women. However, there are women anthropologists who have published alternative viewpoints. Beverly Chinas (1973) describes the way that Zapotec women controlled economic resources, and Carolyn Matthiasson (1974) edited a book in which societies are classified as "manipulative," "complementary," and "ascendant" according to the general nature of the relationships between men and women within the societies. Complementary societies are societies in which men and women have roles defined by gender, but men have responsibility and authority in certain aspects of life, while women have responsibility and authority in complementary aspects of life. Jean Briggs (1974) describes sex role relationships among Eskimo groups in the Canadian Arctic as complementary. Based on my experience in Yup'ik Eskimo communities, I prepared a paper taking the position that gender roles in Yup'ik communities are also complementary (Harrison 1982).

In the years since that paper was written, indigenous women have been publishing their own viewpoints on gender roles. Linda Smith has summarized the work of black women and other "women with labels":

> These groups of women challenged the assumptions of the Western/white women's
> movement that all women shared some universal characteristics and suffered from

universal oppressions which could be understood and described by a group of predominantly white, Western-trained women academics

There are interlocking relationships between race, gender and class which
makes oppression a complex sociological and psychological condition. Many
have argued that this condition cannot be understood or analysed by outsiders or
people who have not experienced, and who have not been born into, this way of
life. (1999: 166–67)

A recurrent theme in the writing of indigenous women is the damage that
was done to women and to indigenous gender roles in the process of colonization. Chiste, for example, states, "First, far from rejecting traditional gender roles in their societies, aboriginal women have repeatedly called for a return to traditional ways and the respect with which they once were held in
their communities. Testimony before the ongoing Royal Commission has
been particularly eloquent in this regard" (1999: 76).

Educated indigenous women in the United States, Canada, New Zealand,
and Australia have demonstrated their awareness of feminist discourse, and
they have formulated their own responses. Formal organizations of indigenous women have been established in all four countries and have asked governments and the general public to support the goals that they have established. Indigenous women expect others to accept their judgments and values
with respect to gender roles in their communities. Medicine has set an example of the kind of acceptance that has sometimes been required of fieldworkers: "Being a native female delineated areas of investigation which were
closed to me. This was aggravated by my prolonged infertility. Conversation
or gossip about such matters as deviant sexual practices, abortions, and preg-
nancy taboos was immediately terminated when I appeared at female gatherings. It was only after ten years of marriage and producing a male child (!)
that I was included in 'womanly' spheres" (1978: 186).

There are situations in indigenous communities in which women accept,
and even support, complementary and well-defined roles for work, responsibility, and authority based on gender. The best guides to what is or is not
working in a particular setting are the opinions of the women of the local
community. A fieldworker who cannot accept this viewpoint should use great
care in choosing an indigenous community in which to work, for uninvited
intervention can quickly sour relationships with the people the fieldworker
needs to collaborate with. Gender roles can provoke emotional discussion,
and there have been problems when well-intentioned outsiders have attempted to intervene. I know of one occasion when a faculty member offered
a course on women's studies in a field-based program in Alaska. All the
Alaska Native students quickly dropped out. They felt that the instructor did
not know anything about gender relationships in their communities. They felt
that she was trying to impose her viewpoints on them. Unless a fieldworker

is an expert on the particular relationships of the people concerned and has been invited to comment, the consequences of intervention can be disastrous.

If a fieldworker is invited to comment or to offer opinions, that is a different matter. There may be situations in which outside experts are invited to do just that. The critical factor in whether or not to offer opinions is the presence or absence of an invitation to speak from local people.

Any number of considerations, values, and issues can make a setting compatible or incompatible for any given fieldworker, and many of these issues are complex. I have included discussions of sex outside of marriage, alcohol, and gender roles because I know of situations in which values regarding these issues have caused irreconcilable conflicts, but these issues do not exhaust the list of potential differences. Short visits to a community are not likely to reveal much about either the physical environment or community values. Every society has ideals for behavior, but actual behavior does not necessarily match the ideals. Only over time is the visitor likely to learn where the discrepancies are. A short visit to a community can provide some indication of potential problems and is well worth the effort for someone considering a move to a new setting, but a short visit will not ensure a successful experience.

There are no pat solutions for dealing with all the complexities. I can only offer a suggestion about the wisest approach for someone about to enter a new setting for the first time. Make your best effort to learn about the community. Evaluate your own feelings and adaptability. Ask for opinions and advice from the people you will be working with. Do not attempt interventions unless you know the situation well and have been invited to intervene.

Be Willing to Collaborate by Sharing Authority, Responsibility, and Credit for Success

It should be self-evident that someone working in a collaborative program should have a positive attitude toward collaboration, but "attitude" can be a fuzzy notion unless there are responses to specific questions. Can the professional person from outside the community share with or even relinquish to people from the local community power, decision-making authority, and credit for work accomplished? Can she or he respect opinions and viewpoints of the community and adapt behavior accordingly? If the answers to these questions are yes, a successful relationship may develop. If the answers are no, the professional should not seek a collaborative setting.

It is not always easy to accept decisions made by members of the local community. I have often given advice regarding educational programs that has been ignored, and I have sometimes found it difficult to proceed with work in a program when I felt that things were moving in the wrong direction. Sometimes the consequences of a decision have been difficult to live with. For example, on one occasion I agreed to have a locally operated printer print a paper that represented an entire year's research effort for me and for other program participants from the local community. It was not quite a disaster, but it would have been a good deal easier and the paper would have been printed a good deal faster, with better quality and less grief, if we had given it to a reputable commercial printer to produce. On another occasion, I told trustees in one program that I believed the manager was diverting small amounts of program funding to his own uses and recommended an investigation. The trustees did not respond, and a few months later they discovered that the manager had absconded with a fairly large sum. Although I was certain that there was a problem, I could do no more than offer advice.

I have learned over time that collaboration does not mean suspending my own judgment about the best ways to proceed. Sharing power with others in the program does not mean that the fieldworker becomes powerless. If the local community did not want professional judgments and opinions, it would not have invited the fieldworker to participate in the program. It would be a waste of participatory effort to have a professional person there and not ask what the professional's judgments and opinions are. Collaboration means discussion between the parties with all opinions—including those of the fieldworker—given respectful consideration and with consensual decision making as the ideal. At the same time, some individuals must be given responsibility and authority for implementing the program. Unless there is a very small number of program participants, it is unrealistic to believe that every participant can share equal responsibility and authority. Structuring of roles for responsibility and authority is discussed in greater depth in the next chapter on program design.

Give Thoughtful Attention to the Ethical Implications of Your Actions

For the first half of the twentieth century, published works by social scientists paid little attention to questions of ethics in research. However, one anthropologist attracted considerable publicity:

> As early as 1919, Franz Boaz [*sic*], in a letter to *The Nation*, challenged the deception of anthropologists who really were acting as spies for the United States government. . . . For his stand against covert research activities, he was censured by the AAA [American Anthropological Association], removed from the governing Council, threatened with expulsion from the Association itself, and pressured into resigning from the National Research Council. . . . Today, the condemnation of clandestine political research, as well as taking positions on other social and ethical issues, has become a major focus of attention in the Association. (Deyhle, Hess, and LeCompte 1992: 617)

Margaret Mead has also presented her views of the ethical position of her colleagues in anthropology in the early years of the century and notes that views on ethics change over time:

> Ethical questions revolved around the obligation, with limited equipment and limited funds, to preserve as much as each one of us could of the small scraps of old beliefs and practices that remained among acculturated, but identifiable peoples, and of the whole range of cultural behavior. . . .
>
> We also became involved in the material and psychological well-being of the peoples we studied. We were sensitive to the impact of heartless or well-meaning regulations imposed by those in power, and alert to the destructiveness of most culture contact. . . .
>
> Where we once tried to widen the general public's understanding of the culturally specific traditions of peoples who they had not learned to respect, today we are accused of stealing these same people's secrets or exposing their mysteries for our own gain. (1978: 427–28)

Anthropologists and other fieldworkers used to write under the assumption that the "subjects" would never know what was written about them, so their writings were not likely to harm them. Educators, health practitioners, agricultural experts, and others also assumed that members of their professions knew what was best for the communities in which they worked, and therefore community members were not necessarily informed about the work and its possible risks and outcomes.

When I first began fieldwork more than twenty years ago, very little attention was paid to questions of ethics. If there were university ethics policies, I was not aware of them. The American Anthropological Association had an ethics policy, but I did not hear about it until several years later. By the time I did read it, it had been revised. It was revised again in the late 1990s.

Virtually every profession involving work with people had developed a statement of professional ethics by the 1990s. Institutions of higher education with departments involved in working with people also had statements of professional ethics. Statements and additional discussion documents about professional ethics have been made available through the websites of the professional organizations and institutions. LeCompte and others (1999: 51–63) have provided a detailed description of the functions of institutional review boards as well as sample information letters and consent forms that can be used in ethnographic research (1999: 72–83). However, not every member of each profession is aware of these ethical statements, and students are sometimes left to discover them on their own.

The Principles of Informed Consent and Confidentiality.

At the end of the twentieth century, ethics policies relating to work with people usually had one central tenet shared among them. This is the principle of "informed consent." This principle states, in essence, that people must be told about the work they are participating in; they must be told about all possible risks if they participate; and they must give consent for their participation. Funding agencies and professional organizations require application of this principle in any research involving human "subjects." The principle is also applied in educational programs, health programs, agricultural programs, and the like. Funding agencies have cautioned experts working in indigenous communities to pay special attention to the rights of individuals to be well informed about the work and about possible risks associated with participating in the work. Experts are required to ask participants for consent to proceed after participants have been informed of the risks.

In some types of research, it is feasible for the researcher to ask for a signed statement of consent from each participant. If there are substantial risks involved in participation, the individual signed consent is essential. In other types of research in which the risks to individual participants are not high and it would be impractical to obtain signed consent forms from everyone who might be involved, the researcher is required to make every effort to inform and gain verbal consent from participants. This may be done through one-to-one meetings, through public meetings, by circulating written announcements, or by submitting drafts of the research or project report to individual participants for review and approval before the report is finalized. In many instances, it is possible to build into the initial agreement or research protocol the requirement for authors to provide copies of draft material to participants for review and comment. The acceptance of the draft material by participants is one way to establish their consent to publish.

Funding agencies often have specific ethics requirements for projects, and indigenous communities or larger organizations such as tribal councils may establish requirements for research in their domains. In some instances, these requirements are reflected in written agreements. Efrat and Mitchell (1974) provide examples of written agreements covering publishing, royalties, publicity, and hiring of assistants. In other situations, however, tribal organizations informally agree on their general requirements but expect to negotiate program-specific written agreements for each program involving outside experts. Written agreements for specific programs are considered in greater detail in the chapter on program design.

A second ethical principle that has been broadly applied to those working with human "subjects" relates to confidentiality. Professional organizations expect their members to respect information given to them in confidence.

Approaching Ethical Issues.

Donna L. Deyhle, G. Alfred Hess Jr., and Margaret D. LeCompte (1992) have discussed the reasons why the extensive statements of ethics of professional

organizations and educational institutions do not resolve all of the ethical issues involved in fieldwork. They summarize five different ethical positions
from the work of W. F. May (1980): the teleological, the utilitarian, the cate-
gorical imperative, critical theory and advocacy, and covenantal ethics. They
point out some of the strengths and weaknesses of the philosophical arguments associated with each position. None of the positions is so clear-cut that
it could satisfy every critic. They conclude that the ethical preferences of individuals may relate to different individual life agendas.

These authors discuss the ethical issues that arise as the result of the special relationships between qualitative researchers and the people they study.
For example, qualitative researchers are likely to establish relationships with
members of opposing groups within particular communities. One or another
among different factions may expect the researcher to support a particular position because of the relationship. But providing support may threaten the
prospects for successful outcomes for the research, and the researcher may
not be able to fulfill relational obligations and expectations.

Reciprocity between the researcher and members of the community can
also raise ethical questions. Deyhle writes that

> she taught university courses for the district's teachers and designed a drop-out study
> to assist the school district in determining who was leaving school and why. When
> tax time came, she became the tax preparer for the local Navajo. She also helped
> with college application forms, translated notes from the schools, helped repair bro-
> ken cars, transported students home to the reservation when buses were missed, and
> worked as a spokesperson between the Navajo parent organization and the school
> district. (Deyhle, Hess, and LeCompte 1992: 628)

I suspect that Deyhle's experiences are fairly typical of the experiences of researchers in indigenous communities in recent years. Several different issues
can be illustrated by this example. One issue is encompassed by the question,
How much should be given by the researcher in exchange for the community's hospitality or for information provided for the research? A researcher
with obligations to complete research objectives cannot spend all of each day
performing services for individuals or the community if the research objectives are to be achieved. Is there an obligation to a funding agency that conflicts with the need or desire to give back to those who are providing information? What are the community's cultural mores about appropriate levels of
exchange, and how are the researcher's actions interpreted within the community? What are the effects of the researcher on the host community? Can
the researcher simply withdraw services when the project ends? Does the researcher have continuing obligations to individuals or communities after the
research ends or in the researcher's home community?

It is unlikely that the ethics statements of any professional organization or institution will provide set answers to any of these questions that will apply in every situation. It is also important to remember that indigenous people have not, on the whole, been involved in the development of professional statements of ethics. Fieldworkers should know about and pay attention to the professional statements, but they would be wise to seek out additional opinions on appropriate ethical behavior from the people of the communities in which they work. At the same time, the fieldworker must keep in mind that opinions from members of the community will not resolve all of the issues either. For example, a fieldworker was once asked to help edit a paper that had been prepared in the local indigenous community. This seemed to be an ideal role for a fieldworker committed to collaborative research. He had been asked to take on what seemed like a clearly defined role in a team project designed by indigenous people. However, after several meetings of the team to review and revise drafts of the paper, the fieldworker realized that a substantial portion of the manuscript had been plagiarized. Local people justified the plagiarism by saying that their ancestors originally gave the material so they did not have to acknowledge the published work. However, the published work contained much more than the oral history interviews. History based on documentary research had formed important components of the book's contents, and the historian was the one who had done the work of bringing it all together. Although the fieldworker could understand the perspective of the locals, after much agonized soul-searching, the fieldworker made the decision to withdraw from the project. The project went ahead without his participation, and the paper was eventually published—with no apparent negative outcomes.

On the other hand, Medicine has described finding herself in a similar situation, but she did not come to the same conclusion as that reached by the fieldworker in the previous example:

> Later, while doing fieldwork on Pine Ridge reservation, I was asked to edit an elder Oglala male's collection of Lakota folktales. . . . As I congratulated him on his excellent collection, he said, "I got them from a book put out by the Bureau of American Ethnology and changed them here and there." This raised issues of ethical consideration which were unimportant at that time, but it also indicated that many native societies had access to previously published data.
>
> At the time, I was not too concerned with his approach. I had already seen anthropologists offering old clothes to natives in exchange for art objects, and I had witnessed courting behavior on the part of male anthropologists with young Indian women. On the other hand, I had seen the equally horrendous scene of a large, aggressive Lakota woman forcing a thin, young, intimidated archeologist to dance with her and buy beer in a border-town tavern. (1978: 188)

These examples demonstrate the ambiguity surrounding many ethical issues. Medicine's example implies that the context was important in determining the appropriate ethics in the given situation. Fieldworkers frequently have to struggle to decide the right course of action and whether to compromise professional or personal ethics in order to meet the expectations of others.

Margaret Mead's comments on the essence of professional ethics may be helpful when considering the types of ethical choices that fieldworkers must make: "The essence of ethics is a human group struggling with new dilemmas. . . . As anthropologists who specialize in the diverse dilemmas of culture-specific situations, we should at least be able to provide for consultation and discussion among ourselves. Realizing the difficulty of the task is at least a step toward better solutions" (1978: 435). Professional associations, colleges, and universities have ethics committees whose members can provide guidance in ambiguous situations, and members of indigenous communities are usually willing to advise fieldworkers, but there are still many situations in which the individual must make his or her own judgment. Fieldworkers can only attend to the credo "First do no harm" and make their best efforts to behave in accordance with the professional, indigenous community, and personal standards of the time.

One final point about professional standards: One should be extremely cautious before offering guarantees of confidentiality to informants. In early 1999, the U.S. Office of Management and Budget proposed to apply public access via the Freedom of Information Act to all data generated from federal research. Professional research organizations opposed this change in policy. However, because of freedom of information legislation, the time may come when researchers of the twenty-first century may be required to disclose data in spite of guarantees of confidentiality that they have personally offered to informants.

Ownership of Intellectual Property

Ownership of intellectual property is one dimension of the ethics of collaboration that needs specific consideration. In the past two or three decades, indigenous people around the world have begun to realize that some of their traditional cultural knowledge has been taken by outsiders and has been used for profit, without compensation to the original owners. Unfortunately, there is little in the way of legal protection for the ownership of traditional cultural knowledge by indigenous people. Tom Greaves notes that, "in the broader world of copyrights and patents, 'intellectual property rights' . . . refers to the legal rights of ownership that individuals and corporations have over the products of individual creativity and inventiveness" (1994: ix). He has elaborated on some of the issues involved for indigenous people. The first issue is whether or not indigenous groups can claim ownership of their cultural knowledge: "Indigenous societies are facing cultural extinction that could be avoided with leadership and cash. Can indigenous societies claim ownership of their cultural knowledge? Can they control whether it may be used by outsiders? Can they claim compensation for its permitted commercial use?" (1994: 3).

A second issue involves the complications resulting from the diversity and complexity of intellectual property:

> If plant extracts and potential pharmaceuticals were the only matters involved, the number of questions to ask would be manageably small. However, native knowledge with commercial possibilities is not limited to medicinals. Other commercially relevant indigenous knowledge includes the location of local mineral and wild plant resources, domesticated plants with interesting genetic properties, musical instruments producing evocative sounds, new ingredients for cosmetics, new foods and spices, art designs and their potential use on all manner of salable products, mythic elements and stories, and sites for tour organizers. The list is enormous, and growing ever longer as entrepreneurs scour the world for remunerative opportunities. The great diversity of externally valuable indigenous knowledge infuses complexity in strategies to protect it. (Greaves 1994: 3–4)

A third issue relates to the protection of knowledge that is central to a people's cultural identity: "Sometimes it is knowledge entrusted only to properly prepared religious specialists. Disclosure to other, unqualified members destroys it. Sometimes it is knowledge shared among all of a society's members, but not with outsiders. Such knowledge charters a society's sense of self; to disclose it loosens the society's self-rationale" (Greaves 1994: 4). Greaves proposes that many of the problems relating to intellectual property for indigenous peoples could be addressed if the indigenous peoples could be formally recognized as owning their property: "Among those of us who seek equity for the world's indigenous peoples the thought arises, why couldn't indigenous peoples *own* their cultural knowledge, and then, if they allow it to be used elsewhere, secure a just share of the money it generates?" (1994: 4).

Article 29 of the Draft Declaration on the Rights of Indigenous Peoples also takes note of the issues surrounding ownership of intellectual property:

> Indigenous peoples are entitled to the recognition of the full ownership, control and protection of their cultural and intellectual property.
> They have the right to special measures to control, develop and protect their sciences, technologies and cultural manifestations, including human and other genetic resources, seeds, medicines, knowledge of the properties of fauna and flora, oral traditions, literatures, designs and visual and performing arts. (Te Puni Kokiri 1994: 24)

In June 1993, another declaration was adopted, this one in New Zealand, dealing specifically with intellectual property rights of indigenous peoples. This declaration begins as follows:

> In 1993, the Nine Tribes of Mataatua in the Bay of Plenty region of Aotearoa New Zealand convened the First International Conference on the Cultural and Intellectual Property Rights of Indigenous Peoples . . . (12–18 June 1993, Whakatane).

> Over 150 delegates from fourteen countries attended, including indigenous repre-
> sentatives from Ainu (Japan), Australia, Cook Islands, Fiji, India, Panama, Peru,
> Philippines, Surinam, USA and Aotearoa.
>
> The Conference met over six days to consider a range of significant issues, in-
> cluding[:] the value of indigenous knowledge, biodiversity and biotechnology, cus-
> tomary environmental management, arts, music, language and other physical and
> spiritual cultural forms. On the final day, the following Declaration was passed by
> the Plenary. (Te Puni Kokiri 1994: 51)

This opening is followed by a preamble containing six points agreed on by
those attending the conference. Recommendations to states, national and international agencies, and the United Nations follow recommendations to indigenous peoples on ways to protect their cultural and intellectual property
rights. This declaration has been circulated among indigenous groups world-
wide, but it does not as yet have legal standing.

Fieldworkers undertaking programs in indigenous communities should inquire locally about procedures for the protection of intellectual property. If no
procedures have been developed, the fieldworker and representatives of the
local community or tribe should consider negotiating a written agreement before the program begins. An agreement should include a statement about the
individuals or organizations that must approve the draft report of the project
before it is published. If representatives from the local community have authority to approve what is published, they can satisfy themselves that nothing
is included in the report that should not be included. They can also ensure that
ownership of intellectual property and of the research outcomes is properly
acknowledged. The question of written agreements is considered in greater
depth in the next chapter.

Fieldworkers should note that, although there is little legal protection for
the intellectual property rights of indigenous people in place at the beginning
of the twenty-first century, nonindigenous professional and legal organizations are acting as advocates for those rights. The Society for Applied Anthropology (Greaves 1994) is one example of such an organization. These organizations could apply considerable pressure on individuals or agencies
taking undue advantage of the intellectual property of indigenous people.

Apply the Concept of Culture in Everyday Working Relationships

A general understanding of the concept of culture can be extremely useful for
a professional person working in a community other than his or her home
community. Without the concept of culture, behavior that is different from
one's own can seem inexplicable, odd, insane, frightening, stupid, or inap-
propriately funny, and it may be explained in ways that are damaging. A cul-

tural framework can provide a positive vehicle for understanding people from groups different from one's own.

However, notions about culture can also be a problem. Published material about the culture of a particular community may be out of date or may have been inaccurate in the first place. Change is occurring rapidly in indigenous communities, accentuating the problem of published reports growing out of date quickly. If a visitor gives too much credence to previously published material, she or he may have problems when expectations do not materialize.

Another difficulty arises when people develop stereotypes based on the concept of culture. If someone believes that a particular cultural trait is characteristic of a group, there may be the expectation that every individual in the group will exhibit the trait and in exactly the same way. In reality, there is always variability within any group, and it is a mistake to expect any individual to behave in stereotypic fashion, cultural or otherwise.

In the nineteenth century, anthropologists traveled to exotic locations in order to study and understand ways of life different from their own. They developed the notion of culture to explain differences in beliefs and behavior between groups of people in different locations. Over the past century, *culture* has come to be used by people in the English-speaking world to explain an ever widening range of phenomena. The term is used by natural scientists to describe a quantity of bacteria grown for study and by people in the arts to mean refined understanding. With respect to social behavior, management specialists write about the culture of organizations. Social scientists refer to complex societies as *multicultural*, and educators speak of *bicultural* (in the case of New Zealand) or *multicultural* (in the case of the United States) education. Philosophers debate about the basic units or "memes" of culture. Sometimes the term seems to be used as a cure-all for everything that ails our complex societies.

Virtually every person who uses the term *culture* has an individual understanding of what the term means in different situations. Sometimes these understandings have come from courses in anthropology, but more often they have been constructed from everyday sources including television, newspapers, magazines, casual conversations, and random observations. The popular definitions often include the assumptions that culture is learned and is something that is shared among identifiable groups of people who form subgroups of complex societies. These assumptions can easily lead to stereotyping, troublesome expectations, and crises in relationships among fieldworkers, program developers, and local communities.

Professional educators are not always as helpful as they might be in defining *culture* for students. For example, in one recent textbook aimed at undergraduates, four definitions drawn from the writings of different educators and social scientists appear in one paragraph. The author of the textbook also provides his own definition, which is different from the variations quoted from the writings of others. Surely, students need greater clarity of presentation if they are to learn to apply the concept in real world situations.

Here is an example of the kinds of difficulties that arise when the term *culture* is used in casual explanations of behavior and is not adequately defined. In the early 1980s, I was working in one of Alaska's regional centers for a field-based university program. The program required travel to villages around the regional center to meet with Alaska Native university students in those villages. Funding was available to hire someone to assist me. My new assistant had a bachelor's degree in the natural sciences—a background that was badly needed in order to provide assistance to students in the required science and math courses—but she had no background in the social sciences.

When the assistant arrived to begin her new job, I spent some time with her going over the expectations for the job and trying to give her some idea of what to expect from the students she would be meeting in the villages. I described some characteristics of Alaska Native culture, including, I think, a tendency for students to be shy at first and a tendency for them to avoid confrontations if there are disagreements. I did not intend to imply that every Alaska Native person is shy under all circumstances or that there are never confrontations. I only meant that some of the students *might* be shy (but not necessarily) and some of them *might* avoid confrontations (but others might be happy to engage in debate). Unfortunately, I did not explain carefully enough what I meant. The assistant left our conversations with the impression that all Alaska Native people were shy and all avoided confrontations. I did not say a word about the general idea of culture. I had been studying and working in cultural groups different from my own for several years. I assumed that *everyone* understood the general idea.

Then, the assistant made her first trip to the villages—and it turned out to be her last trip as well, at least in that job. When she met with students, she told them what I had said about Alaska Native culture, and they interpreted her comments as authoritarian—as though she were trying to tell them what their culture should be. They were deeply offended. They notified the program coordinator in Fairbanks that they did not want her coming to their village again. We made arrangements for her to carry out tasks that did not involve traveling to the villages, but she was unhappy and left the position after only a few weeks.

There are endless examples of similar situations in which individuals have gone to work in communities with cultural traditions different from their own and a lack of understanding of the idea of culture has had unfortunate consequences. There are a number of organizations that send volunteers or paid development workers from First World countries to work in Third World development. These organizations provide training for the volunteers, but the training does not always adequately prepare people to adapt to new cultural settings. Sometimes, anthropologists returning from the field have commented on the "lessons in anthropology 101" that they provided to volunteer workers they met by chance who had been inadequately prepared for particular cultural settings. Teachers, health workers, social workers, and missionaries with little or no orientation to the concept of culture are often hired to work in indigenous communities.

Part of the difficulty in the Alaskan example came about because the assistant understood culture to be something that is shared among groups of people. The poor and incomplete orientation that I gave her was also part of the problem. The question that arises from this example is, If culture is not a set of shared traditions, how should it be defined?

Anthropologists have been debating various definitions of culture for more than a century, but the concept remains elusive (Wolcott 1991: 251). For our purposes, we can accept the basic definition given by Wolcott, quoting Herskovits: "customary ways of thinking and acting" (1991: 257). There are hundreds of different definitions of culture, but there is general agreement that, although groups of people seem to share some common learned characteristics ("customary ways of thinking and acting"), each individual in the group demonstrates his or her individual ways of believing and behaving.

Wolcott (1991: 252–58) summarizes some of the recent theories that attempt to explain the apparent paradox between the shared aspects of culture and individual variation in behavior and belief within any given group. He identifies the theories of A. F. C. Wallace (1970) and Ward Goodenough (1971, 1981) as among the most helpful. Wolcott's article was written primarily to focus attention on the individual and the way that individuals acquire culture. That is not our purpose here. Our purpose is to try to understand how the notion of culture can be helpful to professionals who are not anthropologists, to novice fieldworkers, to teachers, to health, social service, or development workers in communities that are different from their own home communities. Although our purpose is different, Wolcott's analysis can be useful.

Wolcott points out that no one ever learns all of a culture. Each person learns a little bit at a time: "More astounding than the sum of what anyone *does* know, however, is the recognition of how little of the great 'all of it' each individual knows or ever needs to know. *No one has ever acquired culture and no one ever will.* Every human acquires only one particular version covering *some* aspects of a *limited* number of cultural systems" (Wolcott 1991: 265). In other words, each individual makes sense out of his or her experiences and observations in his or her own way. Wolcott asserts that each individual actively incorporates what he or she learns: "The competencies that humans develop are joined in constellations of patterns of thought and action that transcend both the specific behaviors and the specific settings in which they were originally experienced. A metaphor we hear often today refers to the processes of 'constructing.' The metaphor is meant to call up the dynamic imagery of activity in progress" (1991: 266).

In the modern world, individuals can be expected to learn "customary ways of thinking and acting" from more than one group's tradition. Goodenough (1976) has pointed out that multiculturalism is the normal human experience. Virtually everyone comes into contact with groups outside of one's immediate family and neighborhood, learning appropriate ways of believing and behaving from these new groups in the process. This is certainly true of indigenous people. When I was working in isolated Alaskan villages in the late 1970s, nearly everyone in those communities had visited Anchorage or Fairbanks for education, for health care, to visit relatives, to shop, or for other reasons. A few had traveled outside Alaska. Now, in addition, nearly everyone has access to television, rental movies for the VCR, e-mail, and the Internet. Indigenous people from isolated communities have learned appropriate systems of behavior and belief to enable them to function appropriately in urban and electronic settings as well as in their home communities. They share understandings of these settings with mainstream groups. Knowledge of urban and electronic settings does not displace knowledge they have acquired in their home communities. Wolcott points out that "adding new cultural competencies . . . does not require abandoning old ones" (1991: 260–61). Someone can have extensive knowledge from a traditional indigenous culture and can still acquire competencies to function satisfactorily in urban and electronic settings.

Heewon Chang (1999) has written a critique of the assumption that there are fixed geographical boundaries for given cultures. She has given examples of the different multicultural makeup of four people with common ties to Korea. The first was a child born in the United States of a German father and a Korean mother who spent summers with her grandparents in Germany and Korea. The second was born in Korea and was adopted by a Jewish American couple when she was two years old. The third was a fifteen-year-old who was born in the United States to immigrant parents from Korea. The fourth was a Korean woman, fifty years old, who immigrated to the States at the age of twenty to marry a Korean bachelor (Chang 1999: 4–5). Each of these individuals could be expected to have some knowledge of Korean culture and some knowledge of American culture, but each would have integrated different aspects of the two cultures into his or her own "subjective view of the world"—or, in anthropological terms, into his or her own "propriospect"

(Goodenough 1971: 36, quoted in Wolcott 1991: 258). These four could easily be classified by others as Korean American, but it would only be possible to know about each individual's cultural knowledge and traditions by asking each one: "Cultural boundaries within individuals become blurred as components from diverse cultures become incorporated into their individual cultural identity, instead of remaining separate from each other" (Chang 1999: 4).

In summary, then, every individual learns a great deal from the particular groups to which she or he is exposed—family, peer groups, neighborhood clubs, school class, church, e-mail lists, websites, media, and so on—but each individual integrates what is learned into her or his own subjective view of the world. A great deal of what is learned is knowledge that is shared with groups of people based on the group's customary ways of thinking and acting. This knowledge can be called cultural knowledge—but for any given individual, it is impossible to predict what knowledge in particular is shared and with whom.

At the same time, it is terribly important to people in many different societies to acknowledge the value of their traditional cultures and their right to maintain those cultures if they want to. There is no easier way to make enemies in indigenous communities than to suggest that there is no such thing as culture or to suggest that it is not an important concept. Most people in the world can name traditions that belong to their own particular group, traditions that are considered to be essential for the life of the group and which should be maintained by younger generations, so indigenous people are not exceptional in valuing their traditions. Their traditions have been under attack as the result of colonization for generations. It is important for fieldworkers to learn about the traditions that are valued by the community in which they are working and to respect the value that people from the community place on those traditions. Whatever purpose one has in working in the community is much more likely to be achievable if the community's traditions are respected. At the same time, outsiders must keep in mind that there may be individuals within the community who do not adhere to a particular tradition. Some individuals may value a given tradition in the community but not adhere to it themselves, or there may be some who do not value a particular tradition even though the community as a whole values it. Even when one knows about the traditions of a community, one can never assume that the traditions apply to all members of the community. In all probability, there will be exceptions.

It is also important for fieldworkers to realize that they too are bearers of particular "customary ways of thinking and acting," of a particular culture or constellation of cultures. One of the more interesting aspects of culture is that much of it is learned inadvertently. Each of us learns a great many things without really realizing that we are learning them. If one were asked to list all the things that one knows, the list could go on indefinitely and would never be complete. One of the great advantages of living in a cultural group different from one's own is the opportunity for reflection on one's own culture that can be gained in the process.

I would encourage nonanthropologists working in indigenous communities to try to be specific about particular dimensions or aspects of culture that are of interest at a particular moment. One might be interested in language, or traditional beliefs about the environment, or traditional family relationships, or some other specific dimension of culture at a particular point in time. Specifying the dimensions that are of interest may help one to avoid assumptions and generalizations that arise from fuzzy, multiple understandings of what the term *culture* means.

NOTE

1. Linda Tuhiwai Te Rina Mead (1996) is the same person as Linda Tuhiwai Smith (1999).

Chapter Four

Designing Collaborative Programs

Almost by definition, effective collaboration between members of local communities and outside experts is required for success in collaborative programs. However, effective collaboration is not the only essential component for successful programs. Program designers, managers, fieldworkers, and other participants tend to think that the programs they are involved in are so important and useful that the program cannot possibly fail. But programs can and do fail. There have been too many occasions when education, training, social service, or other community change programs have been undertaken in indigenous communities without due consideration to the program components that are necessary for success. Such programs have been destined to fail from the beginning. Program failure can have devastating effects not only on participants but also on communities and on policy relating to future programs. There is a tendency to publish accounts of success but not to publish accounts of failure. As a result, lessons that might have been learned from unsuccessful experiences have not been passed on to others.

There are occasions when researchers enter new settings because employment is available in an innovative program or project, and the researcher believes that she or he can combine research with the employment opportunity. Careful consideration should be given to the way the program has been designed, however. The researcher (or, for that matter, anyone considering employment in a new program) should ask, "Are the critical components in place for a successful program?" If all of the recommendations described below have not been considered for a project, fieldworkers—especially novice fieldworkers—may want to look elsewhere for a program setting.

More than thirty years ago, Goodenough formulated principles for successful development programs:

> Because they reflect actual experience, they are of special interest. We may summarize them as follows:
>
> 1. Development proposals and procedures should be mutually consistent.
> 2. Development agents must have a thorough knowledge of the main values and principal features of the client community's culture.
> 3. Development must take the whole community into account.
> 4. The goals of development must be stated in terms that have positive value to the community's members. They must be something they, as well as the agent, want.
> 5. The community must be an active partner in the development process.
> 6. Agents should start with what the community has in the way of material, organizational, and leadership resources.
> 7. Development procedures must make sense to the community's members at each step.
> 8. The agent must earn the respect of the community's members for himself as a person.
> 9. The agent should try to avoid making himself the indispensable man in the development situation.
> 10. Where there are several agents at work, good communication and coordination between them and their respective agencies is essential. (1963: 22)

Goodenough's principles include guidelines for the individual agent, for relationships between the agent and the community, and for the relationships between the agent and other agencies. I have found it useful to separate guidelines for the individual fieldworker from the recommendations for program design. In the previous chapter, fieldworkers were considered. In this chapter, conditions for the design of programs are considered.

PLANNING FOR BALANCED DEVELOPMENT

Susan Guyette (1996) has written a planning guide for cultural centers, museums, and arts programs. The guide is also of interest to anyone who is considering a large development in an indigenous community. The book was sponsored by the Pueblo of Pojoaque and describes the steps that were undertaken in planning the Poeh Center in New Mexico. It is about methods for cultural preservation and economic development and the way that the two goals were combined whenever possible in the Poeh Center. It is intended for Native American communities and provides information to improve skills in strategic planning, needs assessment, cultural revitalization, business development, tourism development, and generating resources for needed projects. The author does not comment on the role of outside experts in the planning of the Poeh Center. There appear to have been people from outside the community who participated, but the collaboration is not an aspect of the development that the author chose to emphasize in the book.

In 1989 the Administration for Native Americans provided funding to develop a model cultural center: "In the Poeh Center model, a detailed planning process over a six-month period created a strategic plan for approximately twenty cultural preservation projects. Each project was outlined step-by-step" (Guyette 1996: 10). The planning process was based on the belief that sustainable development requires knowledge of the traditional culture and integration of ways to proceed with methods that already work well, rather than introducing development that does not support existing values and activities. The thirteen steps in the strategic plan for the center (Guyette 1996: 9–41) are briefly summarized below:

- Step 1: Create a Vision. A vision shapes the future and pulls people together to create a common focus.
- Step 2: Identify Key Issues. Key issues are those issues seen as a priority to address.
- Step 3: Define a Strategy. A strategy is a central direction used to get a result.
- Step 4: Collect and Analyze Important Data. The process of needs assessment defines the gaps between existing and desired conditions. Guyette's guide discusses techniques for gathering data.
- Step 5: Do a SWOT Analysis. A SWOT analysis identifies strengths, weaknesses, opportunities, and threats.
- Step 6: Create a Mission Statement. A mission statement is a focused expression of long-term purpose.
- Step 7: Form Your Goals. A goal is a long-term outcome and can be general in nature. Objectives are short-term steps.
- Step 8: Define the Projects. The projects needed to carry out the goals are defined next.
- Step 9: Conduct a Resource Audit. It is critical to assess knowledge, managerial and development skills, and fiscal resources.
- Step 10: Calculate Timetables for Development. A time frame for the start and finish of project tasks should be created.
- Step 11: Prepare Financial Projections. Financial projections are invaluable for assessing feasibility.
- Step 12: Write an Executive Summary. Concise summaries of data-gathering processes help to create a focused plan.
- Step 13: Planning for Sequential Development. Architectural, land use, tourism, business, and market plans are effectively used together.

Guyette's model is recommended for communities with the resources to undertake extended planning. There are some limitations to the strategic planning process, however. Guyette notes that "not all cultural groups feel they can shape or influence the future," so these methods may not be appropriate for some communities (1996: 35). Also, funding agencies do not often provide resources for extended planning, and funding is needed to cover the costs of planning. There are also situations in which communities have chosen to undertake smaller scale programs to address specifically identified needs rather than undertaking large-scale, long-term, integrated development programs. And there have also been instances in mainstream organizations (universities, for example) in which the ritual of strategic planning has been undertaken in order to satisfy executives, governing boards, or audit agencies but with no real commitment to the process by participants. In these situations, the strategic plan tends to lack connections to the day-to-day activities of the organization and is largely meaningless. When participants are less than fully committed to the process, planning exercises can waste time and resources.

SMALL-SCALE COMMUNITY INITIATIVES

A set of recommendations for smaller-scale programs is presented below. The recommendations have been derived from the literature and my own experience in programs in indigenous communities. They are intended for programs in which outside experts will collaborate with community representatives, but they can also be considered as basic guidelines for most small-scale community initiatives. The recommendations are presented in a sequence that roughly parallels the likely time available for moving forward from step to step, but the various phases of program development overlap, and the sequence should not be considered as a rigid one.

Fieldworkers and Representatives of the Community Should Collaborate to Develop a Rationale, Philosophy, or Reason for the Establishment of the Particular Program

Ideally, a collaborative program begins with consultation between representatives of an indigenous community and an outside expert. The initial ideas for programs can come from any number of sources. There have been times when someone in a local community or someone from outside the community simply had an idea that seemed to have merit. Sometimes a funding agency has made funding available for a particular type of program, or there may have been academic people who wanted to test a theory. Sometimes, formal needs assessments have provided the initial impetus for the development of programs. In most instances, the structures for collaborative relationships are already in place through formally recognized indigenous organizations (tribal councils, regional councils, traditional councils, city councils, village councils, band councils, chapters, school boards, health advisory councils, village or regional corporations, or formal organizations by any other name).

If the idea has been initiated in the local community, the people who have originated the idea may want to recruit outside experts for collaboration. If they have not already established relationships with consultants from outside, they can network with other communities that can identify appropriate consultants, or they can begin recruiting by contacting local institutions of higher education. They can place notices on their websites and e-mail lists. If an individual or agency outside of the community has initiated the idea, the fieldworker may have to establish a process for community consultation. One of the first steps should be to contact the planning office of the tribal or regional indigenous organization (Guyette 1983: 272). There may be existing plans that should be considered.

If the program is a new one for the tribe, region, or particular community, the fieldworker will need to identify key people who should be consulted. The astute fieldworker will first seek out leaders of the formally recognized indigenous organizations. In most cases, the leaders of formal organizations can provide good advice for identifying key people in the community who should be consulted.

There may also be situations in which there is more than one formally recognized organization with an interest in a program. For example, the vagaries of the law in the United States have resulted in the establishment of legally recognized traditional councils, city councils, and native corporations coexisting in some small Alaskan villages. The same villages may also have school boards and health committees. The presence of more than one organization should be no problem so long as the organizations are willing to cooperate with each other, at least with respect to the particular program. However, if there is more than one organization and the organizations are competitive or in disagreement, the conflict may create insurmountable problems. Conflicts can arise, for example, when a tribal council with authority over a large region is in disagreement with a local community within that region. There have been instances in which a tribal authority has supported the establishment of a particular program but the local community did not agree. Collaboration is only possible in situations in which people are willing to collaborate. If groups in the community or region do not agree on a particular program, the program may be in serious trouble. At the same time, it is important to realize that minor disagreements between indigenous organizations are not uncommon, and programs can achieve their objectives as long as disagreements remain minor.

Program developers have not always given full consideration to the rationale, philosophy, or reason for the existence of a new program, and programs have failed because the underlying assumptions were weak, incorrect, or missing altogether. Some inadequate reasons for initiating programs include

- A funding agency has made funding available. The community is poor and needs the money. The program will provide badly needed jobs for local people.
- Someone in another part of the country or another part of the world ran a successful program, so we should start one like it.
- Facilities are available and we should make good use of them.

Many programs in indigenous communities have been initiated because agencies have provided funding for particular programs. Sometimes these have been job development or vocational training programs. Funding, though, has not led to success *unless the intended program outcomes addressed the needs of some group or groups within the community over and above the provision of employment for individuals who would work in the program.* If a program is started for no other reason than to provide jobs for individuals to run the program, and no other community needs are addressed, the program has little chance of long-term survival. It is possible to have a successful program that trains people for employment outside the program or that develops new employment, but program goals must be based on intended outcomes *in addition to* providing jobs for people who will work in the program.

Many programs in indigenous communities have been based on models drawn from other geographical areas, but program success is very much dependent on local circumstances—including the local culture—so local circumstances must be carefully considered before a new program is undertaken. Are the local circumstances very much the same as the ones where the program operated successfully? What are the similarities and differences in local circumstances, and how might the differences affect the chances of program success? What consequences might the program have in the new circumstances that are unintended and possibly detrimental for the community? These questions need careful attention if chances for success are to be high. New programs must build on the local culture and integrate aspects of the community that already work well.

Facilities (buildings, etc.) must be appropriate for particular programs, but they cannot, by themselves, make successful programs. The major reason for starting a program cannot be based on a building or other facilities. *A successful program in an indigenous community must address perceived needs or desires of a group in the community where the program is to operate. Those needs or desires must be clearly stated, and the characteristics of the population to be served must be described. There should be some evidence to indicate that there are people who will use the program and that they are present in sufficient numbers to justify the cost. Specific goals and objectives should be defined, but the process of defining these should not be carried to extremes.*

Goals and objectives must be clearly stated and a time frame given for their achievement, but demands or requirements for excessively detailed objectives and timelines can actually damage the prospects of the program. The goals and objectives should be stated in terms that all participants can understand. At the same time, there should be an acknowledgment that the program must be flexible and adaptable as perceived needs change over time. Objectives are needed in order to begin the journey, but they must be flexible so that changes can be made based on program experience. Although these prescriptions would seem to be common sense, new programs are initiated again and again without well thought out reasons for their existence.

Look for Sources of Adequate and Dependable Funding

A critical question to ask in the process of generating funding is, "Which comes first, the planning or the search for a funding agency?" The answer is an interplay between the two. An important guideline is to never distort the project to satisfy the funding agency; yet formatting the description of the project according to the specific agency guidelines is essential. In an ideal development setting, the project is first outlined in the community's strategic plan; then the detail is filled in to fit an agency's requirements.

—Guyette 1996: 206

It is easy to agree with Guyette's statement regarding the ideal setting, in which the project is first outlined and then detail is filled in to fit an agency's requirements. Most planners, though, will want to begin investigating funding sources early. There can be no doubt that the availability of funding is an important determinant of the success of the program.

Governments, private foundations, and indigenous organizations have provided funding for innovative programs in indigenous communities in the past. In the United States, there are directories that identify government and private sources of funding. These should be available through university and public libraries. Librarians should be useful sources of additional information on funding. Tribal planning offices often have information on possible sources of funding for new projects, as do government agencies with responsibilities for programs for indigenous people. Planners will need to consider whether it is possible to raise funds within the local community or to generate income from the activities of the program. Not every program can find funding from government or private foundations.

Most funding agencies have their own guidelines for proposals and programs. There have been many instances, however, in which guidelines have been developed based on theoretical models that have been fashionable at the time. Sometimes the theory has been all encompassing, intended to cover every situation no matter what variations might occur in particular local settings. The "management by objectives" theory in education is one example of a theory intended to cover every situation with every group of people. It was prevalent for a time in the United States (see, for example, Wolcott 1977) and in New Zealand (Harrison 1994). Guidelines based on theoretical models have not necessarily taken into consideration local circumstances or real world experience in program operation, and they have sometimes omitted reference to essential dimensions of program design.

Program developers cannot ignore the guidelines of the funding agencies, of course, so the agency's guidelines must be considered in conjunction with the goals and objectives of the local program. Guyette (1996: 205–45) has provided a set of well-informed directions for the preparation of proposals and practical steps for communities to take to ensure that their proposals are favorably received. Some negotiation is usually possible, but the local community often has to choose between adjusting its goals to match those of the funding agency, operating on a voluntary basis, or abandoning the program. If the program is dependent on agency funding, then participants and the funding agency must agree on a set of objectives that are understood by all parties involved. They must agree that the objectives are achievable, that the timelines are realistic, and that the funding available will be sufficient to run the program and is a reasonable sum to commit.

Fieldworkers should not submit proposals to an agency before consulting with the community where the program will take place. There have been occasions when developers have obtained funding for programs only to find that the community was not happy about the program structure. One useful approach may be to prepare a draft proposal to submit for discussion and feedback from community leaders and groups.

Local people often volunteer time to operate service programs in indigenous communities. If programs require full-time regular commitments from workers or resources in addition to volunteered time, then they need funding to operate. Programs have failed when they have not been adequately funded.

There have been instances when underfunding has caused programs to fail when they might well have succeeded if adequate funding had been available. Programs have been known to operate in unsafe facilities without necessary resources and supplies. Staff members in underfunded programs have been known to struggle to maintain programs well beyond the time when they should have given up. Sometimes, failure has been blamed on the participants, on the community, or on the basic philosophy underlying the program when the cause of the failure has been inadequate funding.

Short-term and fluctuating funding can have similar detrimental effects. Government funding tends to fluctuate according to the policies of one political party or another, but the availability of even short-term funding tends to heighten expectations and create false hope for improvement in what are dismal economic and social situations. Uncertainty about funding can cause stress for program designers, managers, other staff, and participants with high staff turnover as a result. Some funding agencies have used "drip feed" systems such that program managers have been required to submit new proposals, evaluations, or other reports so often that the managers have little time for anything else. Anyone considering a formal role in a new program should carefully consider whether there is adequate funding available. If funding is not adequate, it might be best to avoid the heartbreak of working for a program that is destined to fail for this reason.

Confirm That There Is Adequate Support in the Local Community

Program success depends on support from the local community. Research literature in development, management, community psychology, and anthropology contains theory and cases drawing attention to the importance of this point. In spite of this body of literature, government and other funding agencies continue to make decisions about what people need and to develop programs to address the agencies' perceptions of those needs. It should now be quite clear that new programs must address the perceived needs or desires of the people who will participate. Someone from outside the community may be able to propose a rationale for a new program, but if potential program participants do not "buy into" the proposal, there is little hope for success.

There are several different ways to find out about support in the community. In most instances, outside experts need to identify community representatives to work with them in determining the best approaches for surveying opinions and in carrying out the processes. Usually, formal organizations such as tribal or band councils would be contacted and asked for opinions. Individuals in formal leadership roles would also be consulted. Other organizations (school boards, health committees, etc.) would be contacted as appropriate. With permission, presentations can be made at public meetings, or public meetings can be organized specifically to discuss the proposed program. Advertising can be used. Sometimes formal surveys are appropriate—but not in every case.

Procedures for maintaining support within the community should be part of the ongoing program plan. Community support cannot be taken for granted even if support is high in the initial stages of the program. Support must be maintained and assessed throughout the life of the program. One of the most useful means of maintaining support is for program staff to communicate regularly with other community groups and agencies. Program staff who communicate effectively are usually rewarded with high levels of community support.

One of the principles for development proposed by Goodenough (1963: 22) and quoted earlier in this chapter is related to community support: development must take the whole community into account. This principle means that planners need to consider the impact of a program on the entire community as well as its impact on a targeted segment. For example, a program aimed at preparing women for employment might have implications for male employment, for schools or child care facilities, or for other dimensions of community life. The principle does not mean that every single person in the community has to support a program for it to be successful. In all probability, not everyone in a given community will support a proposed program, but there must be a core of support among people who are essential to the program's success. For example, if a program needed the use of space in the school on evenings or weekends, it would be important to have the support of the school board, but support from the health committee might not be of particular significance. If program operation is expected to take place in several communities in a region, support should be gauged in all the communities to be affected, not only in a regional center.

There must be a certain degree of cohesiveness within the community if a program is to succeed. Not every group of people who live in a defined area constitutes a cohesive community. A highly experienced and respected educational researcher once told me that she went looking for the "community" in the neighborhood surrounding her urban university and could not find it. She meant that there were many people in the neighborhood, but they were not socially linked as a community.

In other situations, there can be so much conflict between factions in a community as to make it impossible to succeed with collaborative programs. There is conflict in every community, but if the level of conflict in the community is high or if key leaders or groups do not support a program, program operations can be seriously hampered. Staff from the local community can easily be drawn into factionalism so that conflicts erupt between program participants. There can be pressure on outside experts to support one side or the other. Morale can be damaged, and energies may be diverted away from the program and into the conflicts. Community support necessary to the program's success can wither away.

It is also possible for the introduction of a new program to generate conflict. One example of the kind of conflict that can result occurs when more than one faction wants to control the funding that the program brings with it. Negotiations may be necessary to resolve differences of opinion before a final decision is made to undertake the program. One result of these negotiations may be that new representatives from the community join in the process of collaboration about the program. Another result of negotiations may be that there are changes in the goals, objectives, or general direction of the program—which is fine so long as the funding agency agrees to the changes.

When collecting information on community support, opinions on priorities for research goals should be solicited. Local groups usually want to see specific benefits for their communities rather than placing the priority on abstract or theoretical goals that may be of interest to researchers. In collaborative programs, research goals can be secondary to community goals. Fieldworkers who want to put the emphasis on the research outcomes may add to community conflicts about the program. Anyone who is going to work in a collaborative program should realize that his or her particular goals might not be as important as the goals of others.

There is always the possibility, too, that there will not be enough support for the new program, and the plan is abandoned or the location changed. When people from the local community are involved in planning, managing, and operating collaborative programs, they are much more likely to give support. Program planners, fieldworkers, and community representatives should attempt to determine in advance whether there is support and at what level, but they can only collect information and make a determination about the prospects of success based on their best judgment.

Formulate a Program Plan Including Statements of Roles and Responsibilities, Support Systems for Participants, and Evaluation Procedures

At this point in the design, community representatives and outside experts have developed a clear rationale for the program. They have checked to be certain that their plans do not conflict with existing tribal or other regional plans. They have identified sources of funding, and they have determined that there is sufficient support in the community to proceed. It is now time to consider the details of the program plan. The funding proposal may need to be finalized, incorporating opinions that came from the community during the consultation process just completed. However, the funding proposal will not necessarily be the only document prepared. A separate statement or statements may be needed for participants or for the community.

Unless the program involves a very small number of participants for a very short period of time, it will benefit all parties if agreements are recorded in writing:

> Agreements can be friendly. It is common to look upon a contract or agreement as an indication of a lack of trust. Even with the best of intentions, differences in world view can cause misunderstandings during a project. Whether formal or informal, an agreement provides a plan for services and responsibilities, so that all participants in the cooperative effort share expectations. A contract or agreement can be as formal as the community and researcher need. For example, some tribes implement the policy of a legal contract with academic researchers proposing to conduct research on their reservation. (Guyette 1983: 276)

At the beginning of a new program, it is easy for everyone to assume that there are common expectations regarding collaboration when, in fact, each participant has a different understanding from the others. The funding agency, all program participants, members of governing bodies, advisory groups, and other community members may have different expectations for the program and for fieldworkers. It is hardly ever the case that all expectations are shared in the initial stages, and major problems develop when differences in expectations are not resolved. The program plan can serve as an agreement between the fieldworker and community representatives. Although the program plan is written, it is not "set in concrete." The initial drafts are likely to be rough outlines, nothing more. Program plans and relationships between participants will evolve, and the written versions should be regularly updated as the relationships mature.

There is often intense time pressure at this stage of program design. Funding agencies may have deadlines, and participants may have a sense of urgency about getting program activities under way. However, a written plan, even if it is no more than an outline, is essential for long-term success. There are some fairly simple ways to develop the first agreement. A funding proposal can be the basis for discussions that lead to more detailed plans. Or minutes can be kept of meetings, and someone—perhaps the fieldworker—can use those to outline written plans. Or someone can draft a plan for discussion with others.

The initial section of the plan—the rationale for the program including goals and objectives—should already be in place, although it may need some adjustments based on the community consultations. The remainder of the plan will be composed of descriptions of the actions and operations that will lead to the achievement of the goals and objectives. There should be a clear connection between the program plan and the stated goals and objectives. The program plan should consider the following questions.

Who Will Set Policies for the Program?

Collaboration may involve a straightforward agreement between two parties such as the agreement between a researcher and a school district special projects director (Delgado-Gaitan 1990). Or a new collaborative program might come under the auspices of an existing organization such as a tribal council. Sometimes a new governing body is established for a new program. Usually, new structures take the form of committees, councils, or boards that represent the program's various stakeholders. Guyette suggests that the following factors be considered in forming a balanced committee that includes both community representatives and fieldworkers:

- Age
- Geographical location in community or reservation
- Sex
- Religion
- Speaker of native language
- Clan differences. (1983: 271)

Funding agencies may have requirements for representation on governing bodies, and a research program might need to have representatives with different research specializations. If there are particular skills needed by community representatives, be sure that those skills are identified and that board members have those skills. Training programs for board members may need to be part of the plan if particular skills are lacking.

Community representatives and fieldworkers need to collaborate to determine the best composition for a new governing council, the best procedures for formalizing the council if that is necessary (e.g., becoming a legal entity), and the best procedures for selecting particular individuals for the council. Usually, funding is required to compensate members and for travel to meetings. Members of local groups should be adequately compensated for their contributions. When agencies expect local people to contribute their time without compensation, people are often unable to take time away from income-producing activities, and the groups do not function well.

Procedures for electing officers, setting meeting schedules and agendas, distributing meeting papers in advance of meetings, notifying all of meeting dates/times, and so on should be outlined, although details may be developed later and may be included in supplementary or attached documents. The meeting place for the board or council should be a place where community representatives are comfortable. Most importantly, though, the position of the person responsible for carrying out the tasks necessary for the effective functioning of the group should be identified, and these tasks should be included in that person's position description.

Problems quickly arise when the responsibilities of advisory groups or governing councils are not clearly defined. Unless there is specific agreement, funding agencies or program developers may believe that a group from the local community is simply advisory when group members believe that they have—or should have—decision-making authority. Misunderstandings of this kind can lead to conflicts that damage or destroy programs.

What Procedures Will Be Followed in Setting Policies?

Usually, the governing board instructs program staff to prepare draft policies. The usual procedure is for the board to discuss, change, and adopt policies by majority vote of the governing board.

Who Will Manage the Program? If a Position of Program Manager Is Created, What Authority and Responsibility Will Be Delegated to That Position? What Is the Manager's Relationship to the Governing Body?

Well-defined roles, responsibilities, and relationships are important components in any program, but this is especially true for collaborative programs. Formal written job descriptions are often vague, but even a vague job description can serve as a guide and is better than no job description at all. Timelines and procedures should be established for reviewing and refining job descriptions for all program participants.

There is a tendency for roles for program workers in indigenous communities to be overloaded. When new programs are established, planners often envision work roles that are impossible to carry out. Many programs run into difficulty because staff members are expected to do the work of twice their number or because they feel as though they are expected to do everything single-handedly. This is especially likely to occur in underfunded programs in which the funding to operate the program does not cover the essential tasks that must be performed by staff. Dedicated staff members may try to compensate through personal commitment for lack of funding. In these situations workers tend to burn out quickly, staff turnover is high, and the quality of program offerings is poor.

There can also be problems when there are too few people with formal qualifications working in a program. If the program is to succeed, there must be a good balance between those with qualifications and those who are in training or who are apprenticed to the ones with qualifications. When a staff member has responsibilities that are essential to the running of the program and responsibilities for conducting research too, problems can result. A person in this situation may feel as though she or he is expected to do two jobs at once or may have difficulty in deciding which tasks should have priority. Program planners and prospective staff members should consider carefully whether proposed program responsibilities and research responsibilities can be carried out simultaneously.

Program managers may have responsibilities in any of the following areas:

- hiring, training, supervising, and evaluating staff
- supervising the maintenance of buildings, equipment, and materials
- program planning
- preparing draft policies for the board
- preparing proposals for continuing funding and lobbying the funding agency
- developing relationships with other agencies and public relations
- preparing reports for the governing board, funding agency, general public, and so on
- consulting with the community
- supervising the administration of funding.

The governing board may choose to delegate full authority to the program manager for these responsibilities, or its policies might provide for board members to participate in some dimensions of the program. For example, one or more members might be appointed to sit on selection panels when staff members are hired.

Who Will Administer the Funds? Who Will Prepare the Budget, and Who Will Approve It? Who Will Make Decisions about Particular Expenditures?

One of the most important responsibilities for the program is the responsibility of accounting for and managing the funding. Informed budgets and financial forecasts for the first years of operation are essential components of the program plan. Funding agencies will quickly withdraw support if funds are not properly accounted for or if funds are used for purposes other than the approved purposes. The media is quick to take advantage of every opportunity for headlines implying that public funds have been mismanaged, and media attention is easily drawn to cases where there are questions about funding. Negative media attention can be damaging even when questions are eventually resolved in favor of the program management.

Gibson describes the difficulties that occurred in one project in California where the administration of the grant was delegated to a community-based organization without adequate funding to pay for administration: "Although placement of the grant outside of the research site helped maintain our neutrality in Valleyside Punjabi politics, we also should have considered more fully the ramifications of placing a relatively large research grant within a small service-oriented organization. We should have found some means of building indirect costs into our budget" (1985: 139). Program developers need to be certain that any organization that administers funding has properly trained administrative staff as well as accounting systems in place that will provide accurate, timely financial reports and protection of the funds from misappropriation. Problems relating to management of funding can be avoided if attention is paid to financial planning from the beginning. At least one party in the program must be well qualified in financial management, but this person does not have to be the program manager. Program managers cannot do everything single-handedly. Program managers may have expertise in particular dimensions of the program (education or health, for example) but may not necessarily be well qualified in financial management. The party responsible for finances might be an employee of the program, a consulting accountant, or another agency that will administer the funding. The resources necessary for proper accounting (computers, software, etc.) must be made available, and funding to pay for regular audits is essential.

If community agencies administer funding, they must be compensated for the costs of administration, and they must be in agreement with the aims of the program. There is also the important question of determining who will have authority to decide how funds are spent. Major problems can arise in situations in which the decision-making authority is not clearly stated early on. If the parties cannot agree about delegation of authority and about management of funds, a collaborative program may not be successful in that setting.

What Program Activities Will Be Carried Out in Order to Achieve the Goals and Objectives?

A straightforward statement of planned activities should be set out. A general statement—such as "providing vocational instruction and personal development for youth between the ages of sixteen and twenty-four," for example—is enough for a start, but details should be added as soon as they can be worked out. In the example of vocational instruction, course descriptions should be written and other specifics of the operations added.

Who Will Carry Out These Activities? What Authority and Responsibility Will Each Staff Member Have? What Procedures Will Be Followed for Recruitment, Selection, Orientation, and Training of Staff?

Presumably, staff members of the program will carry out the activities described in the previous step. Job descriptions should be prepared including statements of the responsibilities and authority of each staff member. Very general job descriptions can provide starting points and guidelines for staff members to follow, and greater detail can be added as the program progresses.

The success of the program depends to a great extent on the people who are employed to carry it out. If the procedures for finding the right people are carefully developed, chances for success improve. Procedures for recruitment, selection, orientation, and ongoing staff development and review should be written out, and budgets should be prepared to identify the costs involved with these processes. There are laws that apply to recruitment and selection of employees. Government employment agencies should be able to provide printed information on the legal considerations of employment in the particular setting.

What Support Systems Will Be Provided for Participants?

Program developers do not often consider designing support systems for participants, but experience has shown that such systems are essential for the success of innovative programs. Some of the stresses that participants deal with may include persistently coping with unexpected problems, meeting new people, learning new systems, adapting to new physical and cultural settings, and feelings of uncertainty, isolation, and failure.

What support should be built into innovative programs? Programs should include ways for all participants to

- participate in decision making and program development
- express feelings and opinions
- bring problems to the attention of managers
- develop personal relationships with other participants
- be recognized and rewarded for their efforts
- improve their knowledge and skills
- communicate with others with cultural backgrounds similar to their own.

Programs in a range of settings have included regular staff meetings as well as social and sports gatherings for staff and other participants, provision of counselors, student councils, provision for attendance at professional conferences, staff development programs, provision for family participation and visits from outside experts, and many other strategies.

In small projects, participants may see each other every day. Even in these situations, structures for communication need to be built into programs. For example, particular times need to be set aside for discussion of particular matters. In underfunded programs, where staff are working doubly hard trying to accomplish the impossible, there is even more reason to set time aside to consider the feelings and opinions of all participants.

In some instances, great distances may separate participants. In other instances, communication technology may be out of date or of something less than the standard that professionals have come to expect. Feelings of isolation can intensify in such situations, misunderstandings can multiply, burnout can result, and staff turnover may be high with a negative effect on the quality of the program. There may be little that can be done to improve the situation. It is enough to say that attention needs to be paid to systems of support and communication in the program planning, and potential fieldworkers or other employees of the program need to be certain that they can work effectively where systems of communication are limited.

What Procedures Will Be Followed in Order to Assess the Progress of the Program and to Provide Information to the Local Community, Funding Agency, and Other Interested Parties?

Reasonable procedures for regular evaluation will provide for accountability to the community and to the funding agency. Government and other funding agencies ordinarily require regular evaluations and reports, and these agencies provide details of the processes they require. Unfortunately, funding is not always provided to adequately cover the costs involved in data collection, interpretation, and reporting. Program managers can find themselves with added requirements when available funding has already been allocated. Reasonable procedures for regular evaluation of programs require reasonable funding.

Although funding agencies require reports for their own purposes, there is often no requirement for reporting and feedback at the community level. For the fieldworker or manager in the collaborative situation, it is imperative to obtain feedback from the community or from particular representatives or segments of the community. Written reports may not be the best means of informing the community and seeking feedback. Methods must be tailored to fit particular settings. In the past, local advisory panels have sometimes provided assessments at the local level, but their advice has often gone unheeded. It is not appropriate to ask people to contribute their time to an assessment process unless their advice will be attended to. Reasonable funding must be provided to cover the costs of community consultations.

Who Will Handle Relationships with Other Agencies, and What Authority and Responsibility Will This Person Have with Respect to Other Agencies?

There can be a number of agencies with important relationships to the program. Relationships with funding agencies and media can be sensitive. Agencies with special relationships to the program should be identified, and responsibilities for communicating with those agencies must be spelled out for people in particular positions within the program.

Who Will Prepare Reports for Publication? Who Will Give Formal Presentations and Papers? Who Will Approve Reports for Publication? Are Specific Agreements for the Protection of Intellectual Property Needed? If There Are Profits from Publication of Reports, Who Will Benefit?

Publication of reports can generate disagreement and conflict that lasts for decades. Reports can influence the willingness of indigenous communities to work with people from outside their own communities. Agreements about who will prepare reports and who will be given credit for authoring reports should be put in writing as early as possible in the development of the program. If the governing body or other representatives of the local community want to approve all reports before they are made public, outside experts should be advised of this requirement in writing. Agreements should be made with respect to distribution of any profits from publication.

If formal research goals are part of the program, it is especially important to sort out expectations regarding ownership of intellectual property developed from the research or to be included in the research report. If these expectations are not made clear, the resulting misunderstandings can prove fatal for the research aspects of the project. There has been more than one occasion when a researcher has presented a report only to find that it contained information that the community—or representatives of the community—did not want to publicize. I know of one instance in which an anthropologist asked permission to take photographs while he was living in the community. However, he did not ask permission to *publish* the photos. People who were photographed were deeply offended when his book appeared with photos in it that people had thought were for his personal use only.

What Other Considerations Are Important in the Program Plan?

Even with a well-written program plan, ambiguities will remain. It simply is not possible to consider all the details in advance or to put them all in writing. The collaborative process is a continuing one, and there will be a continuing set of issues and problems for participants to work on. Processes for developing shared understandings and expectations should be considered.

Methods for resolving disagreements should be established and should be written into the program plan.

Are there other people or agencies involved in the program with which formal agreements should be established? For example, researchers may not be members of the governing body or staff members of the program, so written agreements may be necessary to make expectations and relationships explicit and binding. Guyette (1983: 273) feels that researchers have an obligation to anticipate possible consequences of the research and to make those consequences known to participants. While most researchers would agree with her, participants need to be aware that no one can anticipate all of the consequences with absolute certainty. Unintended consequences of the research are always possible.

It is important to recognize reciprocity and to realize that each participant is dependent on the others for the program to succeed. Outside experts have to depend on the knowledge of people from the local community if they are to successfully apply their expertise in the setting, and local people presumably need the expertise of the outside experts either to operate the program or to provide other services needed by the community. Acknowledgment of reciprocity should have a place in the program plan.

It should also be acknowledged (but not necessarily in writing) that all have more than one role in the community where they live and work. Fieldworkers who live in indigenous communities will have roles over and above their work roles, and it can be helpful for program participants to discuss expectations for fieldworkers in the community. For example, fieldworkers may want to participate in recreational activities for which the community has expectations for appropriate behavior. Hunting is an example of the kind of activity that might be attractive as recreation for a fieldworker and for which an indigenous community might have clear-cut expectations for the way the activity is to be carried out. Other examples might relate to family life or parenthood, where the fieldworker may have roles and the community may have expectations for the way the roles should be carried out. Defining one's roles is likely to be an ongoing process for a fieldworker, but the outsider should try to make that process a conscious and deliberate one.

Identify or Recruit Committed Leadership in the Program and, Preferably, in the Funding Agency

In some cases, the community representatives and outside experts who have developed the initial framework for the program will continue to provide leadership in planning and implementation. In other cases, those who initiated the program want to look for other leaders to carry out the plan.

Starting a new program is always a difficult process. There are new systems to be set up, and there are always unexpected problems. Even with the best planning, trial and error can be an essential method for addressing new procedures and problems. Confronting new problems day after day can be stressful for all participants—especially for those in leadership roles—so it is not surprising that there is a tendency toward high turnover in new programs. Difficulties are much harder to overcome if the original program planners are not part of the establishment process or if there is a high turnover rate in leadership. Turnover in leadership often leads to high overall turnover in staff and participants. New leaders may not share in the original philosophy of the program, so new leadership may mean a substantial change of direction. A change of direction might mean repeating some of the steps already undertaken (e.g., a new round of community consultations). New staff should be oriented to the purposes and objectives of the program, but if the original program designers are no longer with the program, there may be no one who can provide the orientation. The original sense of purpose and commitment can be lost, and it may take months or years for a new sense of purpose to develop. In the meantime, participants may feel uncertain and apathetic. These negative feelings can lead to more departures, more new hires, more uncertainty, and eventually the demise of the innovation.

The establishment process usually proceeds more smoothly if the leaders who initiated the program can continue to participate through the establishment phase. Every effort should be made to provide continuity in leadership through that phase.

There have been cases of program success in spite of overwhelming odds when committed leaders persevere. For example, programs have been known to survive when the initial funding is barely sufficient but committed leaders have demonstrated initial success so that funding is eventually increased to reasonable levels. Committed leaders who understand the program philosophy are keystones for the program structure during the establishment phase. Once the program has become well established, with all program participants certain of roles and procedures, it is usually possible for leaders to move on without creating the kind of damage that occurs when key personnel leave before or during the establishment phase.

People selected for leadership in the program—especially people from outside the community—have obligations to fully disclose their intentions if these are not already included in the program plan. How much time will they devote to the program, and over what period? What is expected of them by other agencies, such as the university that employs them or the funding agency? Do any other agreements—such as vacation or leave time—need to be considered? Are they expected to contribute to other projects in the community? If so, how much time is expected from them?

Identify or Recruit Appropriately Qualified Staff

The term *appropriate* does not mean that all staff members need university degrees. Appropriately qualified staff may include elders who bring specialized traditional knowledge, people who are good at resolving conflicts, people who bring a spiritual dimension, or people with "natural" abilities that suit the program.

In most cases, the people with the right educational qualifications and program experience need to be there, too. Traditional social systems in indigenous communities did not require participants to have Western educational qualifications, of course, and those systems can certainly continue to function in traditional ways. However, contemporary education and community development programs usually have goals that require staff who do have formal qualifications. When people with educational qualifications are required, it is risky to try to run a program without them. There have been cases when programs have been staffed entirely by people from the local community who lacked formal qualifications, and the program failed because no one had the expertise necessary for program success. One major purpose of this book is to show that often the best staffing results when people with specialized knowledge of the local culture work in true collaboration with people with Western qualifications from outside the community.

If people from the local community lack the necessary formal qualifications, training programs should be considered so that they can gain qualifications. Apprenticeships, training, or staff development programs can sometimes be set up in such a way as to assist people in the local community to work their way into all the program roles over time. In the meantime, local people can work alongside people from outside the community who do have the qualifications. Good examples of people with educational qualifications working in collaboration with indigenous people can be found in health programs based at *marae* (Maori community centers) in New Zealand. Some of these programs provide integrated general practitioner services, health education run by community health workers, specialist programs like breast cancer screening, and traditional healing through herbal medicines and massage, all within a Maori cultural context.

One further point regarding qualifications: As mentioned earlier, at least one person must have the skills to keep track of program finances and to prepare accurate reports for auditors. Programs cannot be run on good intentions alone, and good intentions will not rescue a program from the chaos that ensues when funding is not properly managed.

Find a Workable Physical Setting

There are many examples of situations in which someone tried to start a new program where the physical setting made program operation difficult or impossible. Program managers often try to "make do" when they are working with budgets that do not include sufficient funds to pay for appropriate facilities. Climate and weather can interfere with program operation. The location of a program in a particular community might mean that access to communication or other technology is limited, thereby creating difficulties for the operation of the program. There have also been occasions when communities wanted to collect rent for the use of facilities that were not really suited to the program purposes.

There have been other occasions when buildings have been constructed but have been too big to operate with the available resources. Inadequate planning allowed for the construction of buildings that could not be successfully operated. This problem can be avoided by long-term planning that includes forecasts of income and operating costs once a building has been completed:

> Budgets were created to anticipate annual operating costs, and income statements were developed to show potential sources of income. This step determined the feasibility of operating a facility of a particular size. This is an important step in avoiding overplanning, that is, creating a facility that is inappropriate to the determined needs or that cannot be successfully operated. Funding agencies that provide construction monies are familiar with incidents where grantees have applied to funding sources, constructed buildings, and then lacked operational funds. Projections, therefore, are very important in showing a tribe, an organization, or a funding agency that adequate planning is in place to operate a cultural center over the long term. (Guyette 1996: 5)

Every effort should be made to identify the best facilities that are available and affordable for a program, coupled with a willingness to make the best of whatever limitations are inevitable.

Attend to the Broader Political and Social Context That Makes It Possible for a Program to Survive

Government bodies fund most education and service programs in indigenous communities. The funding available depends on the opinions of politicians and the general public. If those opinions do not support a specific type of program at a particular point in time, program survival becomes problematic unless opinions change. Opinions of politicians and the general public do change over time, however. Program developers, managers, and participants can have some impact on these opinions, and all participants need to attend to their program's public image. They can prepare written reports, make presentations to groups in the broader community, and lobby legislators.

During the past two decades, the political context has changed with negative effects on funding for programs that can be termed "participatory" or "collaborative." Muhammad Rahman describes the international pressures that have been exerted on strategies and funding for participatory programs in developing countries:

> Mainstream development efforts supported by the great bulk of foreign development assistance remains very much non-participatory, and *poverty-augmenting* rather than *poverty-alleviating*. . . .
>
> Most countries are following the "structural adjustment programme" (SAP) approaches of the World Bank as a condition for the Bank's assistance. SAP is not concerned with PD [participatory development], nor for that matter with poverty alleviation, except as a hypothetical long-run "trickle-down" effect of economic growth. . . .
>
> The presumption of efficient resource allocation under SAP rests solely on the supposed virtue of the "free market," which both in theory and in practice naturally favours the conspicuous consumption urges of the affluent of the society in question rather than the basic needs of the underprivileged. . . .
>
> Taken together, such mainstream development strategies, controlled as they are by these vested interests, can only be expected to increase the "flow of poverty," in the context of which participatory development as a marginal activity supported by limited donor finance may play the role at best of a "safety net" to keep social discontent in check. (1995: 26–28)

And it is not only in the Third World that programs have been adversely affected by shifting political ideologies. Felix Rivera and John Erlich have examined the political context for programs for people of color (including indigenous people) in the United States and have come to similar conclusions about the difficulties of establishing community-level programs at this point in time:

> The struggle to bring about significant social change at the community level continues to be a Herculean task. Despite political rhetoric to the contrary at all levels of government, the gates to social justice are sliding further shut, not open. In the wake of "the end of welfare as we know it," increasing numbers of people of color are being thrown into disadvantage and poverty—homeless, drug addicted, alcoholic, imprisoned, AIDS infected, unemployed, without regular health care, and pushed out of deteriorating schools with few (if any) marketable skills. (1998: 22)

Neither Rahman nor Rivera and Erlich advocate that participatory programs be abandoned because of the political and economic pressures operating against such programs at this point in time. They are only noting the difficulties that developers and program participants face under these conditions.

Part Two

LESSONS LEARNED

The first four chapters describe the historical context for collaborative programs in indigenous communities and the evolution of these programs in the twentieth century. After many generations of European dominance, indigenous peoples in North America, Australia, and New Zealand are trying to regain their right to self-determination. They seek the right to make decisions about the programs that will operate in their communities and the right to determine who will work with them in the programs.

When I began as a fieldworker in 1977, general ideas about collaboration were in circulation, but there were few publications that would provide specific guidance. In each new program where I worked, I learned more about the problems that can arise. After a number of years, I stopped to reflect and realized that I had been dealing with each problem on a case-by-case basis but that guidelines could be useful more generally. A review of the literature supported the suggestion that guidelines for fieldworkers and for program design could be helpful in the development of new programs or in analyzing problems in existing programs. The proposed guidelines are presented here in a sequence roughly parallel to the likely progression of steps in planning, but the various phases of program development overlap, and the sequence should not be considered as a rigid one. The proposed guidelines follow.

FOR THE INDIVIDUAL FIELDWORKER ...

1. Be flexible but recognize that everyone has limits.
2. Be willing to collaborate by sharing authority, responsibility, and credit for success.

3. Give thoughtful attention to the ethical implications of your actions.
4. Apply the concept of culture in everyday working relationships.

FOR DESIGNING COLLABORATIVE PROGRAMS . . .

1. Fieldworkers and representatives of the community should collaborate to develop a rationale, philosophy, or reason for the establishment of the particular program.
2. Look for sources of adequate and dependable funding.
3. Confirm that there is adequate support in the local community.
4. Formulate a program plan including statements of roles and responsibilities, support systems for participants, and evaluation procedures. The plan should consider each of the following questions:

    *   Who will set policies for the program?
    *   What procedures will be followed in setting policies?
    *   Who will manage the program? If a position of program manager is created, what authority and responsibility will be delegated to that position? What is the manager's relationship to the governing body?
    *   Who will administer the funds? Who will prepare the budget, and who will approve it? Who will make decisions about particular expenditures?
    *   What program activities will be carried out in order to achieve the goals and objectives?
    *   Who will carry out these activities? What authority and responsibility will each staff member have? What procedures will be followed for recruitment, selection, orientation, and training for staff?
    *   What support systems will be provided for participants?
    *   What procedures will be followed in order to assess the progress of the program and to provide information to the local community, funding agency, and other interested parties?
    *   Who will handle relationships with other agencies, and what authority and responsibility will this person have with respect to other agencies?
    *   Who will prepare reports for publication? Who will give formal presentations and papers? Who will approve reports for publication? Are specific agreements for the protection of intellectual property needed? If there are profits from publication of reports, who will benefit?
    *   What other considerations are important in the program plan?

5. Identify or recruit committed leadership in the program and, preferably, in the funding agency.

6. Identify or recruit appropriately qualified staff.
7. Find a workable physical setting.
8. Attend to the broader political and social context that makes it possible for a program to survive.

In part 2 I have used these guidelines to reflect on the strengths and weaknesses of a series of programs in which I participated between 1977 and 1996 in Alaska and in New Zealand. The guidelines have only recently been developed and therefore could not have been applied when I was active in the programs. The discussions of the guidelines in terms of each program illustrate both the way the guidelines were developed and the way they can be used in coming to understand what works and what does not in collaborative programs.

In the chapters that follow, I have named some of the communities where the programs took place, but I have not named others. In deciding whether or not to name communities, I followed the protocol that was agreed on during my original work in the community. Some communities originally agreed to be named in program reports, but others did not. Each of the original reports is briefly described in the relevant chapter.

Chapter Five

The Small High Schools Project, 1977–78

In the late 1970s when the Small High Schools Project was undertaken, Alaska's population was about half a million. Alaska Natives representing twenty indigenous culture and language groups made up approximately one-fifth of the total. Archaeological experts believed that the ancestors of the native population crossed the Bering land bridge several thousand years ago, adapting to the new environments they encountered as they migrated. Contact with Europeans began in the eighteenth century when the Russian Vitus Bering sailed along Alaska's southern coastline. The Russian–American Company established outposts on that coastline and along the lower reaches of the Yukon and Kuskokwim Rivers, while the English Hudson's Bay Company established trade in the northeastern regions of the state.

In 1868, the United States purchased Alaska from Russia. Some commercial activities—whaling, fur trading, gold mining—brought outsiders into the territory, but it was not until World War II that the number of nonnatives grew to become larger than the number of the native population. The discovery of oil at Prudhoe Bay in the late 1960s precipitated massive change throughout the state. The oil companies wanted a pipeline from Prudhoe Bay to Valdez, and native land claims had to be settled before construction could begin. The Alaska Native Claims Settlement Act (ANCSA) was passed in 1971, and pipeline construction began a few years later, bringing tens of thousands of workers into the state.

By the late 1970s, the majority of the population lived in the urban centers of Anchorage, Fairbanks, and Juneau, the state capital. The urban populations were predominantly nonnative. Approximately 150,000 people lived in regional centers such as Bethel, Nome, Kotzebue, and Barrow or in villages with populations between 70 and 500. There were about 125 predominantly native villages. Most were inaccessible by road and could be reached only by airplane, sno-go (snowmobile), or boat. Villages generally included a post of-fice, church, school, health clinic, and store in addition to single-family dwellings. Most of the homes had been constructed by their owners, and very few had running water at that time. Satellite telephones had only recently been introduced, and often the only phone was in the village store. Village economies depended on hunting, fishing, and gathering combined with cash income.

Circumstances changed rapidly in the 1970s and 1980s. Pipeline construc-tion workers were recruited from outside the state and were paid high salaries, thus putting pressure on local industries and state agencies to raise the salaries paid to other workers. Oil royalties poured into the state treasury, and state ser-vices such as education expanded. In the early 1980s, a "bust" occurred when international organizations pushed oil prices down, and oil royalties dropped.

Under the terms of ANCSA, Alaska Natives formed regional and village corporations. Village corporations were diligently organizing profit-making and social service activities in the villages where I worked in the 1970s and 1980s. Selection of lands under the terms of ANCSA was also an engrossing issue for local people.

One other major political feature of the 1970s was the Consent Decree signed by the governor of Alaska in 1976 settling a civil class action suit brought against the state. Prior to 1976, most of the small villages had ele-mentary schools but did not have secondary schools. Native Alaskan children had to travel to boarding schools in regional centers or in other states for sec-ondary school education. The Consent Decree mandated that small high schools be established in every village with an elementary school and one or more children available to attend a secondary school. As a result, within the next few years small high schools were established in more than 100 villages.

THE PROGRAM

A program was established through the University of Alaska Fairbanks (UAF) in which graduate assistants would live in Alaska Native villages for one school year while collecting information on the new small high schools being established. The purpose of the study was to document the development of the schools so problems could be addressed earlier rather than later in the process. Each of the graduate assistants was to collect information on the small high school in the community where he or she was spending the year. This information would be gathered through interviews and by attending ac-tivities such as school board meetings. Information to be collected included a history of the school, the number of students, the number of teachers, dropout rates, governance structure, and so forth. At the end of the year, information from all nine sites in the study would be combined so that recommendations could be made.

The responsibilities of the assistantship also included tutoring and otherwise assisting undergraduate university students in the Cross-Cultural Education Development (XCED, pronounced "exceed") Program. The XCED program was a field-based program aimed at preparing students to teach in rural Alaskan schools. The purpose of the program was to train as teachers people who were already residents of rural villages and who would therefore have long-term commitments to the communities in which they were teaching. Rural Alaskan education had long suffered from high teacher turnover and from a lack of understanding by educators of the culture of the native communities. The XCED program was designed to address these problems. The program opened in 1970 and, by 1977, was well established.

XCED originated in 1970 as one of several federally funded Teacher Corps programs, instituted in response to the civil rights movement of the 1960s. One requirement for Teacher Corps funding was for representatives of the targeted minority communities to participate in the governance of the program. As a result, panels of Alaska Native representatives were established in each region with a statewide panel over all. The panels had responsibility for determining policy for the program, and they had a decisive role in the selection of staff. Panel members were recruited through native education networks.

XCED provided a Bachelor of Education curriculum in elementary or secondary school teaching to students in villages around the state. Field coordinators, who were qualified faculty members in the UAF Department of Education, were based in regional centers. Each field coordinator prepared courses that were delivered to all students in the state. Each field coordinator also traveled to villages in his or her region to facilitate studies with students in each village. Students in each region and statewide faculty regularly flew to the regional centers for face-to-face instruction.

The graduate assistants had responsibilities for collecting information on the small high schools and for tutoring undergraduate students. They were also responsible for completing the coursework required for secondary teaching certification and the master's degree. Most courses were essentially correspondence courses that required many hours of reading and the preparation of written assignments, but some of the assignments had to be completed in the classrooms of the local school. Funding to support the graduate assistants came from several sources—from the State of Alaska and from more than one program under the federal government.

Initially, the graduate assistants needed to find placements in one of the nine rural Alaskan villages participating in the study for the 1977–78 academic year. Each village had an advisory committee of university students and other community members who would interview the graduate assistants before approving the placement.

INITIATION

In August 1977, I had just completed a summer course at UAF. This course was the first course in what I planned as a fifth-year elementary school teaching certification. I held a bachelor's degree in sociology and anthropology and planned to become a third grade teacher at University Park School, not far from the university campus.

While glancing through the *Fairbanks Daily News Miner* late one sunny summer afternoon, I saw an advertisement for graduate assistants in the Small High Schools Project. Studying in a village setting simply had to be more interesting than doing a program on campus, I thought. I contacted the program coordinator and applied for a position, thus embarking on an odyssey that has continued for more than twenty years and has crisscrossed Alaska and the Pacific Ocean countless times.

I was offered the option of traveling with another applicant to a village in the interior of Alaska where we would both be interviewed by the local panel. I was extremely uncomfortable with the idea of competing for the placement and asked what my other options were. The second option that was presented to me was a village on the western coast of the state. I clearly remember asking the coordinator about the climate there. "Coastal," he said. I did not ask for more information, but as I would not have to compete with any other applicants, I agreed to go for the interview.

The program began with a one-week orientation on the Fairbanks campus. Then, on about 10 September, I flew to the coastal village with an overnight stay in a regional center on the way. The flight to the coastal village was in a small plane that flew at low altitude through gray mist. The plane circled the village before landing so that I could see the tiny houses sitting on a gravel spit in view of snowy mountains. By the time the plane landed, I was beginning to realize that I might have bitten off more than I could chew.

The population of the coastal village was about 300 people, nearly all of them Alaska Natives whose first language was the indigenous language. The economy of the community was based on marine mammal hunting and fishing.

UAF owned a house in the village, and my instructions were to see if it would be a suitable place for an education center for the program. After inquiring of the local people about the house's location, I hefted my backpack into place, leaned into the wind, and trudged across the gravel to the house, which was some distance from the center of the village.

The house had last been used a few months earlier by some biologists from UAF who had been working on a study relating to local wildlife. These scientists had left what I can only describe as a horrible mess. Trash was piled in the middle of the main room, and no one had taken the time to empty the "honeybucket" (a bucket used as an indoor toilet). The house swarmed with flies, and it stank. Living there for a year meant cleaning up the mess left by the university's scientists and acquiring minimal furnishings. I soon learned too that, in order to heat the house, barrels of heating oil would have to be rolled along the gravel road from the center of the village, one barrel at a time, and all water would have to be hauled to the house.

I settled as best I could the bedroll and one-burner stove I was carrying and arranged to meet with the advisory group. The group was very welcoming, but I think the members were also skeptical about whether a woman could make it alone in that situation. I visited the local store for provisions. As I was bending over a shelf, an old lady in a parka squirrel coat asked what I was doing there. I explained that I had come to live for a year to work with university students in the village. "Alone?" she asked. "Yes," I replied. "Hmpff," she said as she walked out the door. Skepticism from the local people about a woman alone in that setting had a definite effect on me. It contributed to growing skepticism about my ability to do the physical labor necessary to survive in the rugged environment through the year.

One of the local people told me of a recent incident in which a serious accident had occurred. Someone had been badly injured, but, because of bad weather, no planes could get in to move the person to the hospital for several days. I wondered what would happen if I had an appendicitis attack during the year. Did I want to try to get through the year without the modern and immediately available medical care that I was used to?

I returned to Fairbanks for a second week of orientation sessions for the project. By the time I returned to Fairbanks, I felt fairly certain that I could not survive a year in the coastal village without assistance, but I did not know how to make a change.

I went to see the administrator of the UAF unit responsible for the house in the village. He said that the visiting scientists had paid someone from the local community to clean up the house after they left. The local person had failed to fulfill that responsibility, but that was not perceived as the problem of the scientists, the administrator, or his unit of UAF. He had no intention of making any arrangements to clean up the house. Whoever used it next could clean it up.

I was furious, disappointed, and terrified. I went back to the building where our orientation sessions were being held. I went into the women's room, locked myself in a cubicle, and sobbed hysterically for quite a long time. A few years later, when I read the opening passages of *The Women's Room*, in which Marilyn French (1977: 7) describes a similar scene, I realized I was not the only woman of that era to have had this kind of experience.

To this day I do not know just how the program coordinator identified the problem, but he did (maybe it was my red and swollen eyes). He suggested trading locations with a colleague, a man who had visited another village as a possible site. This village was located at the end of a one-hour jet flight from Anchorage, Alaska's largest city. The region was very cold in the winter but did not have high winds to cope with. Because of the jet flights from Anchorage, a wide range of urban amenities was available. One could even buy ice cream in the village store. Fortunately for me, my colleague thought this village was too urbanized. He wanted to spend the year in a more rugged location and was pleased to have the opportunity to go to the coastal village.

There were still the advisory committees in each community to consider. The committee in the more urban village had already accepted my colleague, and the committee in the coastal village had already accepted me. It was agreed that we both needed to visit each community to explain and ask approval for the change. This involved the two of us flying first to one village via Anchorage and meeting with the committee there. Then, we flew back to Anchorage, to the regional center, and to the coastal village and met with that committee. With the approval of both committees, my colleague remained in the coastal village, while I returned to the regional center, Anchorage, and finally the village where I would spend the school year. Unfortunately, by the time I had completed all the travel, I was about ten days behind schedule in completing tasks for the year.

My new home was located in a region that anthropologists call a "transitional region"—its inhabitants were from both Yup'ik and Athabascan cultural groups. Inhabitants of the region often referred to themselves as "natives" rather than identifying with a particular cultural group. Russians were the first Europeans to colonize this region in the 1700s. As a result, the Russian Orthodox Church has remained one of the primary religious organizations in the region, and the personal names of many natives have Russian origins. I did not know any of the history when I arrived in the region and was completely befuddled when I met people named "Sasha" and "Natasha."

People of this region were deeply affected by the epidemics of the early twentieth century. In fact, whole communities were wiped out. Many survivors who had lost their relatives joined predominantly nonnative mining communities. The village where I lived had originally been established as a postal stop, but, by the late 1970s, it had become a hub for passengers and freight traveling to smaller villages in the region. The jets from Anchorage landed in the village, where passengers, freight, and mail were dispersed to smaller planes for transport to the smaller villages.

Although the population was predominantly Alaska Native, a large minority was made up of whites who were employed in transportation, the school district offices, the school, or the regional offices of other agencies. There was little evidence in the everyday activities of the community of anything that might be considered traditional native culture. The general impression of the life of the community was one of Western activities and institutions. Although there were some people who hunted and fished for subsistence, most worked for wages or salaries in the school or school district office, ANCSA corporation offices, stores, Federal Aviation Administration, and so forth. The major forms of entertainment were Western and included basketball, movies, and rock dances.

In 1977, the entire state of Alaska was in the midst of the oil boom. Oil royalties were flowing in, and the state was expanding services. The population of this village, like the populations in many other rural communities, was expanding with the increased flow of state dollars. As a result, housing was difficult to find. Because I expected to spend only eight months in the community as a graduate assistant, I found temporary accommodations in the lodge. The lodge was a local landmark, an old blue two-story house facing the airstrip. Two older men ran it. A plywood barracks of six rooms sat behind the lodge, and I settled into one room there. The barracks had one shower with hot running water—a genuine luxury in rural Alaska in those days. I had breakfast and an evening meal with other guests in the lodge each day.

The field coordinator for the region lived in the regional center about forty-five minutes away by small plane. Like other field coordinators, he traveled to the villages in his region to facilitate all the courses with all the students, and I, along with the other students in the village, flew to the regional center two or three times a year for student meetings.

There were four undergraduate students in the village in 1977–78. One man was Alaska Native, in his mid-thirties. His wife was nonnative. They had one small child of their own and were foster parenting another. The other two students were nonnative. One was a single woman who had recently left a long-term relationship with a local man. The other was a man whose wife was Alaska Native; they had four children.

Funding from federal programs provided a small income for each of the students and their families, but they all lived "on the edge" financially, barely scraping by during that year. All had temporary jobs at some point during the year. Financial worries were major problems for all of them, and, on a daily and continuing basis, the three students in cross-cultural marriages had to confront the conflicts that commonly occur in cross-cultural relationships. Because some of the undergraduate courses required that students undertake assignments in the local school, the attitudes of the local teachers and district personnel were important to the success of the students in the coursework. Teachers and school district personnel were highly skeptical about the quality of instruction in a field-based program. Some expressed skepticism about whether these particular students should be teachers as well.

During the orientation in September, I had learned that my first responsibility was to these students. I was to act as a student advocate as well as a tutor, advocating for the students with the XCED instructors and in the local school. One aspect of that advocacy was meeting with the principal of the school and with teachers, advocating for opportunities that the students needed to do their coursework in the classrooms.

All four students were well motivated and had the skills they needed, and the tutoring aspect of my role was relatively easy. Assisting them with the coursework gave me a sense of instant success. However, the students' financial worries, their personal problems, and the attitudes of the school people drew my constant attention. One or another of the students seemed always to be in the midst of either a personal or a school-related crisis. I had not yet learned that I could not save the world single-handedly. I tried to help with each crisis as it came along. I discovered that I could often be of greatest assistance to the women students by caring for their children so that they would have a chance to study.

SETTLING IN

I quickly settled into a period of solid concentration on the tasks in front of me: working with students, collecting data on the high school, and diligently poring over the mountain of reading and writing assignments that I had carried with me from Fairbanks. "Freeze up"—the weeks in September and October when the temperatures drop and the major rivers and their tributaries freeze over—came and went. The days grew shorter and colder. The first snow fell, and, by November, the Alaskan winter set in. Temperatures sometimes reached fifty below, and sometimes the chill factor was much lower because of the wind. There were times when I did not have to walk from place to place. If I stood firmly with my back to the wind and did not move, the wind was strong enough to blow me along the icy road. After the river froze, sno-goes traveled rapidly up and down the river on the ice, and there were even a few trucks that made their way over the river ice to the regional center.

Once, a family who owned two sno-goes invited me to travel along the river with them to visit another village about ten miles away. I was to ride on the back of one of the sno-goes driven by the teenage daughter in the family. I do not remember much about the ride down the frozen river, but I vividly remember the ride back. It was after dark and very cold, and everyone was anxious to get home. We traveled as fast as the machines, the darkness, and the rough, bumpy trail would allow. I clung for dear life to the young woman in front of me, praying that I would not lose my grip on her. We eventually arrived safely home.

Other forms of entertainment in the village included a small, dilapidated movie theater that showed movies about twice a week. There were regular Saturday night dances. Basketball was an obsession in this village, as it was in many Alaskan villages at the time. Teams of adults competed in the high school gym several times during the week. One evening each week was reserved for women's basketball. I had only been in the village a few days when I was invited to join the women's team. Not having played the game since I was thirteen or fourteen and not having played it very well then, I politely declined. However, the female chairperson of the school board of trustees made a personal visit to invite me to play. "All you have to do is stand under the basket and wave your arms," she said. I agreed and actually played once or twice. However, I did not develop the same passion for the game that the other women had, and I found excuses not to join in. Fortunately, my relationship with the chair of the school board did not suffer as a result.

DISTRACTIONS

The single woman undergraduate student decided in early December to move to Anchorage to live. I was disappointed to "lose" one of my students. Then, a second major event occurred. The deputy superintendent of the school district asked me if I would help out by substitute teaching in the elementary school in one of the smaller villages for a week. A teaching couple had been the teachers in the two-teacher elementary school there. They departed suddenly, and I was asked to fill in for a week so that the school would not have to close. The district's special education teacher would be the second substitute, and the only teacher in the new small high school would help too.

I explained that I had no teaching experience and had only begun my own teacher certification program at the secondary level. That would be no problem, said the district man. "Work on the Christmas program," he said. I agreed to help out for one week, no more. I had other responsibilities to attend to.

The deputy superintendent and I were flown in a small Cessna to a village of about sixty people. This village had begun as a mining camp, but, by 1977, the entire population was Alaska Native except for the storekeeper and the schoolteachers. The elementary school had been built in the style typical of

Chapter Five

the Bureau of Indian Affairs in Alaska—two classrooms with an apartment connected for the teachers. (The apartment was called "the teacherage.") The special education teacher and I were to stay in the teacherage. There were twenty-six elementary students, grades K–8.

The new small high school in this village was in its second year of operation. There were twelve students and one teacher. Classes were held in what was formerly a storage building. Heating was inadequate. In the second year, students had desks, but the school district had not yet purchased textbooks. The high school teacher, an energetic young man, lived in a one-room cabin with a wood stove. One of his major after-school activities was cutting wood for the stove.

And so I began my teaching career. The special education teacher took the older students, and I took the younger group. I went through the motions that I thought were appropriate. We worked on the Christmas program, as we had been instructed to do.

On my first day, I had an inkling that there were major problems in this community. I was introduced to the school's custodian, a native man who had no fingers. I was told that, at some time in the past, he had passed out drunk in the snow, and someone had taken his gloves. His fingers had been frost-bitten and were eventually amputated.

During the evening of my second night in the village, the high school teacher came to the teacherage. Someone had imported a shipment of alcohol to the village. One nearby village had a liquor store, so the alcohol had probably come by sno-go and sled from there. Based on previous experiences, the high school teacher feared violence, and he, the special education teacher, and I locked ourselves in the teacherage. Later that night, we heard loud shouting outside. Someone banged on the school door, but we did not open it. The next day, some of the children arrived an hour or two late for school. One or two put their heads on their desks and fell asleep. As best I could, I continued to work on the Christmas program.

A week later there was still no word from the school district about a replacement teacher. I contacted the school district office by radio and explained, once again, that I had other responsibilities and that I could not stay longer. I felt totally incompetent as a teacher and was certain that "working on the Christmas program" was not contributing substantially to the education of the village's children. I was beginning to believe that it would be in the best interests of the children if the school were closed until competent teachers could be employed, but the school district administration wanted to keep the school open to avoid a confrontation with the community.

Finally, after ten days and no word from the school district, I radioed for a plane to pick me up the next day. That night, another shipment of alcohol was under consumption in the village. Again, the three of us locked ourselves into the school. The next morning, the temperature was forty-five below—too cold for a plane to be flying. At mid-morning, though, a stranger turned up at the school. He was the pilot of the plane sent in response to my radio request. In the village where he was based it was only twenty-eight below, he said, and he had not known it was too cold to fly. I quickly packed my backpack, and we hiked to the airstrip. Another plane was there, a Medivac that had come to pick up the school's custodian. During the previous night, someone had poured gasoline on him and had lit it. He had survived but was being flown to the hospital in the regional center.

After I left, the district closed the school until after Christmas. In January, the school was opened with two new certificated teachers. Later in the spring, I saw the high school teacher when he was attending a meeting in the village where I was living. He told me that four of his twelve high school students had taken overdoses of phenobarbital in an effort to commit suicide. Fortunately, none of them had died. The teacher felt that he had done all he could do and planned to look for another placement for the next school year.

A few years later, though, I heard that there had been a major change in the community. There had been a major effort to restrict alcohol use, and the social climate had improved as a result. The two elementary school teachers who had come that January had been influential in bringing about the change.

I had no doubt after my brief stay in the village that it was a community in crisis. When I discussed my observations with other university staff, they said that similar situations seemed to develop in communities in transitional areas between one major cultural group and another. It was another ten years before there was a general realization that villages throughout the state, and in Canada as well, were suffering in similar ways. Not all villages were impacted in the same way, but some villages in all regions were suffering from the long-term effects of colonization.

OVERLOAD

After I left the smaller village, I spent a week on my assigned tasks and then flew to Anchorage to spend Christmas with friends. Early in January, I continued to Fairbanks to complete some assignments and to participate in a midyear meeting of the XCED staff and the graduate assistants.

When I returned to "my" village toward the end of January, I started the student teaching component of my teacher certification program in the high school. The high school had been established in 1973. The high school building was in a complex with the elementary school and was equipped with a gymnasium and the books, desks, blackboards, and audiovisual equipment that one would expect to find in any mainstream American school.

There were forty-two secondary students in 1977–78, nearly all of them Alaska Natives. All of the certificated teachers for both the elementary and the secondary classrooms were nonnative teachers from other states, many with the distinctive regional accent of Oklahoma. In those days, district superintendents tended to recruit teachers from their own home regions; the superintendent at the time was from Oklahoma.

The curriculum was structured in much the same way as it is in urban schools. The day was divided into fifty-minute periods with students moving from class to class. Subjects taught closely resembled the subjects in urban schools. This structure created a nearly impossible task for teachers because teachers had to do five or more separate preparations for each day's instruction. One vivid memory is of a young energetic man simultaneously teaching a biology class of six students in half of one classroom and a chemistry class of another six students on the other side of the room.

My student teaching assignment was the same as that for other secondary student teachers in urban and rural settings around the state. I was to observe in my cooperating teacher's classrooms for two weeks and then take over one class at a time until I carried the same teaching load that my cooperating teacher carried. Two periods were spent in the seventh and eighth grade classroom and three were in ninth–twelfth grade classrooms. Each class was in a different subject, so I, like the other teachers, struggled to prepare for five different classes each day.

One of the classes was a seventh and eighth grade class on U.S. history. The textbook contained only one column on one page about Native Americans. I recall a sense of utter absurdity in trying to teach Alaska Native children the history of their country when the textbook authors barely acknowledged the existence of the ancestry, history, and traditions of the children I was teaching.

Student teaching held some outstanding experiences for me, though. My cooperating classroom teacher had begun a project based on the Foxfire publications. *Foxfire* was the name of a magazine produced by high school students in Rabun Gap, Georgia, under the supervision of their teacher, Eliot Wigginton. The Georgia students developed the magazine articles by interviewing and photographing people from the local community who were experts in Appalachian crafts and traditions. The project eventually grew into a series of newsletters, books, films, and course guides (Wigginton 1985), and it became a model for high school classrooms in Alaska as well as in other regions of America. In our Alaskan classroom, my cooperating teacher sent older students into the community to tape-record interviews with local people and then transcribe the interviews. The class planned to publish a magazine of student stories called *Echo*. The project had started in September, but students had been bogged down in the tedious details of recording and transcribing the interviews. I suggested to the cooperating teacher that we forget the tape-recording and just have each student talk to and then write about someone or something in the community. This was enough to get the students moving with their articles. The magazine was published by the end of the spring semester. The students, the cooperating teacher, and I were proud and pleased with our work.

Another high point came when the school counselor invited me to assist in chaperoning a group of six high school students on a "career exploration" trip to Anchorage and Fairbanks. She had done an excellent job of organizing and establishing ground rules for the group. There were meetings with students and parents before the trip to ensure that everyone knew what those rules were and what the consequences would be for anyone not abiding by the rules. As a result of her organization and the one-to-three ratio of adults to students on the trip, all went well. We visited the branches of the University of Alaska in Anchorage and Fairbanks as well as several other sites intended to stimulate the kids' interest in one occupation or another. And we visited some fun places, too. I think that my first, and perhaps only, visit to a video game parlor occurred on that trip.

At the same time, student teaching was a full-time job—but I had two other jobs, tutoring the undergraduate XCED students and working on data collection and preparing reports for the project. I continued to conduct interviews, maintain a journal, complete written assignments, and so on throughout the student teaching period. I felt stressed out for much of that semester, and that was reflected in my reactions to the visits of the XCED coordinator from the regional center and the project coordinator from Fairbanks. I remember once that I talked for six hours straight and the field coordinator could not get a word in edgewise.

Once during that semester two friends flew in for a brief visit. One was a pilot with his own Cessna. He and another friend were just flying around one day when they decided to come to visit. They only stayed a couple of days, but it was fun to see them.

I had a week-long break after I finished student teaching. The graduate assistant in the coastal village invited me to visit, so once again I flew to Anchorage, then to another regional center, and then to the coastal village. In my briefcase, I carried four bottles of wine. My colleague had spent the year in a "dry" community. We spent about three days drinking the wine and talking through the events of the year.

I returned to my village to wind up the academic year with the undergraduate students. One of the students was scheduled for student teaching in the fall semester, but he had antagonized the local school principal, and the principal refused to place the student in his school. The field coordinator from the regional center arranged a solution to the problem. He set up a student teaching place for the student in the adjacent school district. However, the student had no resources to pay to move his wife, four children, pets, and all their belongings. The field coordinator chartered a Cessna from the regional center, picked up the student, his family, the pets, and the family's belongings and continued on to the student teaching location. The student completed his degree and teacher certification and has been actively involved in rural Alaskan education ever since.

PREPARING THE REPORT

In summer 1978, the project coordinator, a second faculty member, and the graduate assistants spent six weeks reviewing and compiling the information collected from all the villages. I had loved doing the research, and I loved working to analyze and interpret the findings of the year. A report was completed and issued the following year (Barnhardt et al. 1979).

Unfortunately, the media made a major news story out of aspects of the report that were critical of the small high schools. A political brouhaha ensued. None of the project staff realized that there were political factions in the urban areas of the state that were opposed to the establishment of the small high schools in the villages. When the report became public, these factions and the media made every effort to use the report to their own advantage. Eventually, the outcry died away. By the time the report was published, however, I was well into a new job and a new project. The Small High Schools Project had been funded as a two-year project. It continued through the second year, 1978–79, with a new set of graduate assistants and a second report produced at the end of the second year.

DISCUSSION

There were a number of successful outcomes of the project in 1977–78. The research report was completed and presented to the funding agencies. Three of the four undergraduate XCED students completed their courses for the year. One graduated the following semester and began a long-term career in Alaska Native education. I completed my first formal fieldwork. I felt that it had been a grand experience. I finished my teaching certification and most of the credits required for the master's degree. For the following year, I found employment related to my training.

One of the major reasons for the success of this project was that it was embedded in an existing, well-established program, the XCED program. When this project was undertaken, the term *collaborative research* had not yet come into general use, but the Teacher Corps and the XCED program had established regional and statewide panels of Alaska Native representatives to participate in the governance of the program. There was a general recognition of the need for native participation in decision making and for project staff and local participants to work together in determining the direction the project would take. As a result, there were several collaborative dimensions of the project. The panel of community members and students in each village collaborated with university staff in the appointment of the graduate assistants. Members of the panels assisted the graduate students in finding housing, in providing introductions to various groups, and in data collection. Members of the panels provided information on the history and organization of the communities and schools, and they directed graduate assistants to other sources of information. In my own case, I was as much dependent on the undergraduate students for assistance in the research as they were dependent on me for assistance in completing their studies. The collaborative aspects of this project were among its strengths. Integrating a research component into an existing program in which collaborative relationships had already been established was considerably easier than establishing a new project with no preexisting infrastructure.

However, the project was aimed at collecting information on the schools, and there was no intention to collaborate with the schools to bring about innovation. Over the next two decades, collaborative research projects in indigenous communities changed. Many projects in the 1990s involved representatives of indigenous groups, outside researchers, and schools or other mainstream institutions in collaboration intended to bring about innovation or social change.

The one significant negative outcome of the 1977–78 project was the media coverage stemming from the critical aspects mentioned in the research report. Fortunately, the political effects of the negative publicity were short term. The lesson for researchers was clear: report writers must make every effort to anticipate the media and political response to their reports.

When the report was prepared, all of the project staff collaborated, but we did not realize at the time the importance of collaborating in the write up with at least some of the school participants. If there had been opportunities for some of the school people to comment on drafts of the report, the political uproar might have been avoided, although there is no way of knowing that with certainty, of course. In more recent examples of collaborative research, manuscripts often have been read and critiqued by community members or school personnel before publication.

LESSONS LEARNED

In chapter 3, the characteristics of successful fieldworkers are discussed. My analysis of the actions of the fieldworker in the Small High Schools Project is highly personal—because I was the fieldworker! However, my hope is that my reflections will be helpful to others even though the perspective is a personal one. The guidelines in chapter 3 that relate to the characteristics of fieldworkers are as follows.

The Individual Fieldworker

Be Flexible but Recognize That Everyone Has Limits.

In spite of my great enthusiasm at the beginning of this project, I learned that my flexibility had its limits. I had been living in Alaska for two years before I started on the project. I thought I knew what conditions were like in "bush" or rural Alaska. I realized very quickly, however, that the conditions in the coastal village and in the smaller inland village were new conditions to me, and my best efforts to adapt to these conditions were not likely to lead to success. There are limitations to the flexibility of every human being, I realized.

Once I was in a setting in which I believed I could cope, I was able to make some necessary changes in my lifestyle. I had most of the necessary cold weather clothing and was used to living without a car, walking nearly everywhere I went. Life in the barracks behind the lodge did not require much adjustment; I had lived in dormitories before. I quickly realized, though, that others would know my every move in the small community, and anything that reflected negatively on me would reflect negatively on the project and on the undergraduate students. I avoided parties and dances where alcohol might become a problem, and I became quite circumspect in my relations with members of the opposite sex.

Because my participation in this project was for only one year, there were few, if any, changes in formal policies or university expectations. I did expend a good deal of energy, though, trying to determine what expectations were held by different parties (the university, the field coordinator, the local school and school district, the undergraduate students, other local people) and wondering whose expectations should have priority. Because of the different parties involved and the new situation, I felt ambiguous about the expectations that surrounded me.

I was also in a new job with a new set of tasks and was many miles from anyone who could provide close supervision or instruction. I had received an orientation and appropriate readings to cover. There were letters, a few phone calls, and visits. My undergraduate education in sociology and anthropology had provided some additional clues about the best ways to proceed. Nevertheless, I was very uncertain of myself. I often felt as though I was stumbling along in the dark. Intuitively, I was able to go about the business of conducting research, even when I was not always sure what that entailed, an ability that Wolcott identified as important for fieldworkers nearly twenty years later (1995: 95).

My tolerance for discouragement was severely tested twice during the year. The first incident involved the visit to the coastal village and the seemingly insurmountable dilemma regarding my ability to cope with the physical environment in that location. The second incident occurred when I agreed to substitute teach in the smaller village for one week, when the school district did not make arrangements for me to leave at the end of that commitment. On reflection, I think that, although I survived in the project, I really did not deal very well with those situations.

I am grateful that the program provided me with an opportunity to visit the sites before my commitment for the year was finalized. I can only reiterate my earlier advice with respect to the physical setting: if possible, fieldworkers should visit the field site before making a long-term commitment, to be certain that the physical setting is one that they find manageable.

The values of the village where I spent the year were similar to the values of communities where I had lived all my life. The dominant value system was that of mainstream America. There may have been subgroups within the community with value systems that differed from the mainstream, but the few months that I lived there were too short a period of time for me to explore the value systems in any great depth. I do not recall having to make any major adjustments as the result of conflicts between my values and those of the community.

I would have had great difficulty adjusting to life in the small village where I went to substitute teach in December 1977, however. I did not feel capable of coping effectively with the social problems. The teaching couple who arrived in January 1978 did not have the same response to the situation. They were able to take an active role in developing programs to help to address the problems, but I lacked the training and attributes necessary for me to work productively in that setting.

Be Willing to Collaborate by Sharing Authority, Responsibility, and Credit for Success.

One of the things I found most endearing about the XCED program was the program's stance with respect to collaboration. I had come of age in the 1960s and believed in the right of Alaska Natives to make decisions about research and educational programs in their own communities. Freire's *Pedagogy of the*

Oppressed had been published in 1970, and the book had influenced XCED staff. They advocated "empowerment" and so did I. In the orientation to the program, I was told that I was expected to accept decisions of the local panel. I easily agreed to do so. I do not recall having any difficulty collaborating with local panel members and undergraduate students in the day-to-day activities of research and teaching in the village. I realize now that full collaboration with local people and school, including the write-up phase, would have been more difficult. I talked to local panel members and students regularly about decisions that had to be made, and we worked toward consensus about the best courses of action. I was often asked for my advice, but that is all my opinion amounted to—advice.

Because the local panels were already in place when I arrived in the village, I did not have to identify appropriate people for the panels, and I did not have to establish the principles of collaboration. This was a major advantage for me in completing the tasks for the year.

Give Thoughtful Attention to the Ethical Implications of Your Actions.

I do not recall any instruction regarding research ethics in any of my undergraduate social science courses or in this research project. Some professional associations and the research community in general were slowly recognizing that ethics statements should be explicitly formulated and explicitly taught to undergraduate and graduate students. Up until this time, there had been a general assumption that highly educated researchers, with the best interests of humankind and the advancement of knowledge in mind, would know, without instruction, the best ways to behave.

I do recall cautionary tales discussed in the initial orientation sessions of the project. One such tale is about a school principal in an unnamed village who liked to have a glass of wine after dinner. However, it was a "dry" village, so he did not want the villagers to know that he drank wine. He therefore had a problem disposing of the bottles. He crushed the bottles with a hammer, put the crushed glass in a paper bag, and carried the bag far out on to the tundra to bury it. Villagers observed his movements, and eventually a confrontation came. The villagers thought he had been walking out on the tundra alone so that he could communicate with enemy submarines off the coast. They thought he was a spy for a foreign power!

I do not know what became of this principal, but I do know that there are two lessons for novice fieldworkers in this story. The first is that residents of small communities—particularly residents with some different ways of doing things—should expect to have their movements noticed. It may be possible to remain anonymous in big cities but not in small, isolated communities. The second is that acting in ways contrary to community expectations can lead to detrimental consequences. This tale only touches on the issues involved in ethical expectations for novice researchers. Otherwise, graduate assistants were expected to use good common sense.

Apply the Concept of Culture in Everyday Working Relationships.

The village where I lived that year provides an excellent example of the difficulties involved in applying the concept of culture as an analytical framework. I had a full set of tasks for every day. Those tasks necessitated communicating with and relating to individuals from a range of cultural backgrounds. It was a multicultural community in fairly rapid change because of technological innovations, ANCSA, new money from the state government, and other factors. There were individuals with Yup'ik origins, Athabascan origins, various European origins, and combinations of origins from these cultural groups. Some people had lived in the community for many years, but others were transients who had only recently come from other places. The school staff members who had been recruited from Oklahoma formed one of the most noticeable groups, identified by their distinctive accents.

I found it useful to recognize that each individual's cultural background affected that individual's behavior and viewpoints. It seemed important to understand that each individual was endowed with a particular background that originated in a cultural group. If I knew something about the cultural background of an individual, that knowledge would enhance my understanding, and my work would benefit. Finding out from any one person about his or her background was useful in interpreting that person's viewpoints, but there were too many cultural groups represented for me to be able to generalize about behavior in cultural terms. I had to try to learn about and work with each person on an individual basis.

At the same time, I found it essential to know something about the historical background of the region. I needed that knowledge to help me understand why there were Russian names and a Russian Orthodox Church in the community and why the smaller villages in the region were suffering from extensive social problems. History was something I could learn from books; culture was something that I could only learn from individuals.

Designing Collaborative Programs

Planning for this program occurred before I arrived on the scene, so I can only speculate about the processes. The program coordinator was largely responsible for planning the research and the integration of research tasks with other dimensions of the XCED program. Funding agencies and university administrative staff were involved in planning. The regional field coordinators for the

XCED program and the panel members in the villages must have participated in the planning because they all seemed to know about the role the graduate assistants were to play. A program plan for the year was presented to graduate assistants in the initial orientation, so we knew that a plan was in place. The plan was for a research project addressing specific goals. It was not part of a larger strategic plan. A comparison of the program structure with the recommendations for program design in chapter 4 indicates that the essential components for program success were in place. These recommendations are as follows.

Fieldworkers and Representatives of the Community Should Collaborate to Develop a Rationale, Philosophy, or Reason for the Establishment of the Particular Program.

In this instance, collaboration regarding the rationale for the program had taken place before I joined the project. By the time of the initial orientation for graduate assistants, the goals had been clearly stated and accepted by all the participants. There were three sets of goals and objectives involved in the project that year. The first set focused on research in small high schools in Alaska's rural villages. The second focused on the educational program for the undergraduate students. The third focused on the educational program of the graduate assistants. The rationale for each of the three segments of the project was well developed, but attempting to integrate three separate sets of goals and objectives for a single project created complications for participants.

It was difficult for graduate assistants to balance the three sets of objectives so that all three received appropriate time and attention over the course of the year. The graduate assistants were not always able to find that balance, so in some instances only some of the objectives were addressed. At the same time, there were good reasons for including three sets of goals in the project. In order to get the funding to run the project, funding had to be drawn from several different sources and agencies. The different agencies had different objectives. One set of objectives (research, tutoring, or graduate coursework) would not have resulted in outcomes that would have justified the expense of the project for any one agency.

The project was intended to last for a limited period of time. Over a longer period, problems in balancing the importance of the three sets of objectives would likely have grown, but the reality of the funding structure for the project dictated the complex sets of objectives.

Look for Sources of Adequate and Dependable Funding.

I gave very little consideration to the funding that year, once I was certain that my assistantship would cover my own personal expenses. So far as I was aware, the funding was adequate and was stable for the period of the project. However, the fact that several agencies with differing goals provided funding created complexities that were sometimes difficult to deal with.

Confirm That There Is Adequate Support in the Local Community.

There were people in the local community who supported the project, but there were also people who did not support it; and there were many who did not care one way or the other. The important point in this instance is that there was support in segments of the community that were essential to the success of the project, and only a small number opposed it.

The essential supporters were the undergraduate students and other members of the local panel, the school board, and some of the teachers in the school. The undergraduate students were anxious to have a graduate assistant on site to assist them with their coursework, and they were willing to assist me with the data collection for the research aspects of the project. The school board agreed to have me as a researcher in the school and agreed to have the undergraduate students and me as teacher trainees in the school. Also, some of the teachers were willing to have us as trainees in their classrooms. All of the district and school staff cooperated with my requests for interviews and for other types of information on the school.

The undergraduate students and I believed that the school principal and some staff members in the district offices opposed the XCED program, but there was sufficient support from others in the school and community to offset this opposition. The school and school district offices were staffed primarily by whites from other states whose goals did not necessarily include incorporating field-trained students into the school system. Although I tried to act as a mediator between the school and the undergraduate students, I sometimes had to choose between one faction and the other, and my loyalties lay with the students. I found that the conflicts added to the personal stress of the situation, another factor that might have become harder to cope with if the project had been planned for a longer term. Conflict between school and community factions can also be much harder to deal with in fully collaborative programs in which local representatives, researchers, and the school are attempting to work together.

In this particular situation, in which a requirement of my position was to act as an advocate for the undergraduate students, I could not remain wholly outside of any conflicts between the students and the school or school district. However, it was essential to balance the need to act as advocate with the need to maintain good relationships between the students and the school, for the students needed access to teachers and classrooms in order to complete their course assignments, degrees, and requirements for certification. Acting too aggressively in advocating for the students could have had the effect of antagonizing school personnel to the point at which they might withdraw their assistance for the undergraduate students. This would have had a negative effect on student progress and would have been detrimental to the students.

Formulate a Program Plan Including Statements of Roles and Responsibilities, Support Systems for Participants, and Evaluation Procedures.

I did not participate in the formulation of the program plan, but, by the time I joined the project, most of the essential elements were in place. The project came under the governance structure of the XCED program with policies and procedures determined by the university and the program's panel of Alaska Native and other rural representatives. I had little reason to attend to specific questions of program management or to the responsibilities of any of the other staff members. I liked the XCED staff, and, because the program seemed to run smoothly from my standpoint, I assumed that the program coordinator, field coordinator, and administrative staff knew what they were doing and were administering the funding properly. Fortunately, the year went well in spite of my lack of attention to what I later learned were critical elements of program success.

In this situation, roles were carefully defined. I was told in the initial orientation in Fairbanks that I was expected to work in cooperation with members of the local panel, undergraduate students, the school, and the regional field coordinator. I knew that the local panel had the authority to ask that I be removed from the community if I was not performing. I made every effort to communicate regularly with each group or individual as described in the initial orientation.

At the same time, I took on responsibilities outside of the defined roles (substitute teaching in the smaller village and chaperoning the career exploration trip), and these responsibilities added to a sense of stress and overload, particularly in the second semester of the project. Even without the added responsibilities, the various roles would have been too much for one person over an extended period of time. I worked seven days a week, every waking minute, trying to do the job I thought I was supposed to do. Other graduate assistants coped by doing the same or by focusing on some objectives to the exclusion of others.

Over the years, I have learned to look closely at the requirements of my role in a collaborative program before agreeing to participate. It is often the case that program designers set up role responsibilities that look great on paper but are impossible for a real person to carry out.

The project designers understood the necessity to build systems of personal support into the project, and appropriate funding for support was allocated in the program budget. There were two weeks of orientation at the beginning of the academic year and a one-week meeting in January in Fairbanks for all the graduate assistants and staff. I was visited by Fairbanks academic staff as well as by the sympathetic regional field coordinator. Time was available for me to visit friends and family for the Christmas holidays and at spring break. Personal travel expenses were my responsibility, but the assistantship provided the money I needed to cover them.

Communication was a problem in any rural Alaskan program in the 1970s because many villages were without telephones and the mail was slow. We all had to make adjustments in our expectations to accommodate the difficulties in communication.

Staff members monitored the activities of the graduate assistants, and members of the panel in the local community kept in close touch with graduate assistants throughout the year, informally monitoring their activities. Because this was a short-term project, accountability and evaluation occurred primarily through the project reports. There were no direct profits from publication, and, because the concept of "intellectual property rights" had not yet come into common use, no one involved in the project would have known what to make of the term in relation to the work we were doing. Accountability to the local community could have been improved by incorporating in the project plan a review process for the draft of the final report.

Identify and Recruit Committed Leadership in the Program and, Preferably, in the Funding Agency.

I cannot fault the commitment of the leader of this program. Ray Barnhardt, the Small High Schools Project coordinator, began work on programs in rural Alaska in the late 1960s. His work in Alaska has continued for over thirty years with notable success. He was one of the originators of the XCED program and, in the early 1980s, of the Department of Native and Rural Development at UAF. He has been a Fulbright lecturer in Iceland and has studied on a Fulbright–Hays Award in India. He has worked in British Columbia and in New Zealand while on sabbatical leaves. He has contributed to the development of professional associations of indigenous educators and has organized international conferences of indigenous educators. His publications have appeared in several countries including the United States, Canada, and Australia. In the 1990s, he worked with the Alaska Federation of Natives with funding from the National Science Foundation and the Annenberg Rural Challenge to develop and implement the Alaska Rural Systemic Initiative. In 1999, the Council on Anthropology and Education honored him with the prestigious Spindler Award for outstanding contributions to the field.

Identify and Recruit Appropriately Qualified Staff.

All project staff members who were also staff of the XCED program had graduate-level training and degrees and were experienced in rural Alaska. The graduate assistants had completed bachelor's degrees, but most had little, if any, training in research methods or in education. The orientation at the beginning of the academic year provided minimal preparation for the work we were to do during the year. All of us struggled to acquire the necessary skills on the job. In an ideal world, all of the graduate assistants would have had extensive training in social science research methods or would have been provided with that training before entering the field. Looking back on this situation, though, I cannot see any way to have improved it. The people selected as graduate assistants were the ones with the best qualifications who applied for the positions, and it is unlikely that the State of Alaska would have provided the substantial funding needed for additional training. And I am not at all certain of the extent to which it is possible to train people for the kind of fieldwork we were doing. Fieldwork must be learned through experience, so on-the-job training is an inherent part of learning fieldwork.

All but one of the XCED staff members that year were nonnative. In the years since then, every effort has been made to recruit qualified Alaska Natives to work in the program.

Find a Workable Physical Setting.

Undoubtedly, one of the most important lessons to be learned from the project experience was the importance of choosing a setting that "fit." I have no doubt at all that I would not have completed the academic year in the coastal village, partially because the physical environment was too demanding and partially because a single woman would not have fit easily into the community.

One of the strengths in the design of the program was the option for graduate assistants to visit the prospective villages before making a commitment to live in a particular village for a year. There were travel costs involved because graduate assistants visited the villages and then returned to Fairbanks for the second week of orientation. Travel costs would have been lower if there had been two consecutive weeks of orientation. Also, it would have been less expensive for the program if I had gone to live in the first village I visited. However, the additional costs for travel were essential to the successful completion of the program. As the result of this experience, I always recommend that fieldworkers visit the field site before making a long-term commitment to live there.

Attend to the Broader Political and Social Context That Makes It Possible for a Program to Survive.

The Small High Schools Project was intended to last only two years. It was unlikely that the political climate would have supported a long-term research project. Urban factions opposed to the expenditure of state funds for the small high schools were influencing budget allocations. By 1980 oil revenues to the state began to fall, and funding was soon cut for many state services. Federal funding was declining in the late 1970s, and it declined further with the election of Ronald Reagan as president in 1980.

The XCED program was established in 1970. It began as a federally funded program, but federal policies changed, and by 1980 the state had assumed responsibility. The program's funding was under threat almost from its inception, but rural Alaskans supported XCED through their representatives in the state legislature. Pressure from mainstream university administrators brought about the closure of the program in the late 1990s. It was replaced with the Rural Educator Preparation Partnership. By the year 2000, the political situation had shifted again in support of Alaska Native teacher education, and new university administrators were promising to place high priorities on programs to prepare native teachers in rural areas.

Chapter Six

College Pilot Projects, 1978–81

In August 1978, I went to work for a two-year college affiliated with the University of Alaska system. It was located in one of the regional centers and was responsible for offering technical and academic programs in villages throughout the region as well as in the regional center.

THE PROGRAM, 1978–79

In spring 1978, one XCED field coordinator submitted a proposal to the college for the establishment of a pilot project modeled on XCED. The field coordinator proposed that the college establish two field centers, one in a coastal village and one in an inland village. Field coordinators for the college would be based in these field centers and would travel to other villages to work with students on courses written by college staff in the regional center. The curriculum would follow the two-year college curriculum for the Associate of Arts degree, preparing "First Language Teachers" for the village schools.

In the early 1970s, the Bureau of Indian Affairs (BIA) introduced in some of its Alaskan elementary schools a program in which the first three grades were taught in the indigenous language, with transition to English as part of the curriculum. From fourth grade up, classes were in English. Teachers for the first three grades were from the local communities and were fluent speakers of the indigenous language who went through teacher training programs in conjunction with their classroom teaching. This program was established in villages where children were learning the indigenous language at home as their first language. The BIA established a training program for the First Language Teachers, employing people from the local community and sending them to a university outside Alaska for summer classes to prepare them as teachers.

A few years later, the BIA began to transfer its elementary schools to the state's Rural Education Attendance Areas. The school district with headquarters in the college's regional center continued the First Language Teachers program as it assumed responsibility for the BIA schools in its region, and the college began to assume responsibility for preparing indigenous speakers as teachers. The field coordinator's proposal was intended to make it possible to deliver the program into the villages so that people from the villages would not have to live in the regional center while they attended classes.

INITIATION

The field coordinator suggested that I apply for the college position in a coastal village. He was leaving the XCED program to become the director of the pilot program at the college. If I became the college field coordinator, I would live in the coastal village and would travel by sno-go to one nearby community and by plane to one other village about forty miles away. I believed strongly that the program was a good idea. I applied and was accepted for the position.

The coastal village had a population of about 200. This village was several hundred miles south of the village I had visited in September 1977, and its climate was a good deal warmer. The terrain was marshy, and wooden boardwalks had been constructed so that one could walk from one building to another without sinking into the marsh. In most Alaskan villages, the houses and other buildings are clustered together to minimize the walking distance between them, but in this village buildings were widely separated because the ground was solid enough for construction only in isolated patches. In addition to family dwellings, the village included an elementary school, a church, a community hall in temporary use as a secondary school, two stores, a health clinic, and a post office.

Yup'ik was the dominant language of the community, and children learned Yup'ik as their first language. As children, middle-aged and elderly people had received only a few months or years of schooling in English. Most were not fluent in English.

Wage employment in the village was limited to a few jobs in the school, health clinic, village corporation, and post office. Some villagers held commercial fishing permits, but the economy of the village depended, as it had in earlier times, on hunting for seals, walrus, ducks, and other birds; fishing; and gathering fruits and vegetables from the tundra.

In mid-August 1978, the program director, his Yup'ik assistant, and I flew to the coastal village to meet with the village council. The council approved the establishment of the field center in the village with me as the field coordinator. They agreed to look for housing for me.

After meeting with the village council, the director, his assistant, and I returned to the regional center to finish organizing the program for the fall 1978 semester. College staff should have completed the course outlines by that time, ready for me to carry to students in the villages, but the outlines had not yet been typed. Fortunately for the project, though perhaps unfortunately for me, I was a good typist, so I spent the first week on the job typing the course outlines.

When the materials were ready, I flew back to the village with a backpack and boxes of books, course materials, and other belongings. It was pouring rain when I got off the small plane. I faced a mile and a half walk from the airstrip to the house where I was to live. The only way to transport everything I had with me was to walk into the village, borrow a wheelbarrow, walk back to the airstrip, and push the load along the muddy track back to the little one-room house that would be my home—a total walk of about four and one-half miles. By the time I finished moving in, I was thoroughly chilled and very, very tired.

In 1981, I wrote the following summary of the living and working conditions:

> In spite of my training and previous experience in Alaska, the shock in the first months of that school year was immense. The living conditions, the climate and terrain, the physical stress of the traveling required by the job, and the new teaching situation called for every ounce of adaptability that I had. I moved into a one-room house and had one barrel of water delivered to me each week. I had an oil stove, a one-burner Coleman stove, and electricity that operated only a few hours a day. I walked the mile and a half to the airstrip twice a week with backpack, briefcase, and bags of books. If I wanted to move boxes of books from my house to the school, I borrowed a wheelbarrow. If I wandered off the wooden sidewalks, I found myself in mud up to my knees. As the autumn turned into winter, storms with eighty mile an hour winds blew in off the Bering Sea, and my little house shook in the wind like a popcorn popper. There was no way to know precisely when a plane was coming, and I often spent an hour or two standing in the wind and snow at the airstrip waiting for a plane. In the winter, I bought a sno-go (snowmobile) for travel to a neighboring village. Although I eventually learned to get to that village and back again, I never learned to enjoy being out on the winter tundra alone. (Harrison 1981: 238–39)

After only a few days, I realized that I was sleepwalking. I would wake to find books scattered around my little house or papers rearranged. I thought I was losing my mind. On my next trip to the regional center, I talked to the director and his assistant about it. The Yup'ik woman said that sleepwalking was a common occurrence among Alaska Native students in the Catholic boarding school she had attended. It was one way in which the students responded to the separation from home and to the shock of entering a new cultural milieu. I concluded that my sleepwalking was very much like that of the boarding school students—a response to separation from familiar ways of doing things and to the shock of entering a new cultural milieu.

SETTLING IN

Another adaptation was called for in the first few weeks. I enjoyed a daily glass of wine (or two), and I brought a case with me when I moved into the village. I quickly realized that I had no way to dispose of the empty bottles. The young man who hauled my trash to the village dump could not avoid seeing virtually everything that was in it. I saved the empty bottles and returned them to the packing carton. When all the bottles were back in the case, I mailed it to myself in care of the college in the regional center. When I was next in the regional center, I had the problem of disposing of a case of empty bottles. It was so stressful that I gave up alcoholic beverages for the year except for the occasional Saturday night glass offered to me by the teachers.

There was also the problem of getting my laundry clean without running water. Most of the households in the village had wringer washers. In the winter, ice was cut from frozen lagoons with chain saws, hauled to the houses with sno-goes and sleds, and melted. The water was heated on the stove and was carried outside again after the laundry was complete. I did not have a wringer washer. I washed what I could by hand and carried the rest in my backpack when I flew to another village, to the regional center, or to Anchorage, where automatic washing machines were available.

Another problematic task was emptying the "honeybucket." Each household in the village had prepared a pit where the honeybuckets were emptied. The pit had a wooden cover, and, when one pit was filled, a new one was dug. Someone from each household carried the honeybucket to the pit and emptied it each day. In my household, there was only me to do that odious task. The route from my house to the pit was always muddy or icy and was therefore slippery. In windy weather (which was most of the time), it could be particularly hazardous. There have been few things in my life that I have found as distasteful as that daily walk along the slippery path. Fortunately, though, I always managed to stay on my feet, and the worst thing that I constantly imagined—falling and spilling the contents of the bucket—never happened.

There were communication problems in the new cultural setting, too. I could not tell when people were joking with me. I had employed a young man to assist me with my weekly barrel of water or ice, a monthly barrel of heating oil, and hauling away trash. The village council president had selected a young man to provide this assistance. The council president initially called the young man my "boyfriend." This comment made me extremely nervous until eventually I realized that it was intended as a joke. There were other occasions when I simply could not understand particular comments until someone explained that they were jokes.

There was new communication technology to try to master. Houses in most villages contained CB radios so that people could communicate from house to house in the days before telephones were available. I had a CB radio supplied by the college, but I seemed incapable of learning to use it. Everything broadcast on the CB radio could be heard by everyone in the village, and I was too shy to broadcast anything. Therefore, the college's CB sat unused.

The first language in the village was Yup'ik. English was only used in school or with visiting English speakers. Many of the older people spoke no English. Even though I had begun to study Yup'ik, for practical purposes the only language I spoke was English. Community events centered on the church and were usually conducted in Yup'ik, making it difficult for me to follow what was going on. Young children, seven or eight years old, who were learning Yup'ik and English in school were often willing to translate for me, and they were very good at it. The adult students were fluent in English, and they graciously answered my constant questions about their history and way of life, helping me to understand their language and culture. These students were the best teachers I could have hoped for. I was in the habit of keeping a diary, and I recorded the day's activities along with what I had learned about the Yup'ik culture as each day passed.

It was personally satisfying for me to live and work in Yup'ik cultural settings. The three communities seemed to be cohesive in the way they maintained cooperative approaches to life in their communities. Game brought in by hunters was shared throughout the community, and efforts were made to ensure that all families had adequate incomes. Extended families were closely knit. Village councils strongly opposed the importation of alcohol and drugs, thereby avoiding the social problems that are so often associated with alcohol and drug abuse.

In spite of the difficulties that I had in adapting to the new environment, I enjoyed working with Yup'ik adults in the three communities. Most of them were mature students who were already working in classrooms as first language teachers. They brought relevant experience to the coursework, and they had good reason to be interested in the studies they were completing. They had a demonstrated commitment to teaching the children of their own villages in the Yup'ik language. There were only a few students in each village. I could work with them in small groups or one on one, a very different teaching situation from the on-campus classrooms that I had experienced as a student.

However, there were many problems in trying to implement the pilot program. It was much harder to get from village to village than either the director or I had anticipated. "Freeze up" did not happen that year until mid-December, so sno-go travel was not possible in September, October, and November. The director's instructions were to hire someone to take me by boat the ten miles to the closest village. He did not realize that a small boat with an outboard motor would take two hours traveling along winding streams to cover the ten miles that a goose would fly. The boatman would have to take another two hours to return to his own community. I was able to find someone to do that on one occasion, but on most days the men of the community had better things to do with their time, regardless of the cash payment involved.

The three villages were on the mail plane route, so another plan was to take the mail plane from village to village. However, I discovered that the mail plane could fly the route clockwise or counterclockwise depending mainly on the freight to be delivered. The carrier was not going to go in the direction I wanted to go just because I wanted to go that way. Taking the mail plane could involve many days of waiting for the plane to go in the desired direction, or it could involve taking the plane into the regional center, staying overnight, and flying to the appropriate village the next day—if the planes flew the next day.

Flying at all was never a certainty. Fog, winds, or rain could keep the planes on the ground at any time of the year. The airstrips in the villages were dirt or mud, so the planes could not land in very wet weather. Flights were actually more certain after freeze up, when the airstrips were frozen.

When I was able to get to the village where I was supposed to be, meetings with students could be delayed for several days for a variety of reasons. On one occasion, I arrived in one village to find that the last barges of the season delivering essential supplies to the community for the winter had to be unloaded before they were frozen in. Everyone was helping with the unloading, which lasted about two days. I had no choice but to wait the two days until the barges were unloaded and students were available to work on courses.

On another occasion, I had arranged to meet with a student in her home. When I arrived, I found the student on the floor, surrounded by a flock of recently killed birds that required immediate cleaning so they would not spoil. I agreed that the best thing would be to set a new time to meet to work on courses.

I also realized in the first few weeks of the semester that I had enrolled a number of students who had no idea what was involved in completing a college course. During my initial tour through the three villages to enroll students, I had actively recruited young adults who did not realize that they would be expected to read books and articles and complete written assignments in English. Most withdrew from the courses that semester. When I did my enrollment visits in the second semester, I carefully explained to potential students the requirements of the courses and enrolled a much smaller number. A much higher proportion of those enrolled in the second semester actually completed courses.

After freeze up finally occurred in mid-December, I bought a sno-go—but I was terrified of driving it across the tundra to the nearest village, ten miles away, where there were students whom I was supposed to see on a regular basis. The young man who assisted me with heavy tasks had become a good friend by this time. I asked him to accompany me on my first sno-go trip to the next village, and he agreed to show me the way. Because I was going to continue on to the regional center by plane, he attached a sled to his own sno-go. He would drive on this trip, and I would ride in the sled. When we were just fifteen minutes out of the home community, he stopped to point out to me that one or the other of the villages was always in sight either in front of me or behind me. It would be very hard to get lost in clear weather on this short trip.

And so I began to use the sno-go around my home community and to travel back and forth to the nearby community. The Alaskan winter brought new problems, however, the most memorable one in the form of a blizzard. I had taken my sno-go to the nearby community at the beginning of the second semester at the end of January. When I visited this community, I slept in the home economics room, a room in the old elementary school. I posted notices and had CB radio announcements made that I would be in the high school on a particular evening to enroll students for the new semester. I met with students until about eleven that evening and was the last one to leave the high school, locking the door as I went out.

During the hours that I had been warmly cocooned in the high school, a heavy snowstorm with high winds enveloped the village. I found snow several feet deep drifted against the door of the elementary school where I was going to sleep. I could not get in. I tried digging with my hands and realized that this approach was hopeless. It was pitch dark, and everyone in the village had already gone to bed. It would be hard to make enough noise to wake anyone up. I struggled through the wind and snow back to the high school, hoping that the door had not actually locked when I had closed it, but it was solidly shut. I went back to the elementary school and walked around the building. Hooray! There was a door on the leeward side of the building that was not buried in snow and that opened with the same key as the door I customarily used. Greatly relieved, I curled up in my sleeping bag for a solid night's sleep.

The blizzard continued for two days. I have never been a patient person, and waiting on the weather always drove me crazy. Several of us with itinerant jobs joked that the worst thing that could happen to us was finishing the paperback novel that consumed the hours and days when we were "weathered in." When the novel was finished, there was absolutely nothing to do but wait.

Finally, the winds began to taper off, and I found someone who agreed to accompany me by sno-go back to my home community. I will always remember that ride. Blowing snow obscured any sign that I might have seen of a trail, but the Yup'ik man I was following seemed to know where he was going, so I raced along after him. The wind penetrated through the heavy gloves I was wearing, and my hands felt as though they were freezing. Black patches that appeared on some of my fingers later indicated that my fingers had indeed been mildly frozen; fortunately, the frostbite was not severe, and the black patches disappeared in a few days.

We arrived at the home community, and I left my escort at the school and drove to my little house. I opened the door to find the interior covered in several inches of snow. The blizzard winds had driven the snow right through small cracks around the front door.

It was still about ten below, and I was badly chilled from the sno-go ride. I swept the snow off the stove, lit it, and began to sweep the snow out of the rest of the tiny house. The snow was powdery and so was easy to sweep away, but it still took an hour or so to clean it out. After removing the snow, I climbed into bed to keep warm while the house warmed up. It took eight hours for the oil stove to bring the inside temperature from ten below to seventy above so that I could begin to move around again. The next morning, I walked out to the airstrip. It was time for my regular visit to the third village where I had students.

The physical demands of the job were dramatized when an outside evaluator visited me in April 1979. The evaluator was a woman from an agency in Oregon. She had no experience in Alaska. She arrived on a small plane that landed on skis on a frozen lagoon near the village. I was a little late in meeting the plane. I found her walking across the ice carrying two paper bags of fresh fruit and vegetables as gifts for me. The pilot had dropped her off and had taken off again. She looked terrified and was very glad to see me.

She wanted to meet students, so we walked to the elementary school and then to various students' homes. I estimated that we walked eight miles that day—about what I would walk in a normal workday in the village. Late in the afternoon, she fell asleep in my bed and did not stir until it was time for her to catch her flight out the next day.

Keeping in touch with staff at the college was also a problem. In 1978–79, each of the three villages had one telephone, located in the village store. In my home community, it was a twenty-minute walk to the store. Often, I had to wait in line to use the phone, taking another twenty minutes to get through to the college. It was utterly infuriating to hear a receptionist or secretary say, "He's in a meeting. Please call back." It was another twenty-minute walk back to my house. So there were many occasions when I spent an hour making one phone call and was not even successful at reaching the person I wanted to talk to. If I felt I really needed to get through, two or three hours could be consumed.

Another problem had to do with establishing a village library. Village libraries were part of the proposal for the pilot project. The proposal called for the college to rent a small building and to provide books, materials, and funding for a part-time librarian. The village council and others in my home community agreed that a library would benefit the community, but there was simply no space in the village to accommodate it. The village had a community hall, but it was serving as the temporary site for the high school while a new high school was being constructed. Because no space was available for the library, no library was established that year—but the issue was to surface again two years later.

The director had left the XCED program at the end of the previous academic year and had joined the staff of the college. We were only six weeks into the pilot project in mid-October when he began talking about leaving his new job. I felt quite hopeless about making a success of the pilot project if the key person managing the project was not going to stick with it.

I also found myself at odds with the philosophy of the community college. Its aim was to present a traditional two-year college curriculum in a highly structured format. The situation seemed to me to require nontraditional, culturally appropriate content and method.

BACK TO THE DRAWING BOARD

I had begun the year believing that my master's degree training had prepared me to do well as a teacher in the college position that I had accepted. Before the first semester was over, I realized that I needed to know a great deal more about cross-cultural education before I could begin to solve all the problems I was encountering. As part of its staff development program, the college paid for me to attend a professional meeting. I flew to the American Anthropological Association Annual Meeting in Los Angeles in November. When someone suggested that I begin a doctoral program, I was ready. I applied to and was accepted into a doctoral program in anthropology and education at the University of Oregon under Harry Wolcott's supervision, to begin in June 1979.

However, I had become deeply attached to the people of the village where I worked, and it seemed inevitable that I would return to do the fieldwork for my thesis there. I wanted to do fieldwork that would result in a document useful to Alaskan education and that would build on earlier work in anthropology and education at the same time. I decided on a case study of informal learning that could be published for use in courses for new teachers in Alaska. My thesis supervisor and the director of the Center for Cross-Cultural Studies at the University of Alaska Fairbanks both encouraged me to pursue this line of inquiry.

In September 1979, I wrote to the village council president about a possible return to the village for fieldwork. I received the following letter from the village council in return:

December 4, 1979
Dear Barbara:
Hello, you are welcome anytime this summer, to be here in the village for six months, we will be glad to have you here again.

I know that teachers need to learn more about how Eskimos live, before they come to Alaska. I know a lot of them don't know how we live. I think that the people here will be happy to see you here. I know that they will help you with whatever you will be writing. . . .

If you want to write, you can write to the President and the Council will help you on anything you need.

Thank you for the letter you wrote to us, and we wish you the best of the coming holidays.

Best Regards.

THE PROGRAMS, 1980–81

I did a year of coursework at Oregon and completed my comprehensive examinations before leaving for Alaska in June 1980. I believed that learning the Yup'ik language would be a substantial asset in working in the coastal village. I spent the summer of 1980 studying the language at the Alaska Native Language Institute, UAF. Again, I suffered a rude shock. Learning Yup'ik was a good deal harder than I thought it would be.

Nevertheless, I departed for the village in late August 1980 filled with optimism and enthusiasm for the pending project. One of my most memorable moments occurred as I was walking into the village on my return. A woman whom I had not seen in a year and a half called out, "You've come home!" I did indeed feel that I was coming home.

I planned to use anthropological techniques to learn as much as possible about the way children and adults learned in informal settings so that a summary of my thesis could be published as an orientation document for new teachers arriving in the region. I felt fortunate, too, that I had been approached to work part-time establishing an Adult Basic Education program in the community. I was funding this research out of my meager savings, and I was glad to have the income the work would provide, as well as a well-defined role for the six months I would spend there.

The Adult Basic Education program was well established in the region, but it would be new to this particular village. I knew that I would spend only six months in the village, but the administrator for the program wanted to proceed even if the program would run for only a few months there. Funding was available, and we wanted to use it as best we could. The program's aims were to provide instruction in basic English conversation, literacy, and numeracy to Yup'ik adults. Those students who had completed several years of schooling in English could also prepare for the examinations leading to the General Equivalency Diploma (GED). Someone from the local community who was fluent in Yup'ik and in English was employed to teach beginning English to Yup'ik speakers. I would work with students who were preparing for the GED. The program provided the same teaching resources that were used extensively in other settings, and funding was available to rent space in the village. Regular hours of instruction were established. The program was advertised, and adult students came to enroll.

One of the first things I learned on my return was that the college had discontinued the pilot project that began in 1978. A second field coordinator had come to the village for the 1979–80 academic year. She had many of the same problems that I had coping with the physical demands of the environment, traveling, and poor communication. She left at the end of the year. The community college had new administrators who had decided to abandon the project.

By August 1980, one of the families in the village had built a new house, and the old house was available for rent. It was larger, had better furnishings, and was more comfortable than the last house I had lived in. Construction workers working on the new high school during the summer of 1980 had occupied it. They had cut a hole under the sink to let water drain out rather than carrying the water out as the owners of the house had done when they lived there. Unfortunately, this hole also let cold air and mice in, but it was several weeks into the winter before I identified this problem. Until I realized where the cold air was coming from, I wore my parka and overpants indoors during the day and sometimes had to stop working because of the cold. At night, I would lie awake listening to the mice scampering across the linoleum floors, as I plotted means of eradicating them.

Eventually, my landlord and I discovered the damage under the sink, and the problem was simply solved by covering the hole.

Otherwise, life was physically much less demanding than it had been during my previous stay in the village because I was not trying to travel to other communities. The fieldwork was relatively easy because women who had been my students were extremely helpful in answering my questions and inviting me into their homes to observe their home life and children. Also, children in this village, as in every other village in Alaska, were curious about outsiders and would come to the house after school with the request, "Can we come in?" I had crayons, paper, and games and would observe the way the children learned from each other as they played at my table.

One man in the village objected to my study and accused me of wanting to make money from the book I would write. I went to his house and explained that I did not expect to make any money from a book, but if by any chance I did, I promised to share profits with the community. He was mollified and invited me to supper with his family.

The Adult Basic Education program was not so easy. Again, many people signed up at the beginning of the year, but few of them were aware of the effort it would take to work through the program. The young teaching aide decided very quickly that he did not like the work. I was able to guide two or three students through the studies for the GED examinations during the six-month period but cannot claim that the program was an overwhelming success.

DISTRACTIONS

A problem arose in relation to a village library. In 1978, I had spoken to the village council saying that the college was prepared to rent space for a library, but no space had been available at the time. By 1980, the new high school had been completed, so the community hall was no longer in use as a temporary high school. It was available for rent. However, while I had been in Oregon, there had been a complete change of administrators at the college, and the new administrators felt no obligation to follow through on commitments made previously. The college administration no longer intended to establish village libraries. I argued with the administrators and felt extremely frustrated and angry at the lack of institutional commitment. I was embarrassed to have to explain the lack of commitment.

There had also been high turnover in the elementary and secondary teaching staff in the village. There were four teachers in the elementary school and two in the high school. The BIA administered the elementary school, but the high school was under the state-funded school district. Two two-bedroom apartments were attached to the elementary school for that school's teachers. Two single male teachers lived in one apartment, and a teaching couple with their three children lived in the other. Neither of the single teachers had previous Alaskan experience, but the teaching couple had transferred from another village. Each of the high school teachers rented a house in the village.

Under the best of circumstances, the teaching staff in a village can be cooperative and supportive of the work of one another. In the past, teaching couples were preferred for village assignments for this very reason. However, by 1980, teachers were more or less randomly assigned to village schools. Personality conflicts between the teachers could develop and easily grow out of proportion under these circumstances. Personality conflicts did develop between the teachers that year. I had frequent visits from one teacher or another seeking my support in this disagreement or that. I tried to maintain a neutral position but nevertheless found myself feeling as though I was caught in the middle of their disagreements. I could not seem to get away from their arguments. I was extremely glad to leave them all behind when the time came.

There were some funny times that year, too. The two single teachers in the elementary school introduced the first video recorder to the village. Tapes could be rented by mail from outlets in Anchorage. One Saturday night, I was invited to watch videos with these teachers. Shortly after I arrived at their apartment, I found a glass of Wild Turkey thrust into my hand. The video started—it was a pornographic movie, a genre with which I had little experience. Unsure of just how to react and not wanting to offend my hosts, I drank my drink, watched curiously for a while, apologized for my headache, excused myself, and walked through the snowy darkness to my little house.

I had spent enough time in villages to know that the teachers and I all lived in "glass houses." In small communities in many parts of the world, people tend to know what everyone else is doing all of the time. Villagers were curious about the way of life of strangers and tended to focus even more attention and observation on them than they did on other residents. Under these circumstances, I knew that sex outside of marriage was impossible if I was going to maintain good relationships within the village, and those relationships were important for success in the various tasks I had set for myself during that year. The new teachers had not yet learned this lesson.

This lesson was emphasized for me by a story I was told about a high school teacher who came to the community the year after the incident described above. Before she accepted the position in the village, she was told that villagers frowned on premarital sex. She moved into a small house on the outskirts of the village, and, during the course of the year, villagers began to suspect that young men from the community were staying overnight at her house. She came home from school one day to find the owner of the house in the process of jacking the house up so that it could be moved to a location immediately next door to his own house. The landlord wanted to see exactly who was coming and going and at what times. The teacher left the village at the end of the year. Presumably she found work in a community with more liberal opinions about sexual relations.

Issues surrounding health care became apparent during my second year in the village, too. Programs to provide modern health care to the village had been established in the 1960s and 1970s. Doctors, nurses, and dentists made regular visits to the village, and a health clinic was staffed on a daily basis by local women trained at the college as health aides. Diseases such as hepatitis and tuberculosis continued to cause problems, however.

The Adult Basic Education coordinator who traveled through the villages stayed with me once for two days. On her return to the regional center, she discovered that she had hepatitis. She phoned to say that I should get a shot of gamma globulin as a precautionary measure. I went to the health clinic, but they were out of that particular medication. It had to be ordered from the regional center and did not arrive for a few days—a few days of high anxiety for me. The Adult Basic Education coordinator spent several months recovering from the disease. Fortunately, I escaped infection.

A year or two after I left the village, I learned that there had been an outbreak of tuberculosis. One of my students and her two children had been hospitalized. As soon as I heard this news, I arranged for a TB test. Fortunately, I had again escaped infection.

PREPARING THE REPORT

In February 1981, as planned, I returned to Oregon to complete the write-up of my doctoral thesis. My research had been reasonably successful. In May, after I had drafted the thesis, I sent copies to several people in the village for review and comment and then traveled to the village in June to be certain that I had permission to publish the information that I had included in the draft.

The thesis was completed (Harrison 1981), the doctorate was awarded, and I looked forward to publishing a case study through the Center for Cross-Cultural Studies at UAF. With the encouragement of the acting dean, I began editing the document for publication. Unfortunately, by the time the case study was ready for publication, a new dean had been appointed. He did not approve funding for the publication, and the case study was not published. The edited paper has been circulated informally in Alaska, and, occasionally, I hear from someone who read the thesis or the paper and found it useful. I also developed two articles based on the fieldwork. The first was published in 1982 and describes women's roles in the community and the way those roles influenced their participation in postsecondary education. The second, published in 1984, describes the way that the beliefs of new teachers in the village were influenced by returning teachers.

DISCUSSION

In 1978–79, I spent ten months working on the community college pilot project that provided courses in three villages for adult students in the Associate of Arts degree program. In 1980–81, I spent six additional months working on my doctoral research and the Adult Basic Education program. By June 1981, the thesis was well on the way to completion, but the pilot project and the Adult Basic Education programs had been discontinued, at least for the time being.

There were three major factors that influenced the fate of the programs. First, the physical environment made it very difficult for a staff member to operate effectively. Second, there was a high turnover in staff at the community college, in the Adult Basic Education program, and on my own part as the fieldworker in the village. Third, all of the nonnatives involved in the planning brought assumptions with them that—if there had been greater consultation in the local community—might have been challenged and modified. People in the local community might have provided good advice about transportation, scheduling, and communication as well as about educational needs.

One important factor was related to both the high turnover and to the question of consultation with the local community. There was conflict within the management of the community college about the way the programs should be designed. The dominant faction believed that courses for the Associate of Arts degree should be very much like the same courses in mainstream settings. From this perspective, the local community would have little to contribute to program design. The minority faction within the college believed that courses should be specifically designed to suit the particular cultural context. From the minority perspective, consultation with the local community would be an essential element of program design. Arguments about this issue drained staff energy and led to a sense of powerlessness among those holding the minority viewpoint.

I did not realize at the time the harmful effects that short-term commitments can have. When I first went to work in the village, I talked to village council members and students about the desire of the college to rent space and to start a library. However, institutions do not make commitments, only individuals do. When individuals with an interest in village libraries left their positions at the college, the commitment disappeared. People in the village remembered, though. There were also heightened expectations in the village because of the pilot project and the Adult Basic Education program. These expectations were followed by disappointment when the programs closed. In addition, years later, whenever I saw people from the village in Fairbanks or Anchorage, they would ask when the publication would be ready to help train new teachers for their village. Although I was sometimes able to provide assistance to students from the village who came to Fairbanks to study, I have never gotten over the nagging sense of guilt about offering some things in the village that I could not deliver.

I personally experienced positive lasting effects of my sixteen months in the community. I gained a new perspective on the notions of "rich" and "poor." People in the village did not think of themselves as poor—in fact, they were generally pleased with their material progress in recent years—but when I showed them a photo of my mother standing in front of my family home in California, someone commented, "Your family must be rich!" Before I lived in the village, I had believed that my family had been relatively poor in terms of material wealth. Living in the village made me realize that my own family had been wealthy by comparison with the vast majority of the world's population. To this day, I sing a little hymn of thanksgiving when I get into my hot shower every morning.

Living in the truly communal setting of the village also changed my perspective on mainstream American individualism. People in this village believed that "the land belongs to everyone," and they genuinely shared their resources throughout the community. They demonstrated to me that it was possible for communities to exist in which every individual is cared for.

Also, although I did not become a fluent Yup'ik speaker, I gained a deep respect for people who have learned two or more languages because I know how difficult that is to do. I also know how hard it is to live in a society in which the dominant language is other than one's own first language. I have never fully readapted to mainstream ways of speaking. People in this village were soft-spoken by comparison with the norm for mainstream Americans. In response to that social environment, I became soft-spoken while I lived there and remain so to this day.

LESSONS LEARNED

The community college pilot projects were among the projects that led to the development of the guidelines for fieldworkers and for program design described in chapters 3 and 4. Specific activities and events in the pilot projects contributed to the lessons learned and the formulation of each guideline.

The Individual Fieldworker

Be Flexible but Recognize That Everyone Has Limits.

I made a number of changes to accommodate the physical setting. I used camping skills that I had learned as a youngster, such as cooking on a one-burner stove, but I also had to learn new skills. I learned to light an oil stove for heating my house and use a kerosene lamp for light when the generator was turned off. Because my water supply was limited to one barrel a week, I learned to conserve water in every possible way, including washing my clothes in the same water that I had used to rinse my hair. I learned to drive a sno-go and to follow a trail across the tundra. I also made special efforts to accommodate the social setting, attending church for the first time in many years because church was the focus of community life and abstaining from most alcoholic beverages.

Once again, though, I learned a great deal about my limitations with respect to flexibility. I studied the Yup'ik language but without great success. Physically, I found myself able to cope with the intense cold and with a great deal of walking—but I did not necessarily learn to like either the cold or the excessive exercise. I had a similar reaction to the social isolation that was the result of not knowing the indigenous language and being "marginal" to the community. I could cope with the isolation for periods of time, but I did not necessarily learn to like it. My difficulties in dealing with the physical demands and the social isolation probably contributed to the fact that, although I completed my various contracts, I could not make a long-term commitment to work in the village. In other words, my limitations probably contributed to the short-term nature of the pilot project and Adult Basic Education program.

I did not do well with respect to acceptance of institutional policy changes during my time in this village either. I still believed that every new project must be made to work, no matter what. The pilot project seemed particularly important to me. I was angry when the community college discontinued the pilot project and withdrew its offer of funding for a library in the village. My anger did not contribute constructively to the situation; it only drained my energy and feelings of goodwill.

I frequently experienced a sense of ambiguity and a high degree of frustration. I was constantly trying to "figure out" social relationships and the nature of community expectations for me. I was used to doing things punctually, but people in the village were used to doing things when the time was right, and I could not seem to change my way of doing things. Unless someone went out of his or her way to communicate in English, I could not understand what people were talking about. Even when they spoke English, I could not understand jokes. There were practical problems, too. I had been in the village for several months before I learned how to find out when a plane would arrive, and I never learned to make use of the CB radio.

Villagers needed to be tolerant when dealing with mainstream Americans, including me, of course. I was told a story about a teacher who was hired by the school district and was given little or no information about the community she was coming to. She got off the plane, walked into the village, stayed one night, and then went to the telephone in the store to phone the district superintendent to say she wanted to leave. She was crying during this phone conversation, and everyone in the store could overhear her. There were some elderly ladies in the store at the time who could not speak English, but they burst into tears in sympathy with her unhappiness. The local people loved their way of life, including its hardships, and they were deeply offended when outsiders responded negatively.

I have already stated that I found the physical setting extremely difficult to deal with, in part because my work in the pilot project necessitated regular travel to other villages. There were beautiful moments on the tundra, but my most vivid memories are of trying to fulfill my work obligations in very cold rain or snow. I lacked the stamina to tackle the environment for the long term.

Even though I made a short visit to this village before I went to live there, I had almost no inkling of the community's values and mores until I moved in. Then, as I came to know something about those values, I sometimes had to grapple with them. I had never lived in a community in which resources were so equitably shared, and I greatly admired that dimension of community life. I was unsure, however, about the strict religious aspects of community life. The local church organized nearly all community activities, and there were church-related community activities most nights of the week as well as several times on weekends. Dancing, drinking alcohol, and viewing Hollywood movies were banned. When VCRs came into common use, people could watch anything they wanted to in their homes, but movies still were not shown in community settings. All of this went against my mainstream American belief in the rights of individuals to do pretty much what they want to so long as it does not hurt anyone else.

I came to realize, though, that this community had virtually no social problems. Children were raised in households with two parents and other adult members of the extended family. Family violence, alcoholism, and drug abuse were almost unheard of. I began to understand that there were advantages in the way community social life was organized. I had no difficulty conforming to the community mores for the time that I was there, and I gained respect for the advantages that religious proscriptions can provide. As I have said before, though, this type of community would not be the best place for someone determined to express his or her individual right to drink or to have sex with another consenting adult.

Be Willing to Collaborate by Sharing Authority, Responsibility, and Credit for Success.

At the time of my work in this community, I thought I was doing a fine job of collaborating with local people. On reflection several years later, I realized that the pilot project and Adult Basic Education programs had already been formulated before I started working in them. After I joined the programs, the only collaboration between college staff and the local community occurred when there was a meeting with the village council for approval to run programs that had already been designed by people at the community college. Would the pilot project and Adult Basic Education programs have benefited from greater collaboration with local people in the planning and design? Would local people have identified the problems involved in transportation between the three villages in the pilot project? Could they have given advice about the best approaches to the Adult Basic Education program? I suspect that the answer to these questions is yes. Although my attitude toward collaboration was good, I had not yet learned that collaboration needs to start at the beginning of program design and continue all the way through.

Give Thoughtful Attention to the Ethical Implications of Your Actions.

During my first year in the village, I still did not know that there were formal ethical guidelines for researchers in field settings. However, my doctoral coursework in Oregon included an introduction to ethics in anthropology. As I saw it at the time, the most important aspects for my doctoral research were the concepts of informed consent, confidentiality, and anonymity.

By the time I returned to the village in August 1980, the report of the Small High Schools Project had been published, and media uproar had resulted. I had learned that a research publication can have unpredictable political outcomes. So "subjects" in research studies should be informed that the results of the research will become public and that the researcher cannot always predict the consequences of publication. Even seemingly innocuous research publications can have unintended negative outcomes. The researcher can help to protect "subjects" by maintaining strict confidentiality and by making the subjects as anonymous as possible in the research report, but there is no way to entirely eliminate all risks.

For all three projects—the pilot project, the thesis, and the Adult Basic Education program—permission to proceed was granted by the village council. I asked selected people in the village to review my doctoral thesis before it was finalized in order to ensure that they knew what I had included in the thesis and to ensure that I had their consent to make the contents of the thesis public. I tried to be honest in what I wanted to do and with respect to the probable outcomes of the projects, but I promised more than I could deliver—the report intended for new village teachers was never published, and the funding for the library did not materialize. I am much more cautious now about the promises I make when I work on community projects.

One aspect of the ethics of fieldwork has to do with intimacy between fieldworker and subject (Busier et al. 1997). Any fieldworker with common sense should realize that having sex with a local person will be immediately known in the community and that program work may be negatively affected and might even be destroyed entirely. In other words, it is to the practical benefit of the fieldworker to refrain from sex outside of marriage in that setting. Intimacy, on the other hand, is a matter of degree and does not necessarily involve sex. It would be nearly impossible not to develop some degree of intimacy in the long-term relationships that are inherent to long-term fieldwork. For example, I had some very long conversations covering a wide range of topics with one young man, and a certain intimacy developed between us. Unfortunately, gossip circulated, and local people criticized the young man for spending too much time alone with me. So far as I was concerned, the relationship was totally innocent and the negative effects for the young man were totally unpredictable. But does that mean I was not responsible for the unforeseen consequences? Is a fieldworker responsible for consequences that the fieldworker could not predict? If so, what is an appropriate ethical stance on this matter?

It is important to note that I got what I wanted out of the three projects: salaries for my work in the pilot project and the Adult Basic Education program, a thesis, a doctoral degree, publications, and professional employment at the end of my work in the village. I self-consciously tried not to take unfair advantage of people. For example, a suggestion came to me at one point to study shamanism, but I declined to do so because I knew that local people would not approve of that particular focus. When I started my work in the village, I sincerely believed that my work would have benefits for the community. One might argue that people in the village benefited from the programs even if these programs operated for short periods. One might argue that there were indirect benefits from the papers or from on-campus teaching. This example raises the question, though, Who benefits from research—the researcher or the researched? Should researchers at least be more honest in their reflections and in their presentations to potential "subjects" about the benefits of research?

Apply the Concept of Culture in Everyday Working Relationships.

In this setting, it was extremely useful to know about the concept of culture and to know how to find out about the local culture. With the exception of the schoolteachers, people in the community shared a similar cultural heritage.

All of them spoke Yup'ik as a first language. All of them had been born within a radius of about 200 miles. They had similar schooling experiences. A few had been to boarding high schools, and a few of them had gained experience outside the village in the armed services or higher education. I believe that people in that community shared many dimensions of their worldview, and learning what those shared dimensions were was important in interacting effectively with adult students in that community. Knowing the shared dimensions was also important so that I would know how to behave appropriately.

At the same time, each person was an individual with individual views of the world. It would have been a drastic mistake to make assumptions about the individuals who might have shared particular views. The only way to know the view of one individual was to find out from that person.

One event concerning my investigations into the culture in the village is worth recounting here. Not long after I returned to the community after a year of academic work in Oregon, I asked my young friend, "Tell me about your kinship system." I will never forget the puzzled expression on his face as he tried to figure out what I meant. He could, of course, have told me about his relatives and the way he was related to them and about the way Yup'ik people in general recognized and acknowledged their relatives. However, their "kinship system" was the creation of my culture, not his. The point for novice researchers to remember is that, when you inquire into someone else's culture, you are constructing *your* version of it, but *their* version will always remain theirs.

Designing Collaborative Programs

Fieldworkers and Representatives of the Community Should Collaborate to Develop a Rationale, Philosophy, or Reason for the Establishment of the Particular Program.

There were three different sets of goals involved in my two years of work in this village: one set for the pilot project for the community college, one for the adult education program, and one for my doctoral research. The goals of the pilot project were based on the statewide XCED program goals, but a pilot project is by definition a trial, whereas XCED was already well established. The adult education program goals came from a larger system of adult education programs, and the goals for my doctoral thesis had been developed under the supervision of my doctoral committee at the University of Oregon. Although the village council members had approved all three sets of goals, they were not invited to collaborate in their formulation. In the second year, I combined work in the adult education program with work on my doctoral research, but the goals of the programs were closely related, and I could balance both sets of goals, at least for the six-month period of my fieldwork.

None of the programs was specifically defined as collaborative, but each had collaborative aspects. The village council was consulted about the establishment of each of the programs and about the staff. I was dependent on my adult students for information on how to manage the physical and cultural environments, and they were dependent on me for their coursework. Each of the programs had goals for practical outcomes that would benefit the community, and the pilot project and my doctoral fieldwork had research goals in addition. I asked people in the community to review my doctoral thesis before it was finalized so that they had some authority over the research report. But the question remains: Would these programs have "worked" more effectively if there had been greater collaboration between local people and program developers in the formulation of the rationale? I cannot know for sure, but I suspect that greater collaboration would have resulted in more effective programs.

Look for Sources of Adequate and Dependable Funding.

Funding for the pilot project and the Adult Basic Education program had been budgeted and allocated through the community college before I joined the programs. I applied through various agencies for funding to support my doctoral research but was unsuccessful. Essentially, the salaries for my work in the pilot project and in the Adult Basic Education program paid my expenses for the research.

The major funding problem in these examples was the problem of a village library. As a representative of the community college, I offered funding to establish a library in the village in 1978. Two years later, the offer had been withdrawn, causing some bad feeling and disappointment. I was angry at the time, but I realize now that institutions cannot make commitments except by way of written contracts. As people in institutional roles change, goals and the budgets allocated to reach the goals change. Individuals can follow through on verbal commitments, but institutions are not likely to do so.

Confirm That There Is Adequate Support in the Local Community.

There was sufficient support in the community for each of the three programs. The village council approved the programs and helped to find housing for me and someone to help me with heavy tasks. When a building became available, the council said it could be used for a library and for adult education classes. Students signed up for community college courses and the Adult Basic Education program. Some of them made progress, and some completed units of study. The village council invited me to return to the village to do my doctoral research. My students gave me access to their homes and brought me into their families. The programs were consistent with the goals of the community.

One community member challenged me during my second year and suggested that my motive for doing the research was to make money from a book. However, after I assured him that any profits for me from a book would go to the village council, his objections ceased. As far as I am aware, no one else raised any concerns.

There were factions and disagreements that were related to ANCSA, but so far as I know they were not related to the teaching and research programs. The village corporation opened a store, and there was disagreement about how the store should be managed and about land selections, but those disagreements did not impact the programs I was involved in. I was under no pressure to join one faction or another. On the contrary, villagers' expectations were that the other teachers and I would *not* become involved in these disagreements. These issues were their business, not ours.

On the other hand, I could not avoid the disagreements between the teachers during my second year in the community, and I felt that I was under constant pressure to support one faction or another. I was only able to escape the perceived pressure by leaving the village. I believe that the disagreements only ended when the school year ended and some of the teachers moved out. Although I found these conflicts personally stressful, I felt that they had no direct bearing on the programs.

Formulate a Program Plan Including Statements of Roles and Responsibilities, Support Systems for Participants, and Evaluation Procedures.

Policies and procedures for the pilot project and Adult Basic Education program had been established at the community college before I joined either program. I gave little thought at the time to the processes that brought them about. Program managers had each invited me to apply for the respective positions that I held. I did not have a management role in either the pilot project or the Adult Basic Education program, and I focused almost entirely on the tasks assigned to me. In each case, budgets were established and maintained by well-trained staff at the community college.

The work roles in each program were reasonably well defined, and definitions of roles were not the cause of major problems in the programs. I knew what I was supposed to do in order to fulfill the tasks assigned to me. The designer of the pilot project had worked as a field coordinator in XCED, so he defined the collaboration with the village council, his own role of college coordinator, and my role as field coordinator based on XCED experience. The adult education field coordinator role had been applied successfully in other village settings.

After the village council agreed to have the programs and accepted me as a staff member, there were no further formal requirements for collaboration. However, I was dependent on local people for help in daily tasks and for program success. I heard stories of teachers who had been asked to leave the community because their behavior was unacceptable, and I definitely did not want that to happen. So I maintained ongoing conversations with members of the village council, adult students, teachers, and others in the village regarding issues related to the programs and community life.

It is often difficult for single people to find personal support when they are working in settings in which there are only a few others with similar cultural backgrounds. In the case described above, there were eight people—the elementary and high school teachers and the community college field coordinator (that was me)—with mainstream American backgrounds. On the whole, these people came together in the village by accident. They did not necessarily choose to share each other's company, and they did not necessarily share interests or values with the others in the group. During my second year in the community, there was conflict among the teachers, and this added to other psychological stresses at the time. The fact that I did not speak the dominant language also made it difficult to form close personal friendships with villagers, and the need for confidentiality meant that conversations with others in the village had to be carefully restricted.

Communication problems were related to the issue of personal support. It was hard to learn not to rely on the telephone to reach someone in authority or an adviser. Without telephones, I could not phone relatives and friends in other parts of Alaska or in other states. The main means of personal support came from letters and from trips to the regional center, Anchorage, and other states—far from ideal means of reaching people to talk to. However, the community college program coordinator and his administrator gave me all of the personal support that they could. They patiently listened as I talked about my troubles. The program plan also recognized the need for personal support, and it provided travel funds to a professional conference and for regular visits to the regional center.

The evaluator who wrote a report based on her April 1979 visit to me in the village recommended a more extensive staff development component of the program, which, if implemented, would have provided additional personal support. So far as I know, her report was the only formal assessment that was undertaken for the pilot project. Nowadays, a program of this kind would be likely to incorporate several different types of information gathering in order to assess it.

There was little in the way of discussion about issues relating to the preparation and presentation of reports. When I returned to the village in 1980 to do research, I told the village council and others that people from the community would have the opportunity to read and comment on any reports I prepared. I also assured at least one person that direct profits for me from publications would go to the village council. So far as I am aware, no issues of intellectual property were involved. Agreements were informally arranged, and it has been my personal responsibility to follow through.

Identify or Recruit Committed Leadership in the Program and, Preferably, in the Funding Agency.

The pilot project begun in 1978–79 lasted only two years. Key management staff at the community college left at the end of the first year, and the field coordinator (that was me) left to begin a doctoral program. Program staff who came in for the second year (1979–80) had not been part of the initial planning, and they did not necessarily "buy into" the program goals. By the end of the second year, the project was discontinued.

The adult education program also suffered from staff turnover. The adult education coordinator caught hepatitis in early 1981 and moved to Seattle for long-term treatment. I had agreed to work only for six months and went to Oregon to finish the write-up of my dissertation at the end of that time. The program closed in the village at the end of six months, although the program continued in other villages after that.

I completed the thesis, but it was never published because there was a change of personnel in the position that controlled funding for publication through UAF and the new person did not support publication. Staff turnover in the college and the university were major reasons why the pilot project and adult education programs closed after short periods and why the thesis was not published as intended.

The turnover was not entirely the result of lack of commitment, of course. Illness and other factors made turnover unavoidable. Nevertheless, these examples clearly illustrate the importance of finding leaders for programs and within funding agencies who are willing to make commitments to see new programs through the establishment phase. If key staff members are willing to stay with a program through the initial adjustments and adaptations, the chances of the program's success and long-term survival are enhanced. However, commitment alone cannot make programs successful. Other factors are essential at the same time. There is no single factor that can ensure success.

I did not give much thought to the extent of my own commitments to these programs at the time. I did not realize that short-term commitments to programs can actually damage communities as well as relationships between mainstream and indigenous groups. I can only urge program designers, potential staff, and researchers to treat committed leadership as an essential factor in the design of collaborative programs.

Identify or Recruit Appropriately Qualified Staff.

From the standpoint of the institutions concerned, the staff in these programs had appropriate formal qualifications. However, the first language in the communities was Yup'ik, and my monolingualism was a distinct disadvantage. Also, it would probably have been useful if either the young assistant in the Adult Basic Education program or I had been trained in methods of teaching a second language—but we were not. Hopefully, in the years after these projects were trialed, people from the local community have had opportunities to undertake the education and training necessary to run the Adult Basic Education and community college courses in the village. If bilingual people with long-term commitments to the community can become the staff members of programs like these, staff turnover can be greatly reduced, and program quality should improve.

Find a Workable Physical Setting.

The physical circumstances were extremely difficult and were probably among the major reasons why the pilot project closed. Although I had the assistance of a young man to bring me water and fuel oil, just taking care of basic tasks demanded time and physical labor that I was not accustomed to. Walking everywhere for at least six months of the year, using wheelbarrows and backpacks to transport educational materials, emptying honeybuckets, and heating water to wash oneself and one's clothes are all activities that required more time and personal energy than one would expend to accomplish the same things in an urban situation. It was more difficult to get from one village to another than the original planners envisioned, and it was impossible to maintain a regular schedule for travel. The pilot program depended on regular contact between the field coordinator and the students in each of the three villages, so the transportation and communication problems were significant. Communication was further hampered because telephones were not available. Educational programs ordinarily depend on consistent use of the telephone to keep program staff in contact with one another. The adult education coordinator's hepatitis and the tuberculosis that affected families in the village and school also made the physical location difficult for a field coordinator to deal with.

Looking back on it, I think that neither the program planners nor I gave sufficient consideration to problems relating to the physical location for the pilot project. The pilot project was based on the model of the XCED program. In XCED the field coordinators were based in the regional centers. The regional centers generally had telephones in every house, and because mail plane routes were based out of the regional centers, it was easier to fly to a particular village on a particular day. The larger populations in the regional centers meant that XCED field coordinators had a wider range of people to turn to for personal support.

If the pilot project had more resources and more time, would it have been possible to overcome the problems engendered by the physical location? Perhaps. I will never know the answer with any certainty. Now that satellite telephones and other modern conveniences are more readily available than they were in 1980, would this project be feasible? Again, perhaps. But I also point out that no single factor makes or breaks a new program. Many components are essential for success. In all probability, transportation and communication technologies have improved in the region, and these improvements would make it much easier to run these programs today.

Attend to the Broader Political and Social Context That Makes It Possible for a Program to Survive.

In 1980, Ronald Reagan was elected president of the United States, and a political shift was clearly taking place. Priorities in public education began shifting away from equality of opportunity for ethnic minorities. Federal funding for minority programs was threatened. Oil royalties for the state were high in 1980, but international oil prices dropped soon after that, bringing royalties down with them. The political and social contexts of the closing years of the twentieth century were difficult contexts in which to operate innovative programs for Alaska Native students.

However, the major difficulties of the pilot project were inherent in its physical setting and internal structure. The program did not last long enough to know whether the political and social context would have made it possible for it to survive.

Chapter Seven

Manokotak School, 1983–85

In 1983, a teacher in the school in Manokotak, a village in the Bristol Bay region of Alaska, wrote to a faculty member of the University of Alaska Fairbanks suggesting that a case study of the school in Manokotak be conducted. The teacher's letter said that the school was a successful school. Because there had been persistent negative publicity about small schools in rural Alaskan communities, the teacher suggested that a study of a successful school would be in order. After a series of negotiations with the school district, principal, and Community School Committee, the dean of the College of Rural Alaska at UAF agreed with her, and funding from the Center for Cross-Cultural Studies was made available. I was an assistant professor of cross-cultural education, and the dean asked me to prepare a proposal, which was eventually approved for funding from the College Research Committee. I was ready to begin the program.

THE PROGRAM

I worked with a team of two teachers in the local school, two people from the community, and one person from the school district office in Dillingham. We used participant observation, interviews, and historical research to collect information for our report. Training in research methods was deemed a necessary component of the program because I was the only member of the team with a research background. The teachers and the school district staff person enrolled in a graduate-level research methods course that I was teaching through the XCED program. Data collection for the study was incorporated into their coursework. The two local people were employed as part-time research assistants to conduct interviews in Yup'ik with adults in the community regarding perceptions of the school. I gave the assistants careful instructions about the way the interviews should be conducted. The interview questions were straightforward, and no particular problems came to light in the way the assistants carried out my instructions. The assistants provided the information I wanted, explained it to me, and answered any questions that I asked.

One of the teachers in the school and the two research assistants were Yup'ik, born and raised in the community. The other teacher, the person from the school district, and I came from mainstream middle-class backgrounds, so there were opportunities to incorporate the views of both insiders and outsiders. The Yup'ik teacher prepared a section for the report on the history of the community and the school, while the second teacher prepared descriptions of the curriculum. The school district person contributed contextual information from the district standpoint. I conducted interviews with all of the teachers and the principal. The teacher who wrote the original letter to UAF was one of the teachers on the team, and she collaborated with me on the write-up of the final report. I felt that the five of us worked well as a team, and we shared authorship of the project report. We discussed problems and issues as they came up, but I held the purse strings, awarded the grades to the teachers who were also my students, and carried the major responsibility for the operation and outcomes of the project.

I made three site visits to the school. The first visit was in January 1984 for a period of ten days. The second visit was in March 1984 for five days, and the final visit was in September 1984 for four days. I spent most of summer 1985 on the write-up. The complete case study was published by the Center for Cross-Cultural Studies at UAF (Harrison et al. 1985), and a shorter version was published in *Anthropology and Education Quarterly* (Harrison 1986a). The case study provides descriptions of the village and the development of its school, including the educational history, curriculum, students, staff, and perceptions about the school provided by community members and teachers.

DISCUSSION

The study of the Manokotak School in 1984–85 was one of the few occasions when I set out to study an educational program without trying to incorporate program innovation into the project. Incorporating training in research methods for local teachers and community members was innovative in that particular community at that time, but the approach had been used previously in other settings; I cannot claim any originality for it. It was a useful approach in this particular situation for all concerned, I believe. I do not remember how the team approach to the research came about, but I suspect that it was the result of discussions with colleagues at UAF who had been involved with the Small High Schools Project.

On the whole, the project worked as it was intended to work. There were unexpected problems along the way, but they were not insurmountable. One problem, for example, arose when I went to complete arrangements for the employment of the two research assistants from the local community. During my first visit, I put up notices around the village describing the project and calling for applications. I was delighted when two young women with appropriate English literacy skills applied, for I had worried that I might not be able to identify anyone with the skills and the interest to work with the team. However, the relevant administrator at UAF was not happy with the process because, in order to satisfy affirmative action requirements for all UAF employment, three levels of interview questions were required. I had not completed the formal interviews at three levels, and therefore the administrator wanted me to begin the process again. I was back in Fairbanks after my first site visit, and there was neither the time nor the funding available for me to go to Manokotak to conduct new interviews. I pointed out that there had only been two applicants for two positions, and they were both young women of minority backgrounds. I wanted to employ them both. How could I possibly have discriminated against anyone in the interview process?

Eventually, the administrator relented, and the two women gained places on the payroll. As I recall, though, I had to complete forms with three levels of questions even though the interviews were already over. It seemed to me that the university's affirmative action program had been distilled into a set of rigid and unbendable rules and regulations, and enforcement was unlikely ever to result in the employment of any significant number of people from minority groups. In the decades since this sequence of events occurred, the university's affirmative action policies and procedures have no doubt changed considerably.

One of the lessons I learned from this study was the relative ease of conducting short-term studies of programs as opposed to trying to make new programs work while studying them at the same time. Organizing a short-term study seemed infinitely easier than making a long-term commitment to starting a new program. The outcomes of this project were more than satisfactory. The graduate students learned something about research and completed their research methods course. The two individuals from the community contributed to the project, learned something about research, and made a little money. A report was published specifically for use in Alaska, and a second report was published in a national journal.

One negative comment about the study should be noted. A few years after the study was completed, a faculty member from UAF told me that the Manokotak School was *not* successful. Individual and cultural definitions of success differ, of course, so it would be hard to say whether this faculty member's perception was closer to the truth than the perceptions of the teachers and community members. Our research team did not draw conclusions regarding the school's success. We only provided statements about the perceptions of the school staff and community members.

Perhaps it adds weight to the argument for the success of the Manokotak School, though, to note that a school in another indigenous community used Manokotak as the basis for the design of some of its new programs. This happened a few years after the case study was published. The organization of the small school in a Maori community in New Zealand described in chapter 8 was influenced by the organization of the small school in Manokotak.

LESSONS LEARNED

Once again, specific events and activities in the Manokotak study contributed to the lessons learned and the formulation of the guidelines recommended in chapters 3 and 4.

The Individual Fieldworker

Be Flexible but Recognize That Everyone Has Limits.

Because the visits that I made to the village lasted only a few days, very little adaptation was required on my part. Manokotak was a pleasant place to work. The village had a history of economic development through commercial fishing, and the levels of individual and family material well-being seemed modestly prosperous. Its history had been relatively peaceful, without major conflicts surrounding the school, and many people had finished high school and were fluent English speakers. Yup'ik culture places a strong emphasis on cooperative relationships, and people were interested in the study. School staff, my students, and other community members were consistently helpful and easy to work with.

Be Willing to Collaborate by Sharing Authority, Responsibility, and Credit for Success.

By the time of this study, I had gained some experience in collaborative research and was able to successfully apply collaborative principles to the implementation of the project. The research committee of the relevant unit at UAF, the school district, the principal, and the Community School Committee all gave formal approval. The researchers worked together as a team and shared credit for the final report, while I retained some necessary authority and responsibility.

Give Thoughtful Attention to the Ethical Implications of Your Actions.

It was not difficult to explain the purposes of the study to people in the community and in the school, but there were still ethical issues to deal with. I interviewed all of the teachers, and there were a few who "unloaded" complaints. It is always a matter of the judgment of the researcher as to how much emphasis to place on the comments of individual informants. I grappled with the question of how to deal fairly with the negative comments. I summarized the complaints in the final report, respecting, of course, the assurance of confidentiality that I had given the informants.

Apply the Concept of Culture in Everyday Working Relationships.

My understandings of the notion of culture and, more specifically, of Yup'ik culture were important components in this project. I had a few years of experience living and working in Yup'ik communities by the time of this study, and I brought some knowledge of Yup'ik culture with me into the setting. This helped in my initial adaptation. I was not starting from scratch in learning about the community, and I knew how to communicate appropriately in that setting. Also, the collaborative approach is particularly well suited to Yup'ik settings because of the high value that Yup'ik people place on community cooperation. It might be much more difficult to conduct collaborative projects in settings with higher levels of competition.

Designing Collaborative Programs

Fieldworkers and Representatives of the Community Should Collaborate to Develop a Rationale, Philosophy, or Reason for the Establishment of the Particular Program.

The case study was undertaken because one teacher wrote a letter suggesting a study of a successful rural Alaskan school, the school where she was teaching. Key individuals—UAF faculty members and the dean, the district superintendent, the school principal, and members of the Community School Committee—were supportive of the idea. It was not an elaborate philosophy for a study, but it was sufficient. One reason that it "worked" was the straightforward rationale for doing the study in the first place.

My work in this project came closer to full collaboration than that in the three earlier projects. The Manokotak study originated in the local community, involved teachers and others from the community in data collection, and gave them a place in the authorship of the report.

Look for Sources of Adequate and Dependable Funding.

Funding was limited to $17,000 but was adequate for the study. The funding was used to employ the research assistants, for travel, and for the publication.

Confirm That There Is Adequate Support in the Local Community.

The Community School Committee was composed of individuals from the village. This committee gave its approval to the study. One of the teachers who participated in the data collection and who was enrolled in the research methods course was from the village. The two paid part-time research assistants were from the village. The support of all of these people was important to the success of the study. I did not hear of anyone from the village who opposed the study.

Formulate a Program Plan Including Statements of Roles and Responsibilities, Support Systems for Participants, and Evaluation Procedures.

Others had suggested the major theme for the project, and I wrote a general program plan for the funding proposal. Because the funding came from UAF and I was employed by UAF, the project was subject to university policies. University accounting regulations and staff provided strict guidelines for the way the funding could be spent. There were problems because I did not know about—and therefore did not follow—the correct employment procedures, but these problems were minor. After various approvals were granted for the project to proceed, I had a great deal of leeway to define my own role and to negotiate roles with the other researchers. I wrote formal job descriptions for the assistants because these were required by university employment policies. I also wrote guidelines for the three teachers in my research course because university policy required faculty to provide students with written guidelines for coursework.

The term *collaborative research* had not yet come into vogue, but I had learned in the Small High Schools Project to collaborate with representatives of the local community and with students. I believed that the project would not be successful unless I asked for their viewpoints and took those views into consideration. I had also learned that it helps to promote cooperative relationships within a project if all of the researchers are given credit as coauthors of the reports. However, there were no formal written agreements regarding collaboration or intellectual property rights.

All members of the research team were named as coauthors of the study published by the Center for Cross-Cultural Studies in 1985. Only my name appears on the article that was published in *Anthropology and Education Quarterly*. My justification at the time for claiming sole authorship of the second paper was that I had done all of the writing of the article and had individually developed the case study for a wider audience. If I had it to do over again, I would list all six names of the people who worked on the data collection and write-up on the second paper as well. Their roles in the development of the article could have been acknowledged in this way. The reports constituted the only means of assessing the project.

Fortunately, the school district person, the teachers, and the two research assistants were all able to work on this project with little direct supervision from me. The visits to the community that I made in January, March, and September 1984, supplemented by written materials and phone calls, were sufficient to provide the direction they needed to complete the necessary tasks. The two teachers in the school worked cooperatively on their data collection assignments, supporting each other in the process, and the two research assistants also worked together.

Communication was straightforward by comparison with that in earlier projects. There were phones in most of the homes in the village and in the school. It was relatively simple for me to phone participants from my office or home in Fairbanks or for them to phone me. We were a small group of researchers, so it was easy to meet with each one during my visits to the village.

Identify or Recruit Committed Leadership in the Program and, Preferably, in the Funding Agency.

This was a short-term project, but, as so often happens, it took longer than I had originally planned to complete both of the reports. Fortunately, the leadership of the relevant units of UAF was stable for the duration, and I was able to follow through with my commitment to the study.

Identify or Recruit Appropriately Qualified Staff.

There was a good balance in this project of people with formal qualifications and people with expert knowledge of the school and the community.

Find a Workable Physical Setting.

From my standpoint, the physical location was quite manageable. Manokotak is in one of the milder climatic zones of Alaska. Transportation to the village was by small plane, about fifteen minutes of flying time from the regional center. The weather cooperated during my travel to and from the village. The airstrip was located in easy walking distance from the village. I stayed with the principal, with teachers, or in the homes of community members when I visited. Visits were not long enough for me to wear out my welcome. Telephones were available in the school and in most homes, thus facilitating communication.

Attend to the Broader Political and Social Context That Makes It Possible for a Program to Survive.

One of the advantages of a short-term study is that the researcher does not have to worry about whether or not the project will survive through the various political upheavals that have such influence on long-term programs. The project was not designed with an eye to its survival. A favorable political and social context was required only for a short period of time.

Chapter Eight

Rakaumanga School, 1986–87

I took a sabbatical leave beginning in August 1986. Several years earlier, I had read John Ogbu's *Minority Education and Caste* (1978), which includes case studies of minority education in several different countries. One of the case studies was on the Maori of New Zealand. I was impressed by the similarities between the educational issues confronting Alaska Natives in the Northern Hemisphere and Maori on the other side of the world.

I had visited New Zealand for a two-week vacation in early 1985 and knew that the climate was warm during Alaska's bitter winter months, and the countryside, green and beautiful. Because the dominant language in New Zealand is English, I felt that I could comfortably spend my leave in that country gathering information on Maori education to compare with what I knew about Alaska Native education.

I had met Robert Mahuta,[1] the director of the Centre for Maaori Studies and Research (CMSR)[2] at the University of Waikato, and his wife, Raiha, when they visited Alaska in the summer of 1985. I had discussed with them the possibility of doing a study of a school in a Maori community. I sent them a short research proposal and was accepted as a visiting professor at CMSR for the period of my leave.

INITIATION

I arrived at CMSR in Hamilton, New Zealand, on 1 September 1986. Although I had visited New Zealand a year and a half earlier, I experienced an extreme sense of disorientation during the first few weeks following my arrival. I had left Alaska in midsummer and had stopped to enjoy the tropical

169

beaches of Fiji for a few days on the way to New Zealand. In New Zealand, it was late winter. I had not carried winter clothing with me and was constantly chilled for those first weeks. I rented and then bought a car—which I had to learn to drive on the "wrong" side of the road and in what seemed like the "wrong" direction because of the differences in orientation to the sun in the Southern Hemisphere. Many of New Zealand's place names are Maori—which I could neither pronounce nor remember for any length of time. So I often could not tell people where I had been after I had been there. Although the dominant language is English, I could not understand the New Zealand accent and terminology. I nodded and smiled a great deal, although often I had no idea what people were saying to me. Kiwis—the name by which locals refer to themselves—thought that I was the one with the accent and the odd ways of expressing myself. Shops opened and closed at different times than I expected, and the pattern of holidays was different. There were several occasions when I found myself standing outside a place of business unable to purchase something that I felt was essential at the moment. I felt totally helpless when I discovered that I did not know how to change a lightbulb in New Zealand. American lightbulbs screw into the socket. New Zealand lightbulbs do not. They have a small extension that hooks into the socket. The upshot was that I had to ask for help again and again for even the simplest tasks.

These problems quickly began to resolve, however. Within a week or so, my ear became tuned to New Zealand speech. The weather warmed up, and the luggage I had shipped with warm clothes arrived. I learned to pronounce and remember place names. I used a map and began to relax when driving. I even learned to change the lightbulbs.

Robert Mahuta's home community was Waahi Marae in Huntly, about thirty-five kilometers north of Hamilton. A *marae* can be briefly described as a Maori community center. A marae was usually composed of a *wharenui* (a big house where meetings could be held and where large groups of people could sleep on mattresses on the floor after meetings ended), a large courtyard, and a dining hall opposite the meetinghouse. Many marae such as Waahi had houses and flats adjacent to the main areas. The people who lived in these residences were usually Maori, with a deep commitment to maintaining the marae, not only physically but also as an active Maori social environment.

In mid-September, I moved into a small flat behind the meetinghouse at Waahi. It was pouring rain the day I moved, and I felt the same overwhelming fear of the unknown that I had experienced on the first day that I moved into my little house in the Alaskan coastal village eight years earlier. I was soon to learn, though, that life at Waahi would be very different from life in the coastal village. For one thing, snow *never* fell in this region of New Zealand.

SETTLING IN

I was not the first researcher to live at Waahi. In fact, when buildings at the marae had been modernized at the time of the construction of the Huntly Power Station, two small flats had been built especially for visiting researchers. One of the flats was named "Kimihia" (translated as "go and seek") to acknowledge the purpose of these flats. Robert's view was that, if his people could not afford to visit the world outside the small community, then he would bring the world to them. The "big OE" or overseas experience was a well-established tradition for middle-class youth, but overseas travel was an unaffordable luxury for many Maori.

In the early 1980s, a medical anthropologist from the United States had lived at the marae and had helped to establish a community health program there. A year or two after she left, two doctoral students in anthropology, one Dutch and the other from the University of Chicago, had shared one of the flats while conducting research. Because people from this community had provided orientations to local culture for these visiting researchers, they knew how to go about it. People were more than willing to answer questions and to take me along to various Maori events at the marae and around the region. The local community also had learned what to expect from visiting researchers. They expected those researchers to make a contribution to local development at the same time that the researchers conducted their scholarly studies.

I spent that year at Waahi learning about the local community, its history and traditions, and about Maori education. Because I lived in one of the flats behind the meetinghouse, I became a part of virtually every major social event at the marae. Funerals or *tangi* were among the most frequent events. Maori believe that the soul or spirit does not leave the body until the third day after death. When a Maori person died, the body was taken by the family to the marae, and, for a period of three days, friends and family came to pay respects to the deceased and to comfort the bereaved. Visitors sometimes numbered in the hundreds, and some spent the entire three-day period at the marae, sleeping in the meetinghouse with the deceased and the family. The family of the deceased prepared meals for the visitors in the dining hall, and all members of the extended family felt responsible to help with the cooking and serving of the meals. Even urbanized Maori who were thoroughly integrated into Western lifestyles were drawn to travel from distant locations to fulfill those responsibilities.

As a resident of the marae, I was expected to join one of the parties of visitors to formally pay respects to the family and the deceased during each tangi. I was uncomfortable at the first tangi because, in my own cultural background, people only attend funerals of individuals they had been acquainted with. Attending funerals of strangers could be viewed as morbid. In middle-class America, one would only comfort the relative of a deceased person with a hug and kiss if one had been very close to that person. In the Maori tangi I experienced, however, strangers were warmly welcomed, and "paying respects" meant greeting each of the women relatives with a hug, even if I had never met the person before and even when the individual was sobbing with grief.

When the marae committee chairman, Taitimu Maipi, came to my flat to take me to my first tangi, he had to reassure me several times that it was appropriate for me to be there. In time, however, I came to realize that families really did appreciate it when I came to "pay respects." I also came to know more and more people around the marae, so that I was acquainted with the deceased or the family in more and more instances. I attended dozens of tangi at Waahi and other nearby marae, and I developed a sense of responsibility to pay respects whenever I could.

Children were included in every aspect, but it was expected that they would behave like children and not like adults. As a result, there were likely to be many children playing around the marae during a tangi. I remember one outstanding example when a man in his eighties died. It was said that he had eighty-five grandchildren, and I felt certain that all of those children were playing around the marae for the three days of the tangi.

About three weeks after I moved to Waahi, that marae's annual *poukai* was held. A poukai is an occasion for members of the tribe to come together to honor the Maori queen, to remember their ancestors, and to make contributions to voluntary funds for the welfare of the tribe. There were twenty-eight poukai held on specific dates at marae throughout the Waikato and other regions of the North Island. Waahi's poukai was always held on 8 October, a date that commemorates the coronation of King Koroki, the fifth Maori king. People from the local community spent weeks planning and preparing for the poukai. Distinguished visitors were invited to attend. Gardens were weeded, lawns were mowed, and buildings and fences were repaired and painted. Extra mattresses for the meetinghouse and dishes for the dining hall were sometimes borrowed from other marae in order to cater for the crowds that appeared on poukai day. Food had to be accumulated, and cooking begun well in advance of the event.

In 1986, Rakaumanga School held a family day on 7 October, the day before the poukai at Waahi. Elders and other family members received a formal *powhiri* or welcome to the school. Each class of children entertained the visitors, and lunch was served to everyone.

Visitors from outside the community began to arrive at the marae later in the afternoon. A religious service was held in the meetinghouse in the evening for those who would spend the night there. At 7:00 a.m. the next morning, the flag raising ceremony was held outside the meetinghouse. Visitors who had spent the night and people from the local community gathered for a solemn prayer service, accompanied by the Taniwharau Brass Band, and the raising of the flag that announced that a poukai would be held at Waahi that day.

Several hundred visitors regularly attended the Waahi poukai. The welcoming ceremony for the largest group of visitors began at about 10:00 a.m. with speeches by distinguished visitors and by elders from Waahi. Special invited guests were welcomed after the main party of visitors had been greeted. Everyone present was served an elaborate lunch in the dining hall after the initial greetings and speeches. After lunch, discussion and debate on matters of importance to the community took place on the courtyard of the marae. Late in the afternoon, the flag was lowered to signify the end of that year's poukai at Waahi.

From September 1986 to July 1987, I attended countless social and political events at Waahi and at other marae in the region. This range of social functions could only be carried out with the traditional Maori emphasis on co-operation. Many volunteers were regularly involved in cooking, cleaning, and maintenance work on the marae, and regular fund-raising events helped to support the activities. Extended families used the marae to stage birthday parties for dozens and sometimes hundreds of family and friends, particularly for twenty-first, fiftieth, and sixtieth birthdays. Marriages were held at the marae. Fund-raising events for a variety of causes were also frequent occasions at the marae. The local Taniwharau Rugby League Football Club held special events there. The marae was the venue for a number of political *hui* (meetings or gatherings) during that year, including a hui of the National Youth Council and one for the Maori members of the Public Service Association (PSA).

These two hui—for the National Youth Council and the PSA—were particularly memorable because I found myself in painfully embarrassing situations at both of them. Pakeha (people of European descent) as well as Maori youth attended the National Youth Council hui. At one point, they broke up into two caucuses, one for Maori and one for Pakeha. I had been sufficiently assimilated into the local community so that I went to the caucus with the people from the community that I knew—into the Maori caucus. One of the Pakeha youth called me out and told me that it was inappropriate for me to be in the Maori caucus. According to the local people whom I talked to afterward, the Maori group had been quite comfortable with me there, but I was embarrassed at the time.

I was also asked to leave a planning meeting for the PSA hui. The planning meeting was held a few days in advance of the main hui. The marae committee chairman had insisted that I come. However, the PSA chairman made it clear that only Maori should be involved in this meeting, and I left, wishing I had not agreed to come in the first place.

The PSA hui made national news because Pakeha members of the PSA picketed outside the marae, protesting that the funding was being used so that only Maori could meet. It seemed unfortunate that the people of the marae who were very open to relationships with non-Maori should have experienced the brunt of the bad publicity regarding racism in the Public Service. It was the PSA planning group that insisted that only Maori be involved. The people of the marae were not responsible for that decision. In fact, people from the marae invited the protestors into the dining hall for lunch.

I traveled with people from Waahi by chartered bus to events at other marae around the region, including poukai, the opening of a new dining hall at Maketu Marae in Kawhia, and the opening of a new meetinghouse at Mokau. The ceremony for the opening of new buildings took place at dawn, so the bus left Huntly at 10:00 p.m. or so at night. After driving for several hours, the bus stopped so that people could change into their black clothes in order to commemorate and remember their ancestors during these important events. The bus then drove to the marae, where the passengers disembarked in darkness to await the dawn ceremony, a blessing led by elders and Maori Anglican priests. After the ceremony, a day of celebration, entertainment, and feasting followed. The party from Waahi slept overnight in the meetinghouse before boarding the bus for the return trip to Huntly the following day.

On one occasion, I traveled with staff from the School of Management Studies at the University of Waikato and staff of the Tainui Trust Board to a weekend management workshop in a small community on the east coast. We all stayed in the meetinghouse of a local marae Friday and Saturday nights. I remember that trip especially because one of the party was what the rest of us termed a "world-class snorer." The person who snored seemed to sleep very well, but the rest of us spent each of the two nights marveling at this eighth wonder of the world.

One of my favorite events was the regatta, held in mid-March, on the Waikato River at Turangawaewae Marae in Ngaruawahia, a few miles south of Huntly. Maori ceremonial canoes were the main focus of the regatta, but people also joined races in all sorts of canoes. On the designated Friday, primary school canoe races were held. On Saturday, secondary school races were held. The ceremonial war canoes with as many as sixty adult male rowers in traditional costume performed a salute to the Maori queen on that day, too. Culture groups including children as well as adults performed on a barge on the river throughout the day. Distinguished visitors were invited to join the queen in watching the events. There were also wood chopping contests, carnival attractions, and stalls where local crafts and food were sold.

The final ceremonial event of the year was the Koroneihana, the celebration of the anniversary of the coronation of the Maori queen. The coronation of Te Arikinui Dame Te Atairangikaahu took place on 23 May 1966, and celebrations have marked the anniversary of that date every year. Turangawaewae Marae in Ngaruawahia hosted the events. The celebrations took place over three days and included acknowledgment of tribal members who had died during the previous year, cultural performances, sports events, entertainment, feasting, distinguished visitors, and the queen's annual address to her people.

As in the other marae events I attended during my first year in the region, the coronation celebrations were planned, organized, and carried out by volunteers from the marae and other nearby communities. Thousands of people attended over the three or four days of the coronation celebrations each year. All were welcomed to the marae, and were served meals in the spectacularly carved dining hall at Turangawaewae.

THE PROGRAM

I did not spend the entire year as a touring anthropologist, however. When I applied to CMSR for a visiting position, I had submitted a proposal to conduct a case study of a school in a Maori community. Robert Mahuta recommended that I talk to the principal of Rakaumanga School, the school closest to Waahi, attended by the majority of the children living in and around the marae. The school had only recently received official recognition from the Ministry of Education as a "bilingual school." Staff were in their first year of instituting Maori-immersion schooling for new entrants who were coming as five-year-olds from Maori-immersion preschool programs.

A few days after I moved into my flat at Waahi, I went to visit the principal. He was cautious about a study such as the one I proposed, but I explained that the report would be based on collaboration between the staff of the school, people from the community, and me. I assured him that nothing would be reported without the consent of the school. He discussed it with the staff, who agreed for the study to begin.

The first step would be for me to be formally welcomed into the school community. On 7 October 1986, a family day was held at the school in conjunction with the poukai at Waahi Marae. Elders and other members of the community were formally welcomed into the school. I joined the visiting party outside the school for the welcome. I learned that, after the formal welcome, each visitor individually greeted each member of the home group, with a handshake, a *hongi* (the traditional Maori greeting—touching noses), or a kiss. I discovered that I really liked the kissing part, especially when it allowed me to kiss an attractive man without embarrassment. The formal welcome was followed by a traditional Maori meal prepared in an underground oven at the marae and transported to the school. A gala of fund-raising events was presented in the afternoon attended by parents, children, elders, and others from the community.

Over the next six months, I interviewed teachers, observed in classrooms, attended meetings of the school committee, reviewed historical and policy documentation, and interviewed community members about the history and development of the school. Members of the school staff and community reviewed drafts of the paper I wrote based on these experiences so that, to the greatest extent possible, the final paper represented their viewpoints (Harrison 1987).

One early experience in this project changed my life forever. In November 1986, the principal and staff invited me to attend a hui of bilingual teachers from around the country being held at a marae near Hastings. The teachers were paying the costs themselves, and they insisted that I attend as their guest. A van was rented, and the teachers from Rakaumanga joined teachers from Bernard Fergusson School in Ngaruawahia in a second van to travel together. The drive from Huntly took about six hours, but we stopped for meals, for cups of tea, and to visit one sacred site. Some of the teachers practiced Maori songs and chants as we rode along, using personal handwritten notes as their references. They also spent time talking to me about the background of the Maori language revitalization movement and its place in Maori schooling.

We arrived at the marae around sunset and were welcomed in a formal powhiri. About eighty Maori people were present, including teachers and elders from bilingual schools and Maori staff from the Department of Education. The greetings went on for a couple of hours as the elder from each visiting party gave a formal greeting and was formally greeted by the home party in return. By the time the powhiri was finished and a meal was served, it was 11:00 p.m. We were shown to the sleeping houses. I had just curled up in my sleeping bag on a mattress alongside my fellow travelers when it was announced that the hui would start. We wrapped ourselves in blankets and trooped back to the dining hall where the opening speeches were given. Everything was in Maori. Some of the teachers helped me understand with translations. It was about 1:00 a.m. when the first session of the hui ended and we went to sleep.

Discussions continued after breakfast the next morning and throughout the day. Issues were raised focusing on problems in Maori language programs because of insufficient resources and the best ways to influence the government to provide adequate funding for those programs. The dialogue often became heated, and it seemed that people were saying exactly what was on their minds.

There was another session after dinner. At about 10:00 p.m., the discussions ended. Someone brought out a guitar, and others brought out pitchers of beer. Each tribal group of teachers stood and sang in turn as the guitar was passed from one group to another. At one point, one of the elders who was traveling with my group stood and sang "Old MacDonald" on my behalf (to acknowledge my American background). At about 4:00 a.m., one of the teachers sitting near me told me that I could go to bed if I wanted to. I welcomed the suggestion but could hear the singing continuing well after I was in my sleeping bag.

Maybe it was the acoustics in the hall where the entertainment took place, or maybe it was the beer, but I was deeply moved by the vitality and commitment to their cause of this group of educators. I had attended the Bilingual Conference in Alaska several times in the years preceding this visit to Hastings and was astounded at the differences between the Maori hui and the Alaskan event. In Alaska, the State Department of Education funded the conference and controlled the agenda. As a result, political issues of importance to the indigenous people were not often raised at the formal conference. In the Maori setting, the teachers paid their own expenses, and they controlled the agenda. Political issues were the major focus of the interaction.

We drove back to Huntly after breakfast the next day. I was thoroughly exhausted by the time we reached home, but I knew I had had a life-changing experience. I was strongly attracted to the work under way in Maori education and wanted to be part of it in the future. Before my leave ended six months later, I began to make arrangements to work in the community on a long-term basis.

After a break of several months, I returned to the community and the school. For the next ten years, I sat with the Rakaumanga School Committee, later renamed the Runanga (Board of Trustees), taking the minutes of the meetings and observing as the school became a total-immersion Maori school and as it expanded through the secondary level (see Harrison 1998). Whenever I have been discouraged about other aspects of my work, the school, its staff, the children, and their parents have been a source of encouragement and inspiration for me.

DISTRACTIONS

Late in 1986, the New Zealand Parliament adopted the State Owned Enterprises Act, which dictated that existing government operations in nine areas were to be converted into state-owned "enterprises" on 1 April 1987. The new state-owned enterprises were to be managed by businesspeople on principles of private enterprise. For two or three years prior to the passage of the act, government policy in the Waikato had focused on expansion of energy projects related to coal mining. With the passage of the act, however, managers of what would become the new Coal Corporation announced that coal mining in the Waikato would be curtailed and that as many as 200 people could be made "redundant."

Early in the week of 23 February 1987, Coal Corporation management announced that a mass meeting would be held in Huntly on 26 February where the total number of layoffs would be announced. Virtually the entire adult population of the town attended the meeting where they were informed that nearly 500 would be laid off. Everyone—Pakeha and Maori—in the community of approximately 7,500 was affected because members of both groups were employed in the mines and because other businesses expected to suffer losses as the result of high rates of unemployment and migration out of the community.

Although a "redeployment center" was established by State Coal to offer information related to redundancy and unemployment, staff members in the center were able to offer little factual information to clients. At the time of the announcement, there appeared to be no established policies as to when and how individuals would learn of their job status, standards to be used in determining who would be laid off, what working conditions would exist under the new Coal Corporation, or how rental housing owned by State Coal would be managed after the transition. No advance plans had been made by government departments such as Labour or Social Welfare to increase staffing in Huntly to deal with the impact of the sudden increase in unemployment.

The community was overwhelmed with a sense of uncertainty about the future, and Coal Corporation managers expressed little sympathy for the situation they were creating. The corporation's new chief executive said, in a radio interview that was repeatedly broadcast throughout the region, that the redundant miners should show the same "get-up-and-go" that had brought their ancestors from the United Kingdom to New Zealand's coal mines during the nineteenth and early twentieth centuries. The statement ignored the Maori population, whose ancestors had lived in the region for hundreds of years.

The Tainui Trust Board made submissions to Wellington and sent a delegation of miners to Wellington. At Waahi, the decision was made to establish a resource center to provide assistance to community members who were suffering economic, psychological, and family stress as a result of the employment crisis. A potluck was held in the marae dining hall, and miners and their families were invited. Applications for funding and other assistance went to government agencies. Taitimu Maipi, the marae committee chairman, wrote letters of reference on behalf of coal miners from the local community. A women's meeting was held where women had the chance to discuss stresses within families resulting from the crisis. A delegation was invited from another community where massive unemployment had recently resulted from government "restructuring." This delegation gave a public presentation describing the actions undertaken at the community level in response to the crisis.

At the request of the marae committee chairman, I participated in all of these activities, typing the letters of recommendation, keeping notes and preparing reports, and writing proposals and submissions on behalf of the community. These activities occupied a large part of my time for about three months.

Another program also demanded my time and attention and distracted me from my work on the case study of Rakaumanga School. The Waahi Community Training Centre (CTC) was impossible to avoid because the flat where I was living was immediately adjacent to the CTC facilities at Waahi. This program and its development are described in detail in chapter 9. Even though my primary focus during my first year in New Zealand was the case study of Rakaumanga School, I spent a good deal of time in meetings about the CTC, discussing the program's philosophy and implementation.

PREPARING THE REPORT

I had several problems in preparing the report of the year's work at Rakaumanga School. I had purchased my first home computer a few months before I left Alaska and brought the computer with me. My computer was not compatible with the systems at CMSR, so it seemed to make sense to produce the final version on my machine rather than having it all retyped. But I had never prepared a report for publication this way. The local computer dealer in Hamilton wanted to help, but he had not done anything like this either.

Producing the final text was a struggle. I was not happy with the layout, but I was happy, finally, to have one copy completed, ready for reproduction. There were further difficulties in getting the report printed. The CTC had purchased a printing machine, and program managers wanted to earn a little money for their program by printing my report, but the process was new for them, too. Again, it was a struggle, and, in the end, I was happy just to have it finished. I spent countless hours struggling over the production of the report. I had never had to deal with the actual printing of a report before. I had not realized how important this element of the research process was.

DISCUSSION

What were the outcomes for the year? I learned about the life and culture of the community of Waahi as well as about New Zealand life and culture more generally. I completed two papers for publication: the case study of Rakaumanga School (Harrison 1987) and an article on Alaska Native education, published in two New Zealand journals (Harrison 1986b, 1988). One of the articles on Alaska served as the stimulus for a Maori program developer to initiate new programs for training Maori teachers based on the Alaskan model. This was an unexpected and most satisfactory outcome of the year. Then, in the early 1990s, I drew heavily on my field notes from 1986–87 for a chapter in a book on minority education (Harrison 1993). Several years later, I wrote another article on Rakaumanga using the 1987 report as a starting point (Harrison 1998). This article includes a description of the expansion of the primary school into a combined primary/secondary school with a similar structure to that of the school in Manokotak.

I believe that other work that I did contributed to the welfare of the local community. Looking back on this experience, though, I wonder whether I could have done much more extensive research relating to Rakaumanga School or other aspects of Maori education if I had spent more time on that focus and less time on other work for the community. Perhaps. But I had to honor the priorities of the community if I wanted to do any research at all.

LESSONS LEARNED

The Individual Fieldworker

Be Flexible but Recognize That Everyone Has Limits.

Early in this chapter, I describe the problems that I had in adapting during my first weeks in New Zealand. Problems such as the ones I encountered are common for travelers who have to make simple adaptations as they confront new settings. In most respects, the physical environment was similar to environments that I had known previously, so adaptations to the physical environment were not that difficult. Most modern conveniences—a car, electricity, supermarkets, telephones, and so on—were all readily available.

The Waikato region of New Zealand has a temperate climate. Even so, one visiting American researcher remarked that he got colder in the Waikato winter sitting in unheated buildings for meetings than he ever did while working in Alaska. How well one adapts to a particular physical environment depends on one's expectations and whether one's clothing and equipment are really suitable for that environment. On the whole, after more than ten years in Alaska, it was a great relief for me to be in an environment that was similar to Northern California, where I had grown up. I was very comfortable in my two-room flat behind the meetinghouse at the marae — so comfortable, in fact, that after a six-month visit to Alaska, I returned to stay for four more years before moving into my own house a short distance from the marae.

Maori and Yup'ik peoples hold similar values regarding community cooperation. In both cultural groups, cooperation is upheld as the ideal for community relations. In the Waikato region, I was amazed at the number of programs and projects that were carried out by the cooperative work of Maori volunteers. These included large-scale events involving thousands of participants, such as the regatta at Ngaruawahia in March and the coronation in May, and numerous smaller-scale events such as the poukai on twenty-eight-separate occasions each year at twenty-eight marae. Maori also uphold hospitality and caring for visitors as important ideals. There were other cultural values that appealed to me too, such as the values placed on respect for elders and acceptance of responsibility for care of the environment.

There were some values that required adjustment on my part, though. For example, every individual was expected to have an opinion on issues as they came up, and everyone was expected to express an opinion. This led to frequent arguments and debates on various issues. Ideally, people listened to others' opinions, the debates led to consensus, and amicable decisions were made. I had to learn to expect the arguments and to accept them as part of the normal course of events. Some of these arguments were arguments between factions. There were intricate kin relationships between members of the community, and some disputes between branches of extended families dated back for several generations. Because I was only there for a few months at the time of this study, I was able to learn something about the factions and their history while maintaining a neutral position. My efforts to remain neutral were practical. I sincerely believed that, if I was going to be allowed to stay long enough to complete my research, neutrality was a political necessity. If I identified with one faction or another, I would soon be sent packing. There were members of different factions who were quite insistent that I support one faction or another, but I held my ground.

At the time, there was a good deal of debate and argument between the local community and government representatives. It was not difficult for me to give moral support to the local community when the community argued against government policies. There were also Maori people who were angry about the way the land was confiscated by the government in the 1800s, about continuing injustice in New Zealand society, and about racial discrimination in other countries dominated by people of European descent. There were occasions when Maori expressed their anger verbally, giving me cause to stop and think about my own position in the situation. No one ever seemed angry with me personally. I concluded that the best thing to do was to listen and learn from what they had to say while offering my time and skills to work on projects that I believed might eventually benefit their communities.

There were also people of European descent who told me about their prejudices against Maori (when no Maori were within earshot, of course). Again, I had to think about my response. I concluded that it would be a waste of time for me to try to tell these people what they should believe. If I thought I could have accomplished much by engaging in debate, I might have done so, but I did not think that debate in those circumstances would prove particularly fruitful. I decided to save my energy for projects with greater promise of success.

Government actions, such as the restructuring that led to the sudden unemployment of hundreds of Maori in the local community, tended to unite the community. The Tainui Trust Board's campaign to gain a settlement from the government for the land claims dating from the 1860s also tended to unite the community. So, although there were frequent debates and there were factions, there seemed to be a high degree of unity. I enjoyed living in a community in which there was a sense of people working together toward common goals.

However, I felt moments of stress early in my stay when I attended funerals at the marae when I did not know the families involved. After several years and dozens of funerals, it finally felt natural for me to hug women acquaintances or even strangers who were visibly grieving and weeping over the death of family members. It also took some time for me to adjust to the physical contact—touching, kissing, and hugging—that Maori who lived at the marae took for granted in everyday occasions. When I was introduced to women, a kiss on the cheek was customary along with a handshake. When I was introduced to men, the hongi (nose touching) was appropriate. When sitting in meetings in the meetinghouse, people often sat very close together on mattresses, benches, or the floor, shoulder to shoulder, hip to hip, sometimes with their arms around me to make me feel welcome. And they did make me feel welcome.

I have already mentioned minor embarrassments at two hui. My compulsive punctuality also caused problems for me in this setting as it had in Yup'ik communities. In the Waahi community, though, my punctuality became a joke that we could all laugh about. It was sometimes a struggle, too, to listen to people express differing opinions but to maintain neutrality in my associations with various factions.

Be Willing to Collaborate by Sharing Authority, Responsibility, and Credit for Success.

It was a struggle to balance what the community wanted from me with my commitment to the research project. Collaboration had become almost second nature to me. I had worked successfully in collaborative settings in the past, and I could not imagine any other way of approaching a study. But I often felt the pressure of trying to meet both the community's expectations and my own.

Give Thoughtful Attention to the Ethical Implications of Your Actions.

At the time of the study, my ethical thinking still focused mainly on the issues of informed consent and confidentiality. I made every effort to inform people in the school and in the marae community about my research and to provide them with opportunities to review my written drafts. I also offered time and skills to community projects to reciprocate for the research assistance that the community provided to me.

Looking back on the situation, I have come to realize that there were ethical implications that I had not considered at the time. For example, there were ethical implications to the question of whether to support one faction or another when internal arguments arose. If I had supported any faction and that support had influenced events or relationships *within the community*, then I believe my action would have been ethically questionable. My stated purpose there—the one that I had gone out of my way to inform people about—did not include changing relationships within the community. I continue to believe that neutrality was the best stance, both practically and ethically.

Apply the Concept of Culture in Everyday Working Relationships.

This guideline was especially important to me at Waahi. Very little of the pre-contact material culture remained intact. People interacted in modern economic and political systems with jobs and the cars, television sets, microwaves, and other goods that can be purchased from wage earnings. Nearly everyone had attended English-speaking schools at least to the age of fifteen, and a number had traveled overseas. Everyone in the neighborhood around the marae was Maori, but there was a high degree of integration between Maori and people of European descent in the larger community of Huntly. Maori in the marae community had undergone a diverse range of experiences leading to diversity in the individual viewpoints they expressed and in their reactions to specific situations. There seemed to be a wide range of personalities and of individual responses to any given situation. Some people seemed brash and brazen; others seemed quiet and withdrawn. Initially, it was difficult to identify widely shared cultural characteristics that distinguished people at Waahi from the mainstream.

Over time, I discovered that there were deeply held cultural assumptions and values that characterized the group of people I worked with. For example, in spite of the disagreements and factionalism, everyone expressed loyalty to the Maori queen and the political and spiritual movement that she represented. Even so, I am very cautious about generalizing with regard to aspects of culture that might apply to everyone. If I want to know a particular person's viewpoint, I have to ask.

Designing Collaborative Programs

Fieldworkers and Representatives of the Community Should Collaborate to Develop a Rationale, Philosophy, or Reason for the Establishment of the Particular Program.

Rakaumanga School had a very strong rationale for developing its Maori-immersion program. My reasons for doing a case study of the school were not so explicit. When I was still in Alaska, long before I knew anything about Rakaumanga, I had written a proposal to do a case study of a school and was granted a special sabbatical leave to do the study. CMSR had assisted me in getting permission to come to New Zealand on the basis of the same proposal. Robert Mahuta, director of CMSR, recommended the specific school, Rakaumanga, which he had attended as a child.

I was intensely interested in learning about the way schooling developed when indigenous groups were given the opportunity to run their own schools. I was interested in supporting the efforts of indigenous people in that regard. I knew how to do case studies that focused on analysis of the cultural context of schools, and I liked collaborating with indigenous people in preparing these reports. The school principal and staff agreed to the study. So a case study of Rakaumanga School it would be.

This study was more traditional and less collaborative than the case study of the Manokotak School, partially because I had no funding to hire anyone to work with me. However, it was collaborative in that I explicitly intended to represent the views of the school staff and community members in my portrayal of the school. I asked some of them to comment on drafts of the paper and incorporated their comments into the text, so authority for the report was shared. However, because I did all of the writing, I claimed sole authorship of the paper.

The major collaborative dimension of this study, though, was in my agreement to offer my time and services to various projects in return for the opportunity to learn about the community and to do the study. People from the community—particularly the chairman of the marae committee, Taitimu Maipi, who was also chairman of the school committee—wanted my assistance in achieving goals that had little or nothing to do with my study. People from this community were not about to allow research without achieving some contribution to their own goals in return. So we collaborated.

Look for Sources of Adequate and Dependable Funding.

One great advantage of qualitative research is that it usually does not cost very much. I had a small amount of funding to support my sabbatical leave from the University of Alaska Fairbanks. CMSR agreed to pay for publication of the paper. I paid only a token rental on the flat at the marae. An added advantage was that US$1.00 yielded about NZ$2.00 because of the exchange rate at the time. So someone spending U.S. dollars could live and study very cheaply indeed in New Zealand.

Confirm That There Is Adequate Support in the Local Community.

The director of CMSR had supported extended field stays by several overseas researchers at Waahi. Local people had seen positive outcomes from the work of the overseas researchers, most notably in the establishment of the marae health center, and they were supportive of me when I arrived. Some people in the local community saw me as a resource. For others, an American visitor was an object of particular interest—they were curious and wanted to know more about me. There was some initial concern in the school, but the staff accepted my intention to represent their views and to collaborate on the write-up of the report. If there were objections to the study, I did not hear about them.

Formulate a Program Plan Including Statements of Roles and Responsibilities, Support Systems for Participants, and Evaluation Procedures.

The reader will already have realized, I am sure, that this was the simplest type of research program possible for its time. The successes of this program reinforced the "keep it simple" principle. I was a lone researcher conducting interviews and observations with the intention of presenting the viewpoints of one school's participants. Even though I was associated with two universities—I was on sabbatical from UAF and held an unpaid, visiting position at the University of Waikato—I was not consciously aware of policy constraints from either university. Looking back, the constraints were undoubtedly there, but I did not give them a thought at the time. I collaborated with people in the local community and consulted from time to time with staff of CMSR, and that was the management structure for the project. Funding for the project came mainly from my salary and savings, so I had freedom to spend money as I thought best. The primary means of accountability was through published reports.

My work on the Rakaumanga case study started only a year after I had completed the case study at Manokotak. My assumptions about collaboration had not changed. In order to ensure that I was accurately representing the views of the school's staff and parents, I circulated copies of my drafts for review and comment. I made changes in the text based on their comments. However, I conducted and recorded all of the formal interviews and did all of the other data collection myself. I completed all of the analysis and the writing, so the paper was published under my name as author. At that time, this was acceptable procedure from the standpoint of local people. But times were changing quickly, and issues relating to ownership of intellectual property were to come up for more discussion not long after the study was completed.

The major difficulty in this study arose because of the demands on my time from other community projects. People cared less about my case study of the school than they did about political action and about the economic crisis that erupted when so many employees of State Coal were laid off in April 1987. As far as they were concerned, my typing skills and the output from my computer were far more important than an academic paper about the neighborhood school.

I often felt that I was being pulled in many directions at once. I felt that time for the formal papers had to be carved out in small pieces, and I did not accomplish as much academic study as I had hoped to over the course of the year. However, as an educational anthropologist, it was essential for me to include in my report a substantial understanding of the cultural context of the school. The school did not exist in isolation. Its values and activities reflected its immediate context, including political action and economic crisis. School staff had to decide how to respond when political action and economic crisis affected children and parents, and so I could not ignore these dimensions of school life even if I had wanted to. Also, although I did not realize it at the time, the work on the community projects laid a foundation for the work that I would do in the years that followed.

It is hard to imagine how this community could have provided any more personal support for me than it did. I was invited to every event in and around the marae and to a great many Maori events around the region. People provided explanations, translations, and answers to questions. School staff were cooperative and encouraging. Throughout the community, there was a very strong sense of people working together. Some communication problems continued because I was not familiar with New Zealand English, but they were minor.

Identify or Recruit Committed Leadership in the Program and, Preferably, in the Funding Agency.

The study was short term and small scale. About nine months elapsed from my initial contact with the school to completion of the publication. I was the only staff member involved, and my commitment was sufficient to complete the project as planned.

Identify or Recruit Appropriately Qualified Staff.

I had a good background for this project, and I had the support that I needed from the community.

Find a Workable Physical Setting.

I worked in my flat and at the school.

Attend to the Broader Political and Social Context That Makes It Possible for a Program to Survive.

This was a small-scale, short-term project. There was little reason to be concerned about the impact of the political context on the research. The political context has been terribly important, though, in the development of this Maori-immersion school over the decade following the initial study. The article published in 1998 describes the way that Maori political agitation led to the establishment of a national language policy that supports Maori-language education. The policy in turn has led to funding for the training of Maori-language teachers and Maori-immersion schools.

NOTES

1. On 20 May 1997, the investiture of Sir Robert Mahuta as Knight Companion of the New Zealand Order of Merit recognized his services to the Maori people. This event took place almost a year after it was announced in the Queen's Birthday Honours in 1996. He was addressed as Sir Robert from May 1997 until his death in early 2001.

2. The Centre for Maaori Studies and Research (CMSR) used a double "a" in Maori to indicate that the "a" should be pronounced as a long vowel. CMSR was restructured in 2000 and is now known as the Centre for Maori and Pacific Development Research. The new centre is a unit in the School of Maori and Pacific Development, University of Waikato.

Chapter Nine

The Community Training Centre, 1986–90

The Community Training Centre (CTC) in Huntly opened for the first time in mid-November 1986 with sixteen young adults as trainees and two half-time coordinators as staff members. The center had its origins in a May 1985 hui among officials of the Ministry of Energy, the Tainui Trust Board, and community members at Waahi Marae. The Huntly Power Plant had been constructed on land adjacent to Waahi during the 1970s, but the plant had provided little employment for Maori in the local community. During the early 1980s, the Ministry of Energy was planning expansions of energy development in the Waikato. Local Maori leaders made the point that such expansions would only contribute to Maori economic development if training programs were established with the specific purpose of training Maori young adults for jobs in energy industries.

A year of negotiation between representatives of the Tainui Trust Board and the Ministries of Energy, Education, and Labour followed the 1985 hui and eventually resulted in a memorandum of agreement between those agencies for the establishment of the CTC. Two part-time coordinators were employed in mid-1986, and remodeling of an existing facility at Waahi began in October. Early in November, one of the part-time coordinators talked of leaving the program, saying that he did not belong there, but he continued in the program for the first year.

Members of the local Maori community recommended individuals for the trainee positions, and the trainees began attending on 10 November. Their first task was to assist in the completion of the construction of the building, which was adjacent to the meetinghouse at Waahi. Volunteer carpenters, plasterers, and painters from the marae community supervised and worked with the trainees.

However, before construction of the facility was completed, a major shift in government policy occurred. In December 1986, the State Owned Enterprises Act was adopted by Parliament. Under the terms of this act, State Coal and the Electricity Division of the Ministry of Energy were to become state-owned enterprises on 1 April 1987. The new managers of the state-owned enterprises decided that, rather than expanding energy development in the Waikato, energy development would be curtailed. Nearly half of those employed by State Coal were to be laid off, and no additional power plants were to be constructed.

THE PROGRAM

CTC program coordinators rapidly concluded that the original goal of the CTC—training young Maori adults for positions in energy-related developments—needed revision. Rather than training young people for specific positions, they decided to offer a broadly based educational program that would provide the trainees with exposure to a range of vocational options and experience in management, decision making, Maori language, traditional culture, health, and fitness. The coordinators and members of the local community believed that they would be able to run a program based on the goals that they were devising.

In early 1987, a computer consultant was employed, and a computer laboratory was established for training in computer operation and programming. One trainer opened a full-time module in building trade skills (called the "Handyperson course"). Funding was obtained from another government program for the establishment of a small business specializing in printing and graphic arts. A part-time trainer began offering instruction in Maori language, and each of the part-time coordinators assumed responsibility for specialized training, one in Maori cultural perspectives and one in "life skills."

Because the program was located at a marae and because nearly all of the staff members were Maori, the program operated on principles of Maori protocol. For example, each day began with a prayer and a hymn in Maori, and visitors were formally welcomed in accordance with protocol. The strong Maori cultural influence permeated all of the program operations.

INITIATION

It was in the early stages of the establishment of the CTC that I first became a subject in a research study. A master's degree student from the Department of Community Psychology at the University of Waikato was given permission to conduct an evaluation of the CTC and to use the study as the basis for her thesis. I was not doing a formal study of the CTC at that point, but I was sitting in on organizational meetings and classes as a matter of interest. There were occasions when the graduate student and I had what I thought were informal discussions of the events we were observing. A year later, when her thesis was made public, I discovered that I had been quoted. Effectively, I became a subject in her study. She tried to keep my identity anonymous by describing me as a visiting American researcher and not naming me. There was nothing offensive about her description and nothing offensive about what she had quoted me as saying, but I found that I really disliked being quoted publicly without my express permission, and I did not like becoming a subject in a study without my consent.

In May 1987, both of the coordinators told me that they wanted to leave the CTC and asked if I would take a full-time coordinator's position. I knew enough about the difficulties that the program was facing to realize how much work it would be to try to make the program a success. Initially, I said no, but as the time approached when I was supposed to leave the marae to return to Alaska, I realized that leaving would be hard to do. Eventually, I agreed. I had to go back to Alaska for one semester to complete my contract there, but I promised to return in January 1988.

Toward the end of June 1987, I prepared to leave Waahi. A farewell get-together was organized on my behalf. Chinese food was served in the small club (Kore Mimiti—"Never Run Dry") at the marae. The Rakaumanga School principal, representatives from the CTC, the marae committee chairman, community health workers, and some of the unemployed miners came to say good-bye. Several of them gave speeches thanking me for the work I had done on their behalf. There were gifts, and, in the Maori tradition, a song followed each speech. The tears streamed down my face, and I vowed to return. I departed for Auckland airport the following evening.

I returned to a full-time teaching position at the University of Alaska Fairbanks in early September 1987. That fall semester was one of the most stressful periods of my life. Colleagues convinced me to request a year's leave of absence rather than resigning so that I could return after one year if I wanted to. I was teaching on-campus courses as well as flying to rural villages for short stints of student teaching supervision. I had to arrange to rent my condominium and store most of my belongings. My car seemed to respond to the stress; I had flat tires about once a month, and several male colleagues were called on to change them. I am sure they were glad when I finally left the state.

In order to gain a work permit from the New Zealand government, I needed a letter from the CTC saying that I had been offered a position there and that the CTC had been unable to locate any New Zealander who could fill the position. I telephoned regularly to the one remaining coordinator of the CTC saying that I needed the letter, but no letter arrived. By Christmas, all my other arrangements had been made, but I still had no letter. If I was going to go, I would have to take the chance that I could gain the work permit after I arrived in New Zealand. I very nearly backed out at the last minute, but two friends (the ones who had been changing the tires) encouraged me to take the chance. They drove me to the Fairbanks airport.

I stopped in Southern California for a family visit and made one more call to the CTC regarding the letter. Finally, a short statement was faxed to the New Zealand consulate in Los Angeles. The consulate recommended that I proceed with my travel plans. I would have to apply for the work permit after I arrived in New Zealand, but the letter provided some assurance that a work permit would be granted.

SETTLING IN

I arrived in New Zealand on Saturday, 9 January 1988, and returned to one of the flats at Waahi. I began to "catch up" on all that had happened while I had been away. One of the most important events involved the disappearance of $30,000 of CTC funding. A young Maori man had been given responsibility for managing the funds with little supervision. He had quickly discovered ways to abscond with cash. Discrepancies had been uncovered while I was away, and the situation created a crisis in the management structure. After much discussion, the various parties involved had agreed to transfer responsibility from the Management Committee defined in the original memorandum of agreement to a committee representing several of the local marae under the auspices of the Tainui Trust Board. However, members of the local leadership at the marae did not want the training programs at their marae to be controlled by a committee from other marae. They wanted to maintain control themselves.

Both of the original part-time coordinators had departed in the final months of 1987. A local man with little appropriate background or training had been appointed as manager. In addition, the government had restructured the funding agency into a system known as ACCESS and had delegated responsibility for allocating funding to a Regional Employment and Access Council (REAC). The REAC was composed of individuals representing various constituencies in the community. Much of the real control of the allocation process, however, rested with the ACCESS program manager employed by the Department of Labour. The CTC had submitted course proposals to the REAC, but funding for the continuation of the CTC programs in 1988 had not been approved by the end of 1987.

A visiting researcher at Waahi provided the following description of events just prior to my arrival at Waahi in January 1988:

> Negotiations with REAC
>
> The CTC submitted six proposals for 48 trainees to REAC by mid-December. In its initial response REAC recognised the value of the lead-in period or induction phase when trainees would sample a range of courses. However, REAC requested the CTC to structure the course contracts in such a way that valid performance data would be accessible on a course by course basis. It did not approve two of the proposed courses as they did not anticipate job outcomes in accordance with the required standards. REAC suggested instead to provide a pre-vocational skills course for some twelve trainees running parallel with basic skills training courses for some eighteen trainees.
>
> The letter containing REAC's proposals was received only a few days before the Christmas break. The former coordinator had resigned and the new coordinator did not arrive until after the start of the new year. (Meijl 1988: 7)

On Monday, 11 January, I started to work as the coordinator of the CTC on a two-year contract. The funding for the position was part of the agreement recorded in the original memorandum of agreement and was paid through a two-year technical training institution in Hamilton. My first task was to attend a meeting with the manager of the ACCESS funding agency in Hamilton. The researcher quoted above and the man who had been serving as manager went with me:

> Along with the manager of the CTC, the new coordinator entered the negotiations with REAC from 11 January 1988, barely two days after her arrival. Both the coordinator and the manager as well as the present author went to see the ACCESS coordinator of the region to discuss REAC's comments on the proposals as submitted by the CTC. None of the representatives of the CTC were familiar with the terminology of REAC and the obscure language of the ACCESS coordinator in particular. When the negotiators of the CTC left the meeting with the ACCESS coordinator there was confusion about the requests made to the CTC by the ACCESS coordinator on behalf of REAC. Numerous phone calls for further clarification were needed before the CTC was able to put pen to paper and write a proposal for a pre-vocational course. Basic skills courses had been approved by REAC. In order of preference were computers, automated office and handyperson. No further submissions on these courses were requested.
>
> In addition to a pre-vocational course proposal, REAC requested a list of trainees, a programme schedule, budgets for each course, a payment schedule, and, last but not least, a projection of global outcomes. All the requested material was submitted by 13 January 1988. (Meijl 1988: 7–8)

Looking back, it is hard to believe that the CTC and its new coordinator, me, survived the first half of 1988. There was no coherent system of financial accounting for the program; funding (when it was eventually approved by

REAC) was assured only for six months; there was continuing disagreement between various groups who wanted to control the CTC; the program was staffed with local people who had few qualifications and no training as teachers; and, as the program coordinator, I had virtually no idea how ACCESS was supposed to work.

Nevertheless, we stumbled along for the first three months. We established two major priorities. One was to set up some sort of reasonable system of financial accounting. In the beginning I kept a handwritten cashbook myself, wrote the checks, and prepared monthly statements of income and expenditure to present to the management committee. I was grateful for the many years of secretarial, bookkeeping, and office management experience I had completed before I started graduate study. I had to learn the New Zealand system for reporting payroll taxes and the goods and services tax as well as the banking system. Within a few weeks, we set up a computer accounting system, and I began to train the manager and others in the various tasks involved.

The second major priority was a staff development program for the instructional staff. We met for half an hour early each morning to plan for the day and to discuss issues and problems. We asked for and obtained permission to dismiss trainees early on Friday so that a regular staff development session could be held. One of the previous half-time coordinators and his wife, a distinguished educator, met with the staff on a regular basis. After some months, connections were made with Waikato Polytechnic in Hamilton so that a program leading to a Certificate in Adult Teaching was offered at the marae.

There were countless meetings with the original Management Committee and with the new committee of representatives from several marae. The original Management Committee agreed to disband. The new committee was determined to gain control of the assets, income, and management of the CTC, but the people from the local marae believed that they were the ones who should have authority.

OVERLOAD

In March, a new crisis arose. I had been under the impression that REAC had approved funding to run the courses for six months. I was mistaken. We had been approved to run the courses for three months. Then, a new cohort of trainees was supposed to enroll for a second three-month run of courses. A day or two before the end of the first three-month run, the Labour Department asked for the new enrollment forms, and we frantically scurried about trying to complete the appropriate paperwork.

The next requirement was to report on the outcomes of the first three-month run of courses. The only outcome that made any real difference to AC-CESS was the "into-work outcome"—the number of trainees who found paid employment at the end of the course. I was horrified when I realized the demands being placed on the program by the government. The trainees in the program were almost all Maori who had left school as quickly as possible after reaching fifteen, the age when the law allowed them to leave school. Many could barely read, write, or do basic arithmetic when they entered training. Some had criminal records, and some had been in prison. Some had alcohol or drug problems. The unemployment rate in the Huntly area following the layoffs in the coal mines in 1987 was astronomical. No new jobs were appearing. Yet we were supposed to give the trainees three months of training and put them into long-term employment at the end of that time! And if we did not meet the ACCESS into-work targets, funding would be cut off and the program shut down!

I also became aware that we would have to rewrite and resubmit all the program proposals in June if our funding was to continue beyond the initial six-month allocation. ACCESS wanted specific measurable behavioral objectives for each trainee in each course. The objectives were to be stated in terms of vocational skills. We were not allowed to spend any time teaching basic literacy and computation. Trainees were to be working under the supervision of a trainer from 9:00 a.m. to 4:00 p.m. five days a week. One thing was clear at this point—the government goals as represented by ACCESS were nothing like the original goals as defined in the memorandum of agreement and were even further from the personal development goals defined by the original coordinators.

I felt that we had to fight for the program's survival. If nothing else, the program was providing employment for local people who would otherwise be unemployed, and it was providing rental income for the marae. There was also the hope that we could provide some training that would benefit unemployed youth from the community. I had a firm belief in the ability of small communities to develop and to run their own education and training programs, and I really, really did not want to personally fail in this endeavor. I had risked a great deal in leaving Alaska and the United States to move to New Zealand. I was terrified at the thought of failure.

I was not the only one willing to put up a fight. The other staff and members of the marae community felt as strongly as I did about keeping the program going. Staff members really wanted their jobs, and they really wanted to help trainees acquire education and skills that would benefit them. The community felt that it had a modicum of control over an educational program, and people were willing to fight to maintain that program, even if it meant compromising specific educational goals. One step involved in retaining control of the program was the formation of a charitable trust. A small group from the community formed a charitable trust so that it could legally take responsibility for the management of the program.

One critical element at this point was the support I was receiving from the staff, the CTC trustees, and other members of the community. People listened to what I had to say and worked with me to meet the ACCESS requirements that would maintain the program. People expressed deep affection for me in many ways and on many occasions.

We frantically set about finding and sometimes creating any sort of work we could for the trainees. One of the previous coordinators, the manager of the CTC, and three young women who had been among the original group of sixteen trainees established a small company. I worked with them to write a proposal for a course in small business management for submission to AC-CESS, and the course was funded. Eventually, their company developed a specialization in computer graphics and desktop publishing. Several years later, this company merged with the CTC, and the original group continued to run courses until the year 2000.

The jobs available to most trainees were often short-term laborer positions. Nevertheless, I encouraged trainees into them so that we could meet the into-work outcomes. We employed one or two trainees as assistant trainers. We rewrote proposals for the existing courses over and over again, and we submitted a proposal for one new course, called "Work-Based Training."

We tried to deal with the politics of the situation. We soon realized that each representative on the REAC was supporting proposals submitted by his or her constituency, so we submitted the name of the principal of Rakaumanga School for a position on the REAC. We were fortunate; he was accepted onto the REAC, and that gave us an advocate on that board. I have no doubt that the CTC would have quickly disappeared into oblivion without his advocacy.

In June our best efforts were reviewed by the REAC. They approved funding for an additional three months. During that time, we would have to rewrite and resubmit all of the course proposals again. This process continued for the next year and a half. At one point our funding was approved for six months, but at the end of that six months we were back into the three-month cycle. ACCESS employed staff in the Huntly office to teach us how to write the objectives and proposals, but those staff seemed to know less than we did about how it should be done.

It was extremely difficult to concentrate on other aspects of the quality of the training programs because I was constantly preoccupied with finding the right wording for each objective. One example—out of many examples—will illustrate the problems involved. In the Automated Office course, the first objective on the list was to teach trainees to take an accurate and complete message from a telephone call quickly and efficiently. However, "quickly and efficiently" had to be stated in terms of a specific time frame. When I wrote the objective I said something about one minute. The REAC committee was unsure as to whether it meant a one-minute phone call or that the message was to be completed within one minute after the call ended. They approved three-months funding for the course, but all objectives (not just the one in question) had to be resubmitted before additional funding would be awarded.

I reread my copy of Harry Wolcott's *Teachers versus Technocrats* (1977). It was hard to believe that I was battling the same technocratic mind-set in New Zealand that the teachers in Oregon had fought so hard against many years earlier. Based on the Oregon experience, I knew that the "behavioral objectives" fad in New Zealand would eventually pass. The only question was whether the CTC could survive long enough to see the end of it.

Fortunately, I was not the only program leader who was experiencing difficulty in dealing with the ACCESS system. Within a few months, training program managers and coordinators in Hamilton formed a Training Providers Alliance that developed into a national movement. I attended meetings and talked to other program leaders. It was a great relief to know that I was not alone and that the alliance might be able to lobby for changes in ACCESS policies.

Part of the ACCESS philosophy was to promote competition among training providers. This philosophy was closely linked to the "New Right" political movement that gripped the government at that time. Competition among training providers was disastrous in a small community like Huntly. Small training providers sprouted up around the community, each competing with the others for funding. A cooperative effort on behalf of the entire community would have been much more effective. Fortunately, ACCESS has since changed its policy. Cooperative efforts among training providers have been encouraged in more recent years. In the meantime, however, some of the small training providers have closed, and many trainees suffered the consequences of the underfunded training that resulted from the inefficiencies inherent in the competitive system.

Other problems arose because of the resource-starved conditions under which we were working. The Handyperson course started out in an unused garage on the outskirts of the marae. It was soon apparent that the garage was too small for adequate instruction for the six trainees in the course. Another building was identified as a possible site, but renovation would be required. Over a period of several months, the Handyperson instructor and his trainees renovated the building as part of their instructional program, and eventually the program had a new and better facility.

Another crisis occurred in conjunction with this project. ACCESS insti-tuted a policy whereby staff in Huntly regularly visited each training provider to inspect facilities and procedures. A new ACCESS staff member on his first visit to the program noted that trainees in the Handyperson course were not wearing appropriate safety boots. He was right. Some were wearing thongs, and one or two might have been barefoot, a dangerous situation in a con-struction site. He threatened to close the program down if the situation were not remedied immediately. Each trainee would have to be wearing safety boots within two days.

I sent the trainer and trainees to the nearest outlet selling safety boots. The trainees were all properly outfitted, and the bill was $2,000, a seemingly mas-sive sum from our budget at the time. Everyone wore the boots for the in-spection two days later—and then the boots disappeared, never to be seen again. There was no obvious way to force trainees to wear the boots we had purchased for them. I do not know what the trainees did with the boots. I can only guess that most sold them. Eventually, we negotiated a compromise with ACCESS so that trainees wore shoes or boots of their own, although the foot-gear probably did not meet the preferred standard for safety. The CTC sur-vived another apparent crisis.

Other health and safety problems had to be addressed. The roof in the com-puter room leaked, and we needed special curtains so that reflections off the video display monitors did not damage trainees' eyes. Another requirement was the purchase of chairs designed with appropriate safety features.

We had no source of running water within the CTC facilities. Water for tea, coffee, and washing dishes had to be carried. The area used for tea breaks was covered by a roof but had no walls or other shelter from the winter's constant rain. We installed canvas siding for winter protection.

Other problems arose from the marae setting. Traditionally, when a funeral was held at the marae, out of respect for the family of the deceased, all work on the marae halted for the three-day remembrance. A funeral was held at Waahi every week or two, but we could not shut down the training program for each one. A compromise was worked out so that trainees and staff attended each funeral to pay respects to the family but returned to training after fulfill-ing their obligation. Trainees and staff were instructed to be as quiet as possi-ble through the remainder of the funeral—a hard task for the young people.

Once, trainees were throwing a football around during a midday break. Un-fortunately, their game took place on the marae in front of the meetinghouse. A local resident made a great fuss until I asked the trainees to move the game to the field on the side of the marae. Children who lived in the houses sur-rounding the marae often played ball and other games on the marae, but when the trainees did the same thing, it became a major issue.

Sports equipment and tools for the Handyperson course disappeared almost as quickly as we could purchase them. The computer room was broken into. Disks and accessories disappeared. My flat was broken into three times, once when I was at home. Losses were not great in financial terms—I did not own much worth stealing—but some items of intense sentimental value disappeared. We tried several different systems of security but never completely solved the problem.

Every few months, one of the trainees would be in trouble with the police. On three occasions, trainees asked me to appear in court on their behalf—which I willingly did. I could see no way that a prison term would enrich the lives of any of them.

There were occasional problems with staff and trainees drinking beer and smoking marijuana during working hours, in and around the marae. One staff member repeatedly charged small personal items to the CTC accounts at the local service station. Two staff members were fired, and these conditions seemed to improve.

Conflicts between the CTC trustees and the new management committee continued. I attended weekly meetings with the committee for a year—but then I simply could not stand it any more and another staff member, who was also a member of the CTC trustees, attended in my place. The management committee continued to insist that the assets of the CTC actually belonged to it. There were continuing threats that their staff would come to collect those assets. Staff members did appear at one point with that intention. There was a confrontation between the trustees of the CTC and the management committee staff. It was clear, however, that some of the assets—such as the carpeting—could not easily be removed, and other assets—such as lounge chairs—had already worn out and were of little monetary value to either the CTC or the management committee. Eventually, the CTC trustees agreed to release a photocopier and one computer to the management committee, and the issue finally died a quiet death.

I inadvertently became a subject in a study for a second time while I was working at the CTC. There were two small flats on the marae for visiting researchers. In 1988 when I became coordinator of the CTC, I lived in one of the flats. A European graduate student who was working on his doctoral thesis occupied the second flat. When I read his thesis, there I was. I had not been identified by name, but he had described me in detail. One account in the thesis was based on a private conversation in my flat that the researcher overheard accidentally. The researcher's comments about me were actually quite flattering, but I was offended that he felt he could use any aspect of his neighborly relationship with me without my permission if it suited his purposes. Others who were described or photographed in the thesis had similar complaints.

Later, he published journal articles that are highly critical of some of the people who had given him the most assistance and support during his stay at the marae.

Although there were a great many problems, there were successful moments, too. There were occasional angry outbursts between program participants, but relationships among the trustees, staff, and trainees were generally mutually supportive. Participants felt good about the program, their work, and each other. Some trainees went into long-term jobs when they completed their courses. Staff members were completing recognized courses to obtain Certificates in Adult Teaching. The group that had established the company introduced local people to the use of computers through evening classes using the CTC facilities. The marae benefited from rental income and from the voluntary contributions that trainees and staff made to its upkeep. And the CTC's relationship with ACCESS management began to stabilize.

For me personally, one high point of the experience occurred on 4 July 1989. The staff and trainees of the program organized a surprise party in the dining hall of the marae. A *hangi* (the traditional Maori feast cooked in an underground oven) had been prepared along with all the trimmings. The hall was decorated with an American flag and red, white, and blue streamers. Speeches were made, and I was given a huge bouquet of flowers in the same colors. The Maori queen and her husband attended. It was a marvelous tribute, one I will never forget.

The local man who had been manager when I arrived in January 1988 wanted to move on to other challenges. In early 1989, we selected a trainee in his thirties to begin an individual training program for him to work his way into the manager's position under my supervision. Over the next year, he learned the procedures for handling day-to-day operations: advertising for trainees, completing enrollment forms and Social Welfare Department forms with those people who responded to the ads, filling out the weekly attendance forms and other routine ACCESS requirements, and managing the computer accounting system.

Systems had been set in place such that virtually no cash was handled at the CTC. ACCESS made direct deposits to the CTC account on a regular schedule. Payroll was issued through a system of automatic transfers to employees' bank accounts. Bills were paid by checks that required my signature. The only cash transactions were the trainees' purchases in the Handyperson course. Trainees in that course were allowed to take home items they had made such as bookshelves, picnic tables, or wooden planters, but they had to pay the cost of the materials involved. The manager collected the cash payments and deposited them into the CTC account.

My two-year contract with the CTC was due to expire at the end of 1989. Robert Mahuta, director of the Centre for Maaori Studies and Research at the

University of Waikato, invited me to apply for the position of research fellow at the center. After completing the usual application and interviews, I was employed to begin early in February 1990.

Toward the end of 1989, I realized that I had become lax in checking to see that the new manager had been banking receipts from the furniture income. When I did check, I realized that about $2,000 that should have been deposited through the year had not been deposited. No cash was on hand in the office, and the manager said that no cash had been received. I was convinced that either the manager or one of the office staff had taken the money, but I had no hard evidence to support my conviction. I wrote a report outlining the problem and took the matter to the CTC trustees, but they were not inclined to take the matter seriously. By that time, I was leaving the CTC to begin working at the University of Waikato and left the matter in the hands of the trustees.

In June 1990, I was called to an emergency meeting of the trustees. They had discovered that the new manager had submitted forms to ACCESS to change the bank account number for deposits of income from ACCESS. He had substituted his personal account number for the CTC account number. Payments from ACCESS had been going into his personal account. He was present at the meeting with the trustees and a local police officer. The trustees had arranged with the bank to have the manager's bank account "frozen" so that no further withdrawals could be made. About $5,000 of the CTC funding had already been withdrawn. When confronted with the situation, the new manager said it was all a mistake. He promised to clarify the situation and would meet again with the trustees on the following evening. The trustees relieved him of the keys to the facility and to the vehicles before he left that evening. None of us ever saw him again. Fortunately, the government department that funded the program conceded that it had not followed appropriate procedures for changing the bank account numbers and reimbursed the CTC for the missing money.

For several years, I continued to attend meetings with trustees when I was invited to do so. On the whole, however, the Community Training Centre developed under the guidance of the local trustees and staff and was running training courses when the community entered the new millennium. Unfortunately, the program closed in December 2000 after fourteen years of operation.

DISCUSSION

My role in the establishment of the CTC was one of the most difficult that I have ever undertaken, but the fourteen years of operation of this organization gave me one of my greatest satisfactions. More than any other, this experience impressed on me the importance of thoughtful, detailed planning for programs to succeed. The lessons I learned about the essential components of good programs will last a lifetime.

It is hard to imagine how the circumstances surrounding the initiation of the program could have been more disadvantageous. Government policies fluctuated radically and were often impossible to comprehend. Government policies forced changes in the goals for the program in spite of the preferences of local participants. Policies were rigid and inflexible. There was ongoing local argument about control of the program. After the first year's operation, program plans were in shambles. Funding was minimal and was approved only for short periods of time. The physical facilities were barely adequate. The original coordinators began with half-time positions and short-term commitments. Staff had appropriate training for the skills they were to teach, but they had no training in how to teach. Most of the trainees arrived at the program with histories of low academic achievement. As the program coordinator, I was an American who had little background in New Zealand banking and political systems.

Given the limitations that were faced by participants in the beginning, it is difficult to explain the program's survival and success for as long as fourteen years. I believe there were three critical factors: (1) the determination of community members, staff, and trainees to keep the program going; (2) effective collaboration between an outside professional and the local community; and (3) changes in government policy that made it possible for the program to survive for fourteen years. After I left in December 1989, the trustees, managers, and staff from the local community had to adapt over and over again to changing social circumstances and government policies (including name changes and repeated restructuring in various agencies related to the program). One of their adaptations included the merger of the CTC with the company that had originally been an offshoot of the CTC. They were willing and able to make those adaptations so that they could keep alive a program that provided training and personal development opportunities for disadvantaged Maori youth as well as employment in the community.

Government policies in the late 1980s were consistent in their emphasis on commercial principles of competition as the means for producing successful organizations. These principles almost destroyed the CTC in its early years. By the early 1990s, however, many other small training providers had been forced to close, and government agencies were encouraging training providers to work together in the best interests of trainees. The CTC was able to establish a more reasonable working relationship with the agencies under the new conditions, and funding continued through the 1990s.

While I was working at the CTC, I had no intention of writing about the program for publication, but I was very much in the habit of collecting data.

I kept daily journals of events and my reactions to them. I also filed every scrap of paper that arrived in my hands. I read government publications and journal articles that were relevant. Years after I left my employment at the CTC, I wrote an article for publication (Harrison 1994) analyzing and interpreting the government policies that claimed to provide opportunities for Maori youth while simultaneously ensuring that the opportunities were rigidly limited. I circulated a draft of the article to certain CTC trustees and staff and submitted it with their approval.

My relationship to the CTC trustees was, I believe, totally collaborative. Members of the board joined me in meetings with government agencies and with local organizations. I met regularly with the trustees and discussed every aspect of program operations with them. I did not always agree with the decisions of the trustees, but, after I put forward my arguments, I left the decisions with them. I had little, if any, authority to make decisions about the program on my own. I made every effort to see that staff members had access to training that would eventually give them the skills to run the program without outside assistance.

LESSONS LEARNED

The Individual Fieldworker

Be Flexible but Recognize That Everyone Has Limits.

Once again, I learned as much about my limitations as I did about my ability to adapt. During my previous stay at the marae, I had learned to love life in the community, but during the two years of my employment at the CTC I suffered from persistent anxiety and frustration with respect to the program. I had a very righteous sense of what government policies should be with respect to the program, and I often argued with staff of the agencies concerned. Looking back, I realize that those staff members had no more control over policies than I did. I think my arguments just drained energy that could have been used more productively in other ways. I would have been less anxious and frustrated if I had adapted more readily to the reality of the policy framework that defined the limits of the program.

I was also uncomfortable with the ongoing arguments over control of the program. I have since come to realize that conflict is a normal part of the life of every community. If I had accepted the arguments as a normal part of life, I would have experienced less personal stress, and the energy I devoted to worrying about the conflict might have been better utilized elsewhere.

Be Willing to Collaborate by Sharing Authority, Responsibility, and Credit for Success.

One of my personal successes in this situation was in working collaboratively with the trustees, staff, and trainees from the local community. And I must acknowledge their success in collaborating with me. It was not always easy for any of us, but this collaboration was a critical factor in the survival of the program. If a professional person from outside the community had tried to manage the program dictatorially—without strong collaboration—the program would have failed in its early stages because trustees, staff, and trainees would have withheld their cooperation. They would probably have forced a dictatorial manager out of the program. Our collaborative efforts kept the program going long enough for local people to gain the training they needed so that they could run the program in their own fashion after I left.

Give Thoughtful Attention to the Ethical Implications of Your Actions.

I learned a great deal about ethics from the two researchers who used me as a research "subject" without my permission. It made me feel powerless to be used in this way, and I believe that this has made me more sensitive to the rights of others in research settings. I also learned that there are researchers who give little consideration to ethical issues involved in research with human subjects. Apparently, both of the researchers believed that, once they had been given permission to study a situation, they had permission to use and report anything and everything they observed within that situation. I suspect that the universities that were responsible for the supervision of these students were partially at fault because they had not provided adequate instruction regarding research ethics before the students were allowed to go into the field.

Apply the Concept of Culture in Everyday Working Relationships.

In a situation with an outside professional in an indigenous community, one might expect that problems would arise from a lack of understanding of the indigenous culture. In the situation of the CTC, though, the important problems arose because I did not give sufficient attention to understanding the culture of the bureaucracies we were dealing with. At the time, I tended to blame the individual staff members who were the messengers for government policy. I now believe that all of us would have been better off if I had been able to identify and work within the cultural framework of the institutions that employed those staff members. I might have secretly believed that I was an expert on culture, but I missed this most important point.

Designing Collaborative Programs

Fieldworkers and Representatives of the Community Should Collaborate to Develop a Rationale, Philosophy, or Reason for the Establishment of the Particular Program.

The goals of the CTC changed three times in the first few months of its existence. The program was originally established to train Maori to work in the energy developments planned by the government in 1985. The government changed its plans, and the program coordinators defined the second set of goals in consultation with some members of the local community. These goals focused on personal development and skills training for Maori youth. Government policy changed again, and government agencies dictated that the program teach vocational skills and only vocational skills. The trustees and staff of the CTC agreed to the government's focus on vocational skills, but they also clung to their own goals focusing on the personal development of the trainees. Many of the problems that the program experienced were the result of the conflicts inherent in a situation in which the government insisted on its own agenda and the local community insisted on a different one. As the years passed, the agencies and the community each made some effort to accommodate the other. Hundreds of unemployed Maori, most of them quite young, completed training courses.

Look for Sources of Adequate and Dependable Funding.

I have included in this account descriptions of the problems encountered because funding was uncertain and barely adequate. Countless hours were invested in writing and rewriting specific objectives and in meetings with agency staff. While staff members were involved in the process of preparing paperwork that would lead to continued funding or in meetings to discuss funding issues, they were not available to instruct trainees, develop programs, or attend to their own staff development. The funding process was among the most wasteful I have ever encountered. But we had no choice; without the funding from the government, there would have been no program at all.

Confirm That There Is Adequate Support in the Local Community.

If there is any one single factor that can explain the continuing survival of this program, it is the level of support the program received in the local community.

Formulate a Program Plan Including Statements of Roles and
Responsibilities, Support Systems for Participants, and Evaluation
Procedures.

My experience in the CTC taught me the importance of a program plan that includes processes for policy making, role definitions and relationships, activities, finances, support systems, accountability and assessment, responsibilities for reporting, and other dimensions of program operation. When I started work at the CTC in January 1988, the program was a year into its operations, but none of these components of the program had been well defined. The program plan had yet to be developed. I was not aware of any professional literature that would have helped us establish a program plan, and it did not occur to me to look for any. The government agency was pressuring us to develop behavioral objectives, but agency staff seemed unconcerned about any other aspect of program development. No one in the agency seemed aware that a program consists of more than a collection of objectives.

We developed a coherent program over the next two years, working on various aspects as the need arose. The CTC trustees came into existence to oversee policies for the program, but this was due largely to the local conflict over control. Job descriptions for the coordinator and all other staff were written to reduce chaos; staff needed to know what was expected of them. I set up a financial system based on what I knew from other situations and in consultation with a local accountant (the funding agency required annual audits). One of the program's original coordinators was influential in the establishment of support systems as part of the staff development course that he and his wife introduced. We did not even think about some program components, such as approval processes for professional presentations or papers that might be developed in subsequent years.

One of the difficulties in going about program development in this way is that it seemed for a while as though I was responsible for doing everything from keeping the cashbook to emptying the rubbish bins. Among other things, program coordinator burnout was inevitable, but there were other problems, too. In a collaborative program, everyone in the program needs to share the responsibility as well as the rewards. It took all of the two years of my involvement for the program to develop to the point at which all the participants knew what their roles were and to understand how all of the roles fit together as a whole. By the end of my term as coordinator, I thought I knew how a program should be planned even if I had never been through the process of planning one as complex as this one was. However, with each succeeding program in which I was involved after leaving the CTC, I found that there was always more to learn about planning.

Identify or Recruit Committed Leadership in the Program and, Preferably, in the Funding Agency.

I am not sure how it came about that there were two half-time coordinators in the original coordinator's position when the program opened in 1986. That situation proved to be very difficult for the two people sharing the position and for the development of the program. Each of the coordinators had other commitments at the same time, so neither was fully committed to the CTC. Both of them saw their commitments in the setting as short term. They were fine people, but short-term job sharing is not the best structure for the initial stages of program development. Successful initiation of a new program demands a high level of commitment from those in leadership positions.

The government agencies responsible for the administration of Maori vocational training—along with many other government departments in New Zealand—were restructured countless times in the closing years of the twentieth century because of shifts in the political philosophies driving one government or another. Each restructuring brought about changes in titles and changes in staff in the agencies. These changes meant that there was little consistency in the delivery of policies by the agencies, so it was difficult for program staff at the marae and in other local programs to adapt.

Identify or Recruit Appropriately Qualified Staff.

I learned important lessons at the CTC about qualifications and training for staff in educational programs. I had previously studied school programs in which indigenous people with little training or experience were apprenticed to qualified teachers. Many eventually became excellent teachers through this process. I had not realized, though, that a good balance is needed between qualified teachers and apprentices. In the initial stages of the CTC, we had too many staff members without appropriate qualifications in teaching and management. This was especially true because of the agency's emphasis on written behavioral objectives. There was no way that I could write objectives for skills such as those required for the Handyperson course, for example. Access to the Certificate in Adult Teaching program at the two-year institution in Hamilton was essential to the continuance of the CTC. Without the training in adult teaching, the CTC would not have survived for as long as it did. It was important to the local community to have staff members with backgrounds in the history and culture of the community and who had known many of the trainees since childhood. However, the program was aimed at preparing young people for work in a modern economy, and its aims could not be carried out without staff with formal qualifications. This program provides an excellent example of the way that staff training can be incorporated into program development.

Find a Workable Physical Setting.

I have described the difficulties that arose because of the minimal facilities and because the CTC was located at the marae. As the reader may recall, the trainees had to complete the construction of the building before the program could begin. The roof leaked when it rained, which was often. Drinking water had to be carried in because there was no running water. Because we were at the marae, we had to attend to marae protocol, so we lost training time; furthermore, the mores of the marae were not always clear to us.

Still, there were advantages to the marae location. Most trainees had little sense of the traditional history and culture of the marae. The program's setting at the marae provided an opportunity for them to reestablish connections with their historical culture and language. There was a very strong feeling among Maori, locally and nationally, that their young people would benefit from strengthening these connections. There were many comments from trainees to support that feeling. About a dozen years after the program was established, however, the managers decided to move the program into better facilities on the other side of town.

It is important to note that, although there were difficulties because of flaws in the facilities, these difficulties did not destroy the program. During my time at the CTC, there seemed to be agreement that we would rather not have these difficulties, but we were not going to be overcome by them. The quality of the building and other facilities was not the most important component in the program. In fact, the quality of the physical facilities was well down the list of things to be concerned about.

Attend to the Broader Political and Social Context That Makes It Possible for a Program to Survive.

This case provides a good example of the impact of the political context on program survival. The program was initiated in response to political pressure from the Maori leadership in Huntly because the government was promising employment for Maori in new power stations in the region. Maori needed training so that they could find employment in the promised energy developments. Shortly after the program was initiated, government policy changed. The program was forced to change its goals so that the government would continue to provide funding. Government-imposed procedures seemed to make little sense to many of the individuals who were participating in the program, but people from the local community adapted the program so that they could meet some of their own goals while still accommodating the requirements of the government agency.

During the last decade of the twentieth century, there were several changes of government in New Zealand, but the national system of community-based training programs survived in spite of many problems. Each government in turn realized that it was politically expedient to continue to fund the programs because unemployment and related social problems would increase if the programs were discontinued. It is reasonable to expect the system to continue so long as the funding does.

The continued operation of the CTC in the 1990s is an excellent example of the importance of a favorable political and social context to program survival. However, the managers could not maintain a viable program in the political and social circumstances of the twenty-first century, and the program closed in December 2000.

Chapter Ten

Maori Community Projects, 1990–96

The Centre for Maaori Studies and Research (CMSR) was established at the University of Waikato in 1972. CMSR's primary goal was to "respond to requests from Maaori groups and agencies for research. Its work is best described as research and development in the context of community action: *there should be no development without research and no research without development*" (Centre for Maaori Studies and Research 1994). I began my work as a research fellow at CMSR at the beginning of February 1990. The national holiday of New Zealand is 6 February, the anniversary of the signing of the treaty between the British and Maori chiefs in 1840. It is called Waitangi Day after the name of the site where the treaty was signed. That year, 1990, was the 150th anniversary of the signing of the treaty, and New Zealand was holding a three-day celebration at the Treaty Grounds on the shores of the Bay of Islands. Staff of CMSR and the Tainui Trust Board traveled by car and van to a motel in Russell, a short ferry ride across the bay from the Treaty Grounds.

It was a marvelously inspiring experience. Hundreds of people from tribes around the country attended, bringing their ceremonial canoes and rowers with them as well as their cultural performers. The entire fleet of the Royal New Zealand Navy (consisting of about five ships) was in attendance, as were dozens of private sailing craft. Queen Elizabeth II and Prince Philip were ferried to shore from one of the Navy ships. Maori protestors, a regular feature of Waitangi Day celebrations for the two previous decades, were there too, but protests were restrained in comparison with some in earlier years. The celebrations reflected the mood of great optimism in Maori/Pakeha relations that was prevalent at the time.

The weather was sunny and warm throughout the weekend. I enjoyed it all immensely and concluded the weekend with severe sunburn on my face as the result of that enjoyment. I had paid too much attention to the festivities and not enough to the intensity of the sun.

After that introduction to my new position, I energetically entered into a number of new projects. I suggested a survey of the management committees of the Tainui Trust Board to document changes since publication of *The Tainui Report* in 1983. I wrote proposals for a Maori Student Academic Advisory Centre and an oral history research project. Robert Mahuta, director of CMSR, asked me to begin work on a Tainui tribal health plan. I had no training in any area of health, but I agreed to do what I could. The eventual success of the health plan led to the development of a tribal education strategy.

All of these projects were collaborative. Some were completed within a few months, but there were others that I worked on for several years. I was working on several projects simultaneously. Doing so required that I balance the priorities of the different projects to be sure that the essential tasks in each project were taken care of. I was usually able to do this successfully, but there were times when I simply had too much to do. I was intensely involved in meeting the challenges of these projects for the next several years.

A brief description of each of these projects follows. Because the chapter describes several short projects, I have selected particular illustrative points for discussion rather than analyzing each project according to all the principles relating to fieldworkers and program design.

MANAGEMENT COMMITTEE SURVEY

The first project that I undertook at CMSR was a short one that went well. In 1983, Egan and Mahuta had published *The Tainui Report*, a survey of the needs of the tribe. This report concludes with the recommendation that management committees be established for each local area within the Waikato region under the auspices of the Tainui Trust Board. Each committee was given the responsibility by the board for developing programs that would address needs in education, health, employment, and so forth.

I suggested that we follow the plan and procedures used in the original survey, conducting group interviews with people from each of the local areas. One member of the Tainui Trust Board, Taitimu Maipi, agreed to go with me to visit each of the nine management committees. Committees were made up of volunteers from the local area, but some of the committees had been able to acquire funding to pay staff by submitting applications to government programs. The trust board member had participated in the team that conducted the needs survey in the early 1980s. He arranged the meetings with the management committees. We developed an interview schedule and interviewed committee members and staff about the structure of each committee and about the programs under way. I summarized the responses to the interviews. Reports were prepared and presented to the trust board.

One might wish that all research projects could be so cleanly and swiftly completed. Not surprisingly, this project reinforces the point that simply designed, straightforward projects are easier to accomplish than more complicated projects. A small project like this one did not need much adaptation on my part or an elaborate program plan. Collaboration was the key to success in this case. I could have accomplished nothing on my own because the management committees would not have agreed to meet with me alone. Partnership with the trust board member, a person well known in the local community, was essential.

TAINUI HEALTH PLAN

In the early 1980s, a visiting medical anthropologist, Corrine Shear-Wood, had helped to establish a community health center at Waahi Marae. The government provided funding to employ and train two Maori women from the local marae to provide "preventative health" services. They were trained to do such things as blood pressure and diabetes screenings and to encourage healthy practices of fitness and diet for the local community. Space for the health center was located at the marae, in a building adjacent to the dining hall.

In the next few years, other marae in the region also established marae-based health centers, but different priorities were established at different centers. Some of the centers incorporated Maori traditional health practices into their programs.

By 1990, a Tainui Health Task Force had been established under the auspices of the Tainui Trust Board. The task force was composed of representatives from the local management committees of the board. These representatives were usually people who were involved in the marae-based health initiatives. A member of the Tainui Trust Board chaired the task force. He was the same board member who worked with me on the survey of management committees. The task force had begun to discuss possibilities for a tribal health plan.

Everyone on the task force wanted to develop a tribal health plan to improve the health of the tribe, but none of us had any idea what the next steps should be. At that point, a small miracle occurred. Paul Florin arrived at CMSR on a sabbatical leave from the University of Rhode Island. Paul is a specialist in community-based health initiatives.

The program is described in the Tainui Health Plan:

> The Tainui Health Plan was a joint project between the Tainui Health Task Force (a subcommittee of the Tainui Maaori Trust Board) and the staff of the Centre for Maaori Studies and Research, University of Waikato. Paul Florin, a Visiting Professor from the University of Rhode Island, was the principal writer of the plan, but the plan itself was developed in a series of hui with the Health Task Force.
>
> At the first hui of all participants, the Task Force requested that a survey of all Management Committee health delegates be conducted to describe the present health activities within each region, the aspirations for future programmes, and the resources needed to achieve future plans.
>
> The survey was completed during March and April, 1990, and a first draft of the plan was prepared based upon the findings of the survey. A series of discussions was held between the Task Force, the Trust Board and CMSR staff to refine the initial draft and to reach a consensus on the plan. . . .
>
> In the course of the survey, it was found that several Management Committees had already prepared proposals for plans for their particular regions. (Tainui Maaori Trust Board 1990: ii–iii)[1]

Taitimu Maipi was chairperson of the task force. He, Paul Florin, and I visited each of the Tainui health committees in the region. We discussed the priorities that each committee had for health development in that local community and took notes on the discussion. Paul then drafted a plan for the tribe that included two health resource centers, one in South Auckland and one in the Waikato region, that would coordinate health developments throughout the tribal region.

There was one unpleasant experience in a meeting with one health committee. An older Maori woman verbally attacked Paul and me for interfering in Maori affairs. Although I understood the historical background that led to the woman's comments and although I had heard the same sort of abrasive accusation in the past, I was upset on this occasion. Paul and I had been invited by members of the local tribe to assist in the development of the health plan, and we had been invited to the particular meeting. More importantly, Paul was volunteering many hours of his time to the development of this plan—he was not getting paid for his work—and I thought his contribution should have been acknowledged. I expressed my annoyance rather loudly. I do not remember exactly how the issue was resolved, but somehow the woman's outburst and mine were both forgotten. Work on the health plan went forward.

Paul's leave ended, and he returned to the United States. Other CMSR staff members and I edited Paul's draft and prepared the report for publication. This plan was presented to the Waikato Area Health Board in October 1990, and a second small miracle occurred. There was strong support from the Area Health Board for Maori health initiatives, and the Area Health Board granted approximately \$100,000 a year for salaries and operating expenses and agreed to build a Tainui Resource Center adjacent to Turangawaewae Marae, the largest marae in the region.

At this point, other fortuitous events occurred. First, a Tainui man with a degree in management studies who had been in a senior management position with the Area Health Board decided to leave the Area Health Board to work for the tribal health plan. The tribe would have one of their own who was professionally trained to lead the health plan. As soon as this man took on the leadership role, I moved out of the health field and back into projects for which I had greater expertise. Tainui people managed the health program from then on.

This collaborative research project was as successful as anyone could ever hope. A tribal health plan was developed and published. Initial funding was granted, and local people took charge of the program. Extensions of that initial program have continued to operate into the twenty-first century.

A number of factors contributed to success. One factor was good luck in having qualified people available at the right time. A professional person with the right background arrived for a visit just when the project was getting under way, and a qualified Maori was available to take over after initial funding was granted.

Other factors contributing to the success of this project include the prior development of an infrastructure for a tribal health plan through marae health initiatives and the management committees of the trust board. There was virtually no conflict within the community about health developments at the time, although conflicts arose at later stages. Also, the research was not particularly physically or emotionally demanding for those who were working on the plan. There were only minor individual stresses to cope with.

Another advantage was the political context. If the health plan had been developed either a few years earlier or a few years later, it would have been impossible to gain the initial funding that started the program off. In 1990, government policies meshed with Maori community goals regarding health, but the 1990 election brought in a new government with new policies for the health system.

I should point out that there was no cohesive overall plan for conducting this project. We worked our way through one step at a time. In this case, it worked. We were blessed. There may be other situations in which good fortune will lead to success, but I cannot recommend that program developers rely on good fortune as a general rule.

THE MAORI STUDENT ACADEMIC ADVISORY CENTRE

Early in 1990, an announcement was circulated at the University of Waikato that proposals for new projects promoting social equity were being accepted. The proposal I prepared was based on the model of the Rural Student Services program at the University of Alaska Fairbanks, where I had worked in the early 1980s. Rural Student Services provided a wide range of counseling and advice primarily to Alaska Native students on the Fairbanks campus. The proposal that I wrote presented a plan for establishing the same range of services for Maori students at the University of Waikato.

However, when funding was granted for the Maori Student Academic Advisory Centre (MSAAC) at the beginning of the 1991 academic year, it was clear that we would have to narrow the focus of the new project because the funding would not cover the range of services proposed. The director of CMSR decided that the most important priority was to improve the academic performance of Maori students. That became the focus of the program.

We planned to employ a full-time coordinator to organize a program of tutoring to be provided by advanced undergraduate and graduate students, all Maori, each working six hours a week. The coordinator would work under my supervision. The part-time tutors were to be called academic advisers. The aim would be to improve Maori student retention rates, especially for first-year students, the students with the highest dropout rates.

As often happens with new programs, there were people who thought that they should have a role in managing this program, so I organized an advisory group of Maori staff from different departments on campus. Our first task was to employ the coordinator. The position was advertised, the advisory group interviewed candidates, and the group recommended one person for appointment.

Shortly after the selection was announced, the sole male candidate for the position (who was not the candidate selected) filed a complaint with the Personnel Department of the university. All of the members of the panel who conducted the interviews had been female, and the male candidate believed that he had been discriminated against on the basis of gender. I wrote a response to the complaint pointing out that appropriate procedures had been followed. I had learned from my experience in hiring staff for the project in Manokotak. I had formulated three levels of questions, and all candidates were asked exactly the same questions. Candidates' responses had been recorded and compared by the interviewing panel. No gender bias was evident in the process. The issue quietly passed into history.

More problems were to follow, however. Funding for the new program did not become available until after the academic year had begun. By the time we selected and trained advanced Maori students as part-time tutors, set up systems and procedures, and advertised the program on campus so that students would know that services were available, it was nearly midyear.

We were, of course, expected to spend all of the first year's funding in the first academic year, and we were expected to show measurable outcomes at the end of the year if additional funding was to be granted. By the end of the first year, we issued a report showing the number of students who had received services. This number would have been much greater if we had been notified earlier that the program had been approved, so that the program could have started at the beginning of the academic year rather than halfway through it.

Another problem was finding suitable space for the project. The only rooms available were two windowless converted storerooms in the basement. The staff of MSAAC made the best of this bad situation for many months until rooms became available above ground.

The funding agency did not intend to provide funding indefinitely. The agency intended to provide start-up funds for programs that the university would eventually fund if the initial programs were successful. For the second year, a much smaller amount would be available. Therefore, one of the major tasks of the program coordinator in the first year was to seek supplemental funding to continue the program in the second and succeeding years. The coordinator began visiting the deans of the seven schools of study within the university to beg for money. Some schools were willing to allocate small amounts to the program. In order to continue the program in the second year, CMSR made $15,000 available. Later in the year, the national Maori development agency provided that amount so that the original $15,000 could be repaid to CMSR. The funding from the agency was granted only once and would not be available a second time.

The coordinator continued her visits to the deans during the second year. At the same time, the number of Maori students being served climbed dramatically, so the need for the MSAAC services became clearly evident. All the schools of study contributed to the funding for the third year.

Services were expanded in the second year when the university's counseling office agreed that the Maori counselor would spend one day a week meeting with students on the premises of MSAAC. Thus, the MSAAC academic advisers could easily refer students to the Maori counselor when such referrals seemed appropriate. The academic advisers also volunteered time to participate in a program recruiting Maori secondary school students for the university.

The original coordinator left at the end of the second year. We could no longer afford a full-time coordinator. A graduate student was employed to run the program on a part-time basis. Even as the available funding decreased, demands on MSAAC increased. The university asked students when they enrolled each year to indicate their ethnic backgrounds, but very little had been done to accumulate statistical information about Maori students. MSAAC took on the task and began producing annual reports of statistics on Maori students. Many divisions and departments within the university used these reports for program planning.

As the years have gone on, the numbers of students utilizing the services of MSAAC have increased, and academic staff around the university have been able to see the progress that students have made as the result of the services offered. The university has allocated ongoing funding for the operation of MSAAC, but the range of services has been limited by the funding available. Annual reports of statistics on Maori students have been produced for all divisions and departments of the university. The coordinator of MSAAC now reports to the dean of the School of Maori and Pacific Development within the university.

This project was another success. Although the funding has never been available to offer the range of services that I originally envisioned, the number of students requesting and receiving individual tutoring has increased each year, and so has the range of services available. The work that the original coordinator did in bringing issues of Maori student retention and achievement to the notice of deans in the early 1990s was important because several schools within the university then developed their own Maori liaison and support programs.

The major problem in the establishment of this program was to find adequate and stable funding. The instability of funding in the early years was a major problem, for resources had to be used to secure funding rather than for program development. Given the difficulties in the early years of operation, it is not surprising that the original coordinator left after two years.

Collaboration in this project was not particularly effective. I initiated the advisory committee of Maori staff more or less out of habit, without thinking much about what the committee's role would be. I knew that, in order to gain long-term funding, we needed support from across the university, and we were more likely to get that support if Maori staff had opportunities to express their opinions. At the same time, authority for the project was lodged with the director of CMSR, and there was no way to legitimately distribute that authority to a committee. Our willingness to communicate with Maori staff in many departments through the advisory committee contributed to the support we needed. I was dismayed when the committee wanted to appoint a candidate for the coordinator's position who was not the candidate I would have chosen, but I was glad that the committee was there to help me sort out the complaint of the male candidate who did not get the job. The advisory committee met for about a year after the project started, but it eventually disbanded. When the staff had been selected and the program set in place, there was little reason for Maori staff to spend time in advisory meetings.

ORAL HISTORIES PROJECT

In 1990, another academic staff member of the university approached me and asked me to write a proposal for funding for a project to collect and publish life histories of Maori elders. The staff member's idea was to train a group of community people to conduct interviews with the elders in Maori so that the life histories could be published in Maori. I had enjoyed reading published life histories of women from other indigenous groups, and I supported the notion of community-based research and publication in Maori. I thought the staff member's idea was a great one. She was a fluent Maori speaker with high academic standing, so I assumed that she had the necessary knowledge and commitment to lead the program. I set about preparing plans and proposals to various agencies.

Before these proposals were submitted, I made a critical error, an error for which I would pay a very high price. Originally, I put the name of the other staff member on the proposals as the principal investigator. I was invited to add my name so that we would be co–principal investigators. Driven by vanity, I added my name. I did not take into consideration that, because I was not a speaker of Maori, it would be next to impossible to carry through the project alone if my co–principal investigator were to withdraw.

Eventually, we were granted sufficient funding to begin the project. However, the grant did not cover all of our objectives. We would have to work for one year conducting and recording interviews, but we would have to submit a new proposal to cover costs for transcription, translation, and publication of the interviews during the second year of the project.

My co–principal investigator gathered a team together, and the project got under way. It was launched with a luncheon, and a noted photographer took photos of each of the elders to be interviewed. The luncheon was well attended by people from the community.

The other investigator and I began to meet with the people she had selected as the research team. We gave each of them a list of topics to discuss with the elders during the interviews. We discovered that no one knew much about videotaping, which was the method we had selected for documenting the interviews. We also discovered that the CMSR equipment was not in working condition, and we would have to rent equipment, an item I had not budgeted for. These problems were surmounted, and interviews began.

At each meeting of the research team we watched some of the tapes. Because I did not speak Maori, it was essential for the other investigator to review each of the tapes carefully to be sure that the interviewers were getting relevant information and to be sure that the quality of the tapes was such that they could be transcribed. Unfortunately, my co–principal investigator was busy with other projects. I was never quite certain that the reviews were taking place.

When transcription of the tapes started, we discovered that it took much longer to transcribe tapes recorded in Maori than tapes in English, even when our transcribers were fluent in Maori. It was going to cost much more for transcriptions than we had budgeted. One interviewer turned in time sheets for time she had not actually worked. I felt that it was necessary to confront the interviewer, and I did. Her work on the project ended abruptly, but there was no way to retrieve the funds that had been paid to her.

Unfortunately, at about this point the other co–principal investigator more or less abandoned the project because of some complicated political circumstances that had nothing to do with the project itself. Because I could not speak the language, I could do none of the interviewing, transcribing, translating, or reviewing of the videotapes myself. I could not assist the interviewers by observing during the interviews. I had no way of knowing what was on the tapes and could not judge the quality of the material we were working with. Were the interviewers actually obtaining life histories, or were they chatting about irrelevant topics? I had no way of knowing. I could not tell if the Maori transcriptions were grammatically correct or if the words were spelled correctly. I could not edit the transcriptions. The beautiful vision with which I had started the project had turned into a nightmare. Nevertheless, I had signed a contract with the funding agency and felt compelled to complete the project if it was humanly possible.

It took several years, but, because local people volunteered many hours to the project, the objectives were eventually met, and two of the life histories were published (Kukutai n.d.; Turner 1995, 1996). The adult daughter of one of the elders gave many voluntary hours to the project. Without her efforts and the efforts of other volunteers, the publications would never have been finished.

In many of the projects in which I had worked in the past, I could blame other people for flaws in the program design or for poor leadership. In this project, everything that could go wrong did go wrong, and I had to accept much of the blame. Although the co–principal investigator left me "holding the bag" so to speak, I made the mistake of accepting responsibility for a project that I could not carry out alone. There were also many things that I should have checked before submitting the original proposals, such as the state of the video equipment, the amount of time it would take to transcribe tapes in Maori, and the existing skills of the potential researchers from the community.

This project provides an example of the pitfalls inherent in collaboration. In collaborative projects there is no way to guarantee that all the participants will carry out the responsibilities agreed on, so there is always the danger that a project will suffer because some of the collaborators do not follow through. At the same time, collaboration was the project's strength. Without the collaboration of the volunteers who worked on the project, it would have failed entirely.

This project also illustrates the importance of committed leadership. The person who initiated the project later abandoned it, but the determination of several volunteers, along with my own, made it possible to complete it. This project is also an example of the importance of having appropriately qualified staff in the project. In spite of my education, training, and previous research experience, I was not appropriately qualified because of one critical condition: I did not speak the language. If I had it to do over again, I would complete the proposals on behalf of the staff member who requested them and would provide some training in interviewing techniques for the group, but I would leave it at that. Live and learn.

THE TAINUI EDUCATION STRATEGY

Because the Tainui health plan had worked so well, the Education Committee of the Tainui Trust Board decided to take the same approach—develop a plan for the tribe's education and present it to an agency or agencies with a request for financial support. The Education Committee was composed of about fifteen Tainui people who were employed in various agencies of the education system ranging from early childhood through university level and including people in special education, the Education Review Office, and the Ministry of Education. Most of the members of the committee had been professionally trained in particular areas of educational expertise, but some had no formal qualifications.

A hui was held at Waahi Marae in October 1990, and work began on a written strategy statement. A series of weekend meetings was held during 1991 in which the committee worked on goals and objectives for each level of the education system: early childhood, primary schools, secondary schools, polytechnics, universities, and special education. The draft included a proposal for the establishment of a Tainui resource center, similar to the Tainui health center, which would coordinate tribal education activities throughout the region. After each meeting I rewrote the draft plan, taking into consideration the discussions during the meeting. A new draft was presented to the committee at each meeting for discussion and review.

The plan was completed in mid-1991 (Tainui Maaori Trust Board 1991). A delegation from the Tainui Trust Board traveled to Wellington to present the plan to four ministers of government agencies: Maori Affairs, Education, Health, and Finance. Because members of the Tainui committee worked in every level of educational institution, they were aware that some objectives could be achieved through the normal funding channels of the Ministry of Education and other agencies but that funding for other objectives was not available in the same way. The Tainui delegation requested that a working party composed of government officials and Tainui representatives meet to discuss implementation of the plan.

Two months later, the manager of the Maori section of the Ministry of Education flew from Wellington to Hamilton to meet with the Tainui Education Committee. He presented the ministry's "Ten-Point Plan" for Maori education. Point Ten on the plan proposed support for tribal education plans. The Ten-Point Plan was to be widely circulated by the ministry and was promoted as the ministry's response to the needs of Maori in education. The members of the Education Committee were greatly encouraged by the meeting. It was not until five years later in early 1996 that we learned that the Ten-Point Plan had never been adopted as Ministry of Education policy. No funding was allocated for tribal education plans during the 1990s.

At the time, we thought that there was real hope for support from the ministry. The ministry delegated responsibility for the working party to the regional manager of the Hamilton office. A series of meetings then took place between the regional manager and members of the Education Committee. The Education Committee proposed that the ministry allocate approximately $100,000 for the establishment of the Tainui resource center as described in the Tainui education strategy.

After several meetings between the Education Committee and the regional manager of the Ministry of Education, we were told that the funding system would not allow any substantial allocations for a tribal resource center but that the regional manager would make $2,000 available for the establishment of a Maori education database in the region. A student with specialist skills was employed to work with the Maori liaison officer in the regional office. A questionnaire was sent to all schools in the Tainui region.

Toward the end of that year, under the supervision of the Maori liaison officer, the data from the questionnaires were entered into a computer in the Hamilton office of the Ministry of Education. Then, a tragedy occurred. The Maori liaison officer developed gangrene in one of his toes. He went into the hospital for surgery, but the gangrene spread. There was more surgery and more gangrene. In March of the following year, he passed away. He was deeply loved. The committee members were shocked at the circumstances of his death and grieved for some time afterward.

As a consequence of his death, there was no progress on the Maori education database for several months. Finally, another meeting was held between the regional manager and Education Committee members. Two main issues were discussed: filling the position left vacant by the Maori liaison officer's death and the Maori education database. The regional manager had decided that the liaison officer's position would become a half-time position and the Ministry of Education would define the duties of the position. The members of the Education Committee disagreed with those decisions, believing that a full-time position in the Hamilton office should be allocated and the duties of the position should be negotiated with the tribal representatives.

In addition, it was discovered that the computer record of the previous year's questionnaire responses had been lost, although the original questionnaires were still on file. Work on the database would have to begin again. The regional manager allocated $1,000 to employ someone to reenter the data from the first questionnaire and to design, distribute, and collate information from a second questionnaire. Eventually, a report on Maori participation in primary and secondary schools in the region was produced.

No Tainui education resource centers have ever been established, but there has been progress on other dimensions of the strategy. The numbers of Maori-immersion preschools and primary schools increased in the region. One Maori-immersion school, Rakaumanga, expanded into a composite school (primary and secondary instruction in one institution). A School of Maori and Pacific Development was established at the University of Waikato. The Tainui Trust Board achieved a settlement with the government of its century-old land claim and so could establish a substantial program of university scholarships. The tribe's postgraduate college opened in early 2000.

This case illustrates the importance of the political context for the success of a proposed program. In the case of the Tainui health plan, the plan was produced at a moment in time when the local Area Health Board had adopted public goals regarding Maori health and also had the authority to allocate funding in support of a tribal health plan that addressed those goals. In the case of the education strategy, politicians and the Ministry of Education publicly proclaimed their intention to address the problems of Maori under-achievement but gave little more than lip service to funding for tribal education strategies even though tribal strategies were included in the ministry's Ten-Point Plan. The Ministry of Education examined, approved, and funded changes in Maori education as cheaply and sometimes as grudgingly as possible, one at a time.

The Tainui education strategy was a valuable effort. It helped Maori teachers and other professionals in the region to develop a shared vision of the education system that they wanted. The shared vision helped to promote the implementation of some, but not all, of the objectives of the strategy in the final decade of the twentieth century. There is every reason to believe that, heartened by their successes, Maori educators will continue their efforts to identify new and better strategies for Maori education.

NOTE

1. The Tainui Maaori Trust Board used a double "a" in Maori to indicate that the "a" should be pronounced as a long vowel. The organization was phased out toward the end of the 1990s and was replaced by the Waikato Raupatu Lands Trust.

Chapter Eleven

Collaborative Programs in Indigenous Communities

As the twenty-first century began, indigenous people tended to view researchers with suspicion because the people could not see how previous research had contributed to the welfare of their communities. Many indigenous communities also had histories of inadequate or failed educational and social programs that had been designed by outsiders. However, they could often see promise when outside experts collaborated with them in the development of programs, and they supported research linked to these programs. Collaborative programs between indigenous peoples and outside experts evolved in the second half of the twentieth century as a means of empowering indigenous communities. During that time, the willingness of outside professionals to share responsibility and authority with indigenous peoples increased dramatically.

Collaborative programs sometimes seemed like ideal solutions, but certain issues have been pervasive over several decades of collaborative work, appearing in published reports and in my own program experiences as well. Efrat and Mitchell (1974) found that the indigenous group they worked with wanted Indian-designed activities that the researchers had not intended. Gibson (1985) and Delgado-Gaitan (1990) added goals to their programs as requested by the communities where their programs were based. The people of Waahi Marae wanted me to work on their programs as well as on the research I originally intended to focus on.

The researcher's goal of publishing for professional audiences has sometimes been in conflict with community goals. Watahomigie and Yamamoto (1987) point out that there were sometimes delays in publishing research findings so that the applied goals of collaborative programs could be achieved first. I found in the Rakaumanga case that it was more important to the community to have the research paper printed locally than to have it available to a professional audience.

Gibson (1985) found that not every participant could share equally in decision making for collaborative programs, that good systems for administration of funding were critical to success, and that conflicts between community factions could be detrimental. Stull, Schultz, and Cadue (1987) describe a program that suffered from shifting government policies and funding as well as from factional community conflict. The issues described by Gibson and by Stull, Schultz, and Cadue reappeared in the Community Training Centre where I worked in the late 1980s.

Debates about the ethics of research have been ongoing throughout the twentieth century and have included questions of the personal position of the researcher, as discussed by LeCompte (1995). Issues of ethics are related to the issue of discrepancies between the insider's view and the outsider's view, which has received greater attention in recent years. Each new publication by indigenous researchers adds to our knowledge of the issues they face because of their unique perspective and their continuing community relationships.

At the same time and in spite of the problems, collaborative programs have had many successful outcomes. In chapters 5 to 10, I have described my experience in two decades of work in collaborative programs. Reports were published in conjunction with almost all of the programs. Some of the reports were for academic audiences, but others were intended to benefit indigenous communities. One, the report on the Manokotak School (Harrison et al. 1985), has been used in training teachers for rural Alaskan schools, and it provided a helpful model for Rakaumanga School in New Zealand when the latter was considering the establishment of its own small high school. Two of the reports, the *Tainui Health Plan* and the *Tainui Education Strategy*, provide guidelines for the Tainui tribe in the development of their own programs. Both reports have been used as models by other tribes. In most of the programs, indigenous people benefited directly in various roles as university students or employees and in personal development or vocational training.

The programs also illustrate the way that guidelines for fieldworkers and for program design can be used to explore the strengths and weaknesses of programs, either planned or in operation. The guidelines address some issues with respect to individual fieldworkers and some issues related to program design.

FOR THE INDIVIDUAL FIELDWORKER ...

Be Flexible but Recognize That Everyone Has Limits

With respect to fieldworkers, my experiences demonstrate that, although flexibility is a desirable trait in a fieldworker, there are always limitations in one's ability to be flexible. In the Small High Schools Project, I made short visits to two communities where I probably could not have worked successfully even for an academic year. I completed a year of fieldwork that year because I found a setting in a physical and social environment in which I could cope. In the college pilot projects, I was able to cope with the physical environment a few months at a time, but the environment made it difficult to run the program, and the physical demands were hard on me. I walked several miles each day in wind, rain, or snow and transported teaching materials in wheelbarrows. Even when I was wearing proper cold weather gear, I needed unusual energy just to keep warm. I could not make a long-term commitment to work in a program in such a difficult environment. When I was working on the study of Rakaumanga School, I learned that the way one adapts to a particular physical environment may depend to a certain extent on one's expectations. In the Community Training Centre, I learned that I needed to be able to change rapidly because the policy context changed rapidly. In virtually all of the programs, a higher tolerance for ambiguity and a better ability to tolerate moments of discouragement would have helped me to maintain a healthy emotional balance while I worked.

Be Willing to Collaborate by Sharing Authority, Responsibility, and Credit for Success

Although I learned early in my research career that collaboration can have positive effects on program development, I was not always as collaborative as I might have been. Staff of the community college designed both of the college pilot projects without much collaboration with villagers. Some of the problems of the programs might have been avoided if local people had been allowed greater participation in program development. In every program, I was dependent on people from the local communities to get the job done. Even in New Zealand, where life was very much like that in mainstream America, I had to ask for help again and again with simple tasks. However, when I was working on the Rakaumanga study, demands from the community nearly overwhelmed the research. I learned that fieldworkers cannot collaborate with everyone. Responsibilities and authority have to be delegated to one person or to a small group of people.

Give Thoughtful Attention to the Ethical Implications of Your Actions

Consideration of the ethics of collaboration emerged as a major theme in the programs. Formal statements of research ethics only touch the surface of the questions that arose time and again in each of the programs. In the Small High Schools Project and the college pilot projects, I learned that the fieldworker cannot always predict the outcomes. "Subjects" need to be informed of that risk, along with other more obvious issues. I have been more careful in later programs to offer only what I can deliver. In the college pilot projects, I learned that intimacy is almost inevitable in long-term work in indigenous communities and that there are personal consequences. I wondered if I was responsible for consequences that I could not have predicted.

In the Manokotak study, I had to ponder ethical means for presenting the complaints of some teachers. In the Rakaumanga study, I wondered about the ethics of supporting one community faction or another. I concluded that it was essential for me to work within the program goals and boundaries that I had announced to the community; interference in internal relations was not part of the plan. In the CTC program, two other researchers used conversations with me in their reports without my permission. From these experiences, I learned the importance of gaining permission to use material given by informants. As time went on, I realized that ethical questions are ongoing, constant considerations not only for researchers but also for other fieldworkers in indigenous settings.

Apply the Concept of Culture in Everyday Working Relationships

When I began fieldwork in 1977, I thought that I had a good working knowledge of the concept of culture. As I moved from one field setting to another, my reservations about that knowledge increased. Eventually, I came to two major conclusions. First, I realized that I would have to be cautious when using culture as a framework for understanding the individuals with whom I was working. Most indigenous people have had experience in a wide range of cultural settings. Their backgrounds cannot be categorized easily. Fieldworkers must attend to the backgrounds and idiosyncrasies of individuals if their programs are going to work. Second, I realized that fieldworkers have to pay almost as much attention to the culture of government bureaucracies and other institutions associated with their programs as they pay to the indigenous cultures where they work. I tended to blame individuals in the bureaucracies for problems when I should have had a better grasp of the culture of institutions.

FOR DESIGNING COLLABORATIVE PROGRAMS . . .

The lessons for program planning that emerged from my program experiences are also significant.

Fieldworkers and Representatives of the Community Should Collaborate to Develop a Rationale, Philosophy, or Reason for the Establishment of the Particular Program

The first guideline that emerged is that fieldworkers and representatives of the community should collaborate to develop a rationale, philosophy, or reason for the establishment of the particular program. All of the programs in my experience included well-developed reasons for their existence. In the Small High Schools Project, a collaborative research project was embedded into an existing collaborative program. This contributed to the success of the project, but multiple goals made it difficult for the graduate assistants to carry out the tasks assigned to them. In the college pilot projects, the low level of collaboration between college staff and local people may have contributed to the early demise of the programs. Some problems might have been avoided with better collaboration. The Manokotak case study demonstrates that straightforward goals make collaboration relatively easy to achieve. In the Rakaumanga case study, a different sort of collaboration emerged; I gave time to community projects, but the community projects then nearly overwhelmed the research. In the CTC, the rationale changed during the early phases of the program. Collaboration in the CTC, the Tainui health plan, and the Maori Student Academic Advisory Centre led to the establishment of long-term Maori-operated programs. In the oral histories project, collaboration from Maori volunteers rescued the project from abject failure.

Look for Sources of Adequate and Dependable Funding

The second guideline recommends that program developers establish adequate and preferably stable sources of funding. Most of the programs had adequate levels of dependable funding, but the CTC case illustrates the difficulties that program managers and other staff experience when funding is short term and always in jeopardy. During the two years that I was associated with the program, it was impossible to concentrate on developing program quality because so much time was committed to rewriting objectives in order to keep the funding coming in. In the oral histories project, there was no way to go back to the funding agency for more money when unforeseen circumstances arose. The project was only completed because of the work of volunteers. It seems quite clear that adequate and stable funding must be central concerns in program design.

Confirm That There Is Adequate Support in the Local Community

The third recommendation for program designers is to confirm that there is adequate support in the local community. The Small High Schools Project demonstrates that its success did not depend on support from the whole community, but it did depend on support from specific people in key positions, including classroom teachers and the local school board. The CTC shows that a program can survive even when there are disagreements and arguments about it, although I am certain that very high levels of disagreement can be damaging. This project also shows that the determination of staff and community members can be critical to the long-term survival of programs.

Formulate a Program Plan Including Statements of Roles and Responsibilities, Support Systems for Participants, and Evaluation Procedures

The fourth recommendation for planners is to formulate a program plan including statements of roles and responsibilities, support systems for participants, and evaluation procedures. In the programs in which a solid plan was in place, there was little reason to wonder whether the plan was important or not. Sometimes—as in the Small High Schools Project—I was hardly aware that a plan was operating. However, when I found that little detailed planning had taken place for the CTC, I was overwhelmed by the need for planning. Because I was primarily responsible for developing the plan, I learned by experience to think about the specific dimensions of new programs that are given in the detailed guidelines. My experience at the CTC demonstrates that administration of funding needs special attention in program planning.

In the Manokotak study, I learned that simple and straightforward plans are easier to carry out than more complicated plans. This principle was reinforced in the Rakaumanga study. The Rakaumanga study also shows that the preparation of the report can be problematic, and so provision for completing it should be carefully included in the program plan. The Manokotak study and the CTC incorporated different kinds of training for local people as part of the program plans, and the training contributed to the success of the programs. In the Tainui health plan, I learned that under fortuitous circumstances, programs can move from step to step without overall planning. However, I do not recommend that developers take the risks involved without careful consideration of the possible consequences. The project summaries from the 1990s show that straightforward plans with small numbers of participants and short-term, small budgets can be successful, but the oral histories project demonstrates the consequences if one party in the collaboration does not follow through.

Identify or Recruit Committed Leadership in the Program and, Preferably, in the Funding Agency

The fifth guideline recommends that program developers identify or recruit committed leadership in the program and in the funding agency. The importance of this guideline emerges from the college pilot projects wherein high staff turnover and short-term commitments contributed to the close of the projects in the village. The part-time job sharing arrangement of the coordinators also contributed to the initial problems of the CTC. In the other programs in which leaders were present who were committed at least for the time necessary to get the operation off the ground, it was easy to take their leadership for granted. The importance of committed leadership was most noticeable in its absence.

Identify or Recruit Appropriately Qualified Staff

The sixth guideline recommends that program developers identify and recruit appropriately qualified staff members. The oral histories project, more than any of the other examples, shows the need for recruiting staff members with appropriate qualifications. Although I had a doctorate and a number of years of relevant experience, I was not qualified for the project because I did not speak, read, or write Maori. The Manokotak study and the CTC demonstrate some ways whereby training for local people can be incorporated into the projects so that they can gain the needed skills.

Find a Workable Physical Setting

The seventh guideline recommends that program planners find a workable physical setting. My experiences demonstrate that an appropriate physical setting is an important element in program success, but the physical facilities do not have to be elaborate or luxurious. Although the physical environment made it extremely difficult to run the college pilot projects, the physical setting is not likely to be the most important component of programs in more temperate climates. The CTC operated for several years in facilities that could be described as minimal. The physical setting needs to be given thoughtful attention but only after a program plan is in place. The program should determine the location and kind of facilities that are needed, not the reverse.

Attend to the Broader Political and Social Context That Makes It Possible for a Program to Survive

The final guideline recommends that attention be paid to the broader political and social context that makes it possible for a program to survive. Although this guideline is the last one given, it is the most important for any long-term program and for the future of collaborative programs in general. Several of the programs—the Small High Schools, Manokotak, Rakaumanga, and the oral histories project and the management committee surveys—were intended as short-term projects. The college pilot projects, the CTC, the MSAAC, and the Tainui health and education plans were intended for the long term. The long-term operation of the CTC, the MSAAC, and the Tainui health plan has depended on the continuation of policies that have supported funding for these programs. In all likelihood, government policies in the twenty-first century will support funding for collaborative programs in indigenous communities, and collaborative programs will continue and expand. If government policies do not support funding for collaborative programs, the future of such programs is bleak. The broader political context will be the most important determinant of the long-term success of collaborative programs partially because it is the political context that determines whether programs will receive government funding.

Indigenous people in the United States, Canada, Australia, and New Zealand face similar problems because of histories of European conquest, because of similar government policies from country to country, and because they hold similar visions for their own futures. Government policy frameworks relating to indigenous peoples in the four countries have similarities because the frameworks grew out of the same origins in European law and history. Indigenous peoples have maintained continuing commitments to achieving self-determination in all dimensions of life including economic development, education, health, families, religion, land and other natural resources, language, and arts. Government polices have tended to acknowledge the notion of indigenous self-determination, but government agencies have tended to control the design and funding of programs. Similarity of the political contexts in all four countries have led to similarities in the way programs were designed, funded, and managed.

Throughout the history of contact, relationships between indigenous peoples and the governments in the four countries have been dynamic and changing. Ongoing debate, argument, and negotiation were the normal contexts for program development in the twentieth century. The goals of the indigenous people were often at odds with those of the bureaucracies that held the purse strings. As a result, fieldworkers in programs in indigenous communities had to attend to the goals of the indigenous communities, the goals of the government bureaucracies, and the dynamic context of argument and negotiation between the two.

THE FUTURE ROLE OF
UNIVERSITIES IN COLLABORATIVE PROGRAMS

University politics add another dimension to the context of collaborative programs. The civil rights movements of the 1960s and 1970s provided the basis for some university researchers to enter into collaborative programs with the hope that the reports published for indigenous audiences would be recognized and rewarded by the universities that employed them. By the end of the century, however, a political shift had taken place. Universities internationally were using rigid and limited definitions of research that did not include work in collaborative development programs unless reports of the programs appeared in academic publications. Reports prepared for indigenous communities did not "count." At the University of Waikato in New Zealand, for example, research was defined by a list of items in a point system, with high priority given to academic publications or books. Academic staff members were told that the system was used internationally and therefore reflected the practices of universities in several countries. Checklists like Waikato's grew out of the assumption that the quality of research could be measured quantitatively and simply. The theoretical literature demystifying this belief is extensive, but the belief prevailed nevertheless, even among academics who should have known better.

A second relevant shift occurred in the politics of university research toward the end of the twentieth century. In the early years of the century, the stated goals of most Western universities included the goal of supporting research. By the end of the century, however, public funding for universities had declined so that the institutions were drawing large proportions of their income from government-funded research contracts. The tables had turned. Instead of universities supporting research, researchers were expected to support universities by bringing in funding through research contracts. The Foundation for Research, Science and Technology, the major government science-funding agency in New Zealand, requires that researchers collaborate with "end users." Projects funded by this agency in indigenous communities have had to be collaborative. Although the University of Waikato was extremely anxious to obtain the agency's funding, the agency's requirements for collaboration had no impact on the checklist approach to assessing the quality of research. Commissioned reports were low on the priority list, and problems relating to academic publication of collaborative work would not be taken into consideration when the university assigned points for research to an individual or a unit within the university.

These shifts ignore the practical necessities of research in indigenous communities in the twenty-first century. In the opening chapters of this book, I discuss the reasons why it has become essential for researchers to offer some specific benefits to the communities in which they conduct their studies. Indigenous communities insist that there must be benefits for the "subjects" of the research. They also insist that programs enhance self-determination in their communities. Researchers who have attended to self-determination for indigenous communities sometimes had to delay publication or not publish at all. Researchers sometimes wondered—as I did in the college pilot projects and thereafter—who benefited from the research. Were the primary beneficiaries the researchers, the communities, or the universities? The twenty-first-century university requirements generate unreasonable ethical burdens for researchers trying to attend to the welfare of the people while meeting the goals of the universities at the same time.

One would expect the changes in university definitions and funding structures to have a strong influence on the specific activities of researchers. Researchers who chose to work in collaborative programs had to attend to the goals of the communities, the goals of the bureaucracies that funded social programs and research, the goals of the universities that employed them, and the dynamic context of argument and negotiation among all of these elements. Older tenured academic staff had the option of collaborative work with indigenous peoples regardless of university sanctions. Younger untenured academic staff had to choose between producing contracts and publications to satisfy the universities, trying to satisfy indigenous communities as well as universities, and ending their academic careers prematurely. These shifts in university policies could easily discourage younger researchers from entering into collaborative relationships in which academic publication is not a high priority for indigenous collaborators.

I have already pointed out that programs with clear-cut goals are more likely to be successful than programs in which there are too many different goals or there are contradictions among the goals of different stakeholders. University-based fieldworkers would be wise to carefully examine the goals of the stakeholders (including the universities that employ them) before making commitments to collaborative programs in indigenous communities. If there are too many stakeholders with too many different goals, the program may not survive for long.

My experiences in collaborative programs have shown the practical value of research skills for fieldworkers, but collaborative programs are not dependent on university researchers. Many programs have attracted outside experts—educators, social service workers, health workers, and other program developers—who were not employed by universities but who received their training in universities. Universities will continue to have important roles in training collaborative fieldworkers; but given the restrictions that are imposed on researchers by university politics and the preferences of indigenous people, the outside experts who work in future programs are more likely to be employed by government agencies or by tribal organizations than by universities. Hopefully, changes in the political context will eventually bring about a broadening of the vision of research within universities so that researchers can attend to the welfare of the people with whom they work as well as to their own career advancement and the goals of the universities.

COLLABORATIVE PROGRAMS
FOR THE TWENTY-FIRST CENTURY

The following excerpts from a media release of the Aboriginal and Torres Strait Islander Commission (ATSIC) in Australia clearly convey the sense of urgency that indigenous people feel:

Media Release—Aboriginal and Torres Strait Islander Commission
Date: Fri, 3 Mar 2000
As the indigenous community of Mornington Island and across the Gulf and Mt Isa region struggles to come to grips with the tragic death by suicide of five more young indigenous people in the last two months, ATSIC's new Regional Council Chairman asks:
How long will this tragedy be allowed to continue?
In a passionate plea to governments and the wider community, Noel Sarmardin, speaks out about the frustration and anger of his community.
He is calling for "unprecedented, sustained action" by governments to help put an end to the continuing trail of youth suicides among his people. . . .
Indigenous people are crying out for an end to all this—we need help here—but there seems to be no answers from the health system, from government programs that don't work. . . .
How many more reports and inquiries do governments need?
. . . We need plane loads of doctors, health workers, counsellors, with funding for programs.
With funding for discrete centres, infrastructure where people can get counselling and help without everyone knowing.
We need education and preventative programs and help on the ground seven days a week, 12 months a year.
They should be out at Mornington, meeting with the indigenous health centre people, the community council and elders.
To develop a sustained, long-term approach to rebuilding these communities from the bottom up.
We are asking them—begging them to help our communities do this.
We need job and training programs, housing, recreation and sports facilities.
We need indigenous people trained and running and delivering and developing these programs in conjunction with our communities.
We need a sustained whole of government—whole of community approach to this.
One that tackles all the fundamental, underlying issues of unemployment, health, dispossession, lack of housing, lack of self respect, lack of education, low self esteem, alcoholism, violence.

Responding to what our communities and people say they need. . . .
Noel Sarmardin
Chairman
Gulf and Western Queensland ATSIC Regional Council

Sometimes, collaborative program development has to move ahead even when policy directions are murky, with the hope that agency support will be there when it is needed. Collaborative programs can be successful when they are carefully planned, when the political context is supportive, and when adequate funding is available. I cannot predict the direction of majority sentiment in the future, but I am hopeful that the mainstream public will lean toward support for collaborative programs in indigenous communities and that government policy and funding will follow.

I conclude with two important recommendations. The first has to do with fieldworkers, and the second, with program planning. My experiences have clearly shown the importance of training and orientation for fieldworkers before they move into indigenous communities to begin collaborative work on programs. Fieldworkers need to know as much as possible about the communities in which they will live. Research skills can be extremely useful for fieldworkers who are learning about the community and its needs even if the fieldworker is not intending to conduct formal research. Courses aimed at providing research skills should be available whenever possible. Fieldworkers need to learn about the physical environment, the general concepts of culture and collaboration, and how to work with these concepts in indigenous as well as bureaucratic interactions. Fieldworkers need to be able to look for and balance the goals of various stakeholders in the program setting. Orientations should provide fieldworkers with the opportunity to think about ethical questions in their work and about their own capacities to be flexible.

My second recommendation has to do with program planning. I receive regular announcements of the inauguration of new education, health, economic development, and social service programs in indigenous communities in the United States, Canada, Australia, and New Zealand. Over and over again, I see programs start up with almost no planning at all or with rigid direction by government agencies. Often, there is a sense of urgency about getting a new program started. The need in the community is so great that there seems to be no time for careful planning. In other situations, one particular theory for program success is accepted with almost religious fervor by an agency, and agency staff become such true believers that they are unwilling to perceive any defects in their approach. True believers in theories make it virtually impossible for local communities to exercise self-determination in program planning. The programs described in this book demonstrate that careful planning and genuine collaboration are essential features of successful programs in indigenous communities. Don't start without them.

Appendix

Draft Declaration on the Rights of Indigenous Peoples

1. AFFIRMING that indigenous peoples are equal in dignity and rights to all other peoples, while recognizing the right of all peoples to be different, to consider themselves different, and to be respected as such.
2. AFFIRMING ALSO that all peoples contribute to the diversity and richness of civilizations and cultures, which constitute the common heritage of humankind.
3. AFFIRMING FURTHER that all doctrines, policies and practices based on or advocating superiority of peoples or individuals on the basis of national origin, racial, religious, ethnic or cultural differences are racist, scientifically false, legally invalid, morally condemnable and socially unjust.
4. REAFFIRMING also that indigenous peoples, in the exercise of their rights, should be free from discrimination of any kind.
5. CONCERNED that indigenous peoples have been deprived of their human rights and fundamental freedoms, resulting, inter alia, in their colonization and dispossession of their lands, territories and resources, thus preventing them from exercising, in particular, their right to development in accordance with their own needs and interests.
6. RECOGNIZING the urgent need to respect and promote the inherent rights and characteristics of indigenous peoples, especially their rights to their lands, territories and resources, which derive from their political, economic and social structures and from their cultures, spiritual traditions, histories and philosophies.
7. WELCOMING the fact that indigenous peoples are organizing themselves for political, economic, social and cultural enhancement and in order to bring an end to all forms of discrimination and oppression wherever they occur.

8. CONVINCED that control by indigenous peoples over developments affecting them and their lands, territories and resources will enable them to maintain and strengthen their institutions, cultures and traditions, and to promote their development in accordance with their aspirations and needs.
9. RECOGNIZING also that respect for indigenous knowledge, cultures and traditional practices contributes to sustainable and equitable development and proper management of the environment.
10. EMPHASIZING the need for demilitarization of the lands and territories of indigenous peoples, which will contribute to peace, economic and social progress and development, understanding and friendly relations among nations and peoples of the world.
11. RECOGNIZING in particular the right of indigenous families and communities to retain shared responsibility for the upbringing, training, education and well-being of their children.
12. RECOGNIZING ALSO that indigenous peoples have the right freely to determine their relationship with States in a spirit of coexistence, mutual benefit and full respect.
13. CONSIDERING that treaties, agreements and other arrangements between States and indigenous peoples are properly matters of international concern and responsibility.
14. ACKNOWLEDGING that the Charter of the United Nations, the International Covenant on Economic, Social and Cultural Rights and the International Covenant on Civil and Political Rights affirm the fundamental importance of the right of self-determination of all peoples, by virtue of which they freely determine their political status and freely pursue their economic, social and cultural development.
15. BEARING IN MIND that nothing in this Declaration may be used to deny any peoples their right of self-determination.
16. ENCOURAGING States to comply with and effectively implement all international instruments, in particular those related to human rights, as they apply to indigenous peoples, in consultation and cooperation with the peoples concerned.
17. EMPHASIZING that the United Nations has an important and continuing role to play in promoting and protecting the rights of indigenous peoples.
18. BELIEVING that this Declaration is a further important step forward for the recognition, promotion and protection of the rights and freedoms of indigenous peoples and in the development of relevant activities of the United Nations system in this field.

Solemnly proclaims the following United Nations Declaration on the Rights of Indigenous Peoples.

PART I

ARTICLE 1

Indigenous peoples have the right to the full and effective enjoyment of all human rights and fundamental freedoms recognized in the Charter of the United Nations, the Universal Declaration of Human Rights and international human rights law.

ARTICLE 2

Indigenous individuals and peoples are free and equal to all other individuals and peoples in dignity and rights, and have the right to be free from any kind of adverse discrimination, in particular that based on their indigenous origin or identity.

ARTICLE 3

Indigenous peoples have the right of self-determination. By virtue of that right they freely determine their political status and freely pursue their economic, social and cultural development.

ARTICLE 4

Indigenous peoples have the right to maintain and strengthen their distinct political, economic, social and cultural characteristics, as well as their legal systems, while retaining their rights to participate fully, if they so choose, in the political, economic, social and cultural life of the State.

ARTICLE 5

Every indigenous individual has the right to a nationality.

PART II

ARTICLE 6

Indigenous peoples have the collective right to live in freedom, peace and security as distinct peoples and to full guarantees against genocide or any other act of violence, including the removal of indigenous children from their families and communities under any pretext.

In addition, they have the individual rights to life, physical and mental integrity, liberty and security of person.

ARTICLE 7

Indigenous peoples have the collective and individual right not to be subjected to ethnocide and cultural genocide, including prevention of and redress for:

a. any action which has the aim or effect of depriving them of their integrity as distinct peoples, or of their cultural values or ethnic identities;
b. any action which has the aim or effect of dispossessing them of their lands, territories or resources;
c. any form of population transfer which has the aim or effect of violating or undermining any of their rights;
d. any form of assimilation or integration by other cultures or ways of life imposed on them by legislative, administrative or other measures;
e. any form of propaganda directed against them.

ARTICLE 8

Indigenous peoples have the collective and individual right to maintain and develop their distinct identities and characteristics, including the right to identify themselves as indigenous and to be recognized as such.

ARTICLE 9

Indigenous peoples and individuals have the right to belong to an indigenous community or nation, in accordance with the traditions and customs of the community or nation concerned. No disadvantage of any kind may arise from the exercise of such a right.

ARTICLE 10

Indigenous peoples shall not be forcibly removed from their lands or territories. No relocation shall take place without the free and informed consent of the indigenous peoples concerned and after agreement on just and fair compensation and, where possible, with the option of return.

ARTICLE 11

Indigenous peoples have the right to special protection and security in periods of armed conflict.

States shall observe international standards, in particular the Fourth Geneva Convention of 1949, for the protection of civilian populations in circumstances of emergency and armed conflict, and shall not:

a. recruit indigenous individuals against their will into the armed forces and, in particular, for use against other indigenous peoples;
b. recruit indigenous children into the armed forces under any circumstances;
c. force indigenous individuals to abandon their lands, territories or means of subsistence, or relocate them in special centres for military purposes;
d. force indigenous individuals to work for military purposes under any discriminatory conditions.

PART III

ARTICLE 12

Indigenous peoples have the right to practice and revitalize their cultural traditions and customs. This includes the right to maintain, protect and develop the past, present and future manifestations of their cultures, such as archaeological and historical sites, artifacts, designs, ceremonies, technologies and visual and performing arts and literature, as well as the right to the restitution of cultural, intellectual, religious and spiritual property taken without their free and informed consent or in violation of their laws, traditions and customs.

ARTICLE 13

Indigenous peoples have the right to manifest, practice, develop and teach their spiritual and religious traditions, customs and ceremonies; the right to maintain, protect, and have access in privacy to their religious and cultural sites; the right to the use and control of ceremonial objects; and the right to the repatriation of human remains.

States shall take effective measures, in conjunction with the indigenous peoples concerned, to ensure that indigenous sacred places, including burial sites, be preserved, respected and protected.

ARTICLE 14

Indigenous peoples have the right to revitalize, use, develop and transmit to future generations their histories, languages, oral traditions, philosophies, writing systems and literatures, and to designate and retain their own names for communities, places and persons.

States shall take effective measures, whenever any right of indigenous peoples may be threatened, to ensure this right is protected and also to ensure that they can understand and be understood in political, legal and administrative proceedings, where necessary through the provision of interpretation or by other appropriate means.

PART IV

ARTICLE 15

Indigenous children have the right to all levels and forms of education of the State. All indigenous peoples also have this right and the right to establish and control their educational systems and institutions providing education in their own languages, in a manner appropriate to their cultural methods of teaching and learning.

Indigenous children living outside their communities have the right to be provided access to education in their own culture and language.

States shall take effective measures to provide appropriate resources for these purposes.

ARTICLE 16

Indigenous peoples have the right to have the dignity and diversity of their cultures, traditions, histories and aspirations appropriately reflected in all forms of education and public information.

States shall take effective measures, in consultation with the indigenous peoples concerned, to eliminate prejudice and discrimination and to promote tolerance, understanding and good relations among indigenous peoples and all segments of society.

ARTICLE 17

Indigenous peoples have the right to establish their own media in their own language. They also have the right to equal access to all forms of non-indigenous media.

States shall take effective measures to ensure that State-owned media duly reflect indigenous cultural diversity.

ARTICLE 18

Indigenous peoples have the right to enjoy fully all rights established under international labour law and national labour legislation.

Indigenous individuals have the right not to be subjected to any discriminatory conditions of labour, employment or salary.

PART V

ARTICLE 19

Indigenous peoples have the right to participate fully, if they so choose, at all levels of decision-making in matters which may affect their rights, lives and destinies through representatives chosen by themselves in accordance with their own procedures, as well as to maintain and develop their own indigenous decision-making institutions.

ARTICLE 20

Indigenous peoples have the right to participate fully, if they so choose, through procedures determined by them, in devising legislative or administrative measures that may affect them.

States shall obtain the free and informed consent of the peoples concerned before adopting and implementing such measures.

ARTICLE 21

Indigenous peoples have the right to maintain and develop their political, economic and social systems, to be secure in the enjoyment of their own means of subsistence and development, and to engage freely in all their traditional and other economic activities. Indigenous peoples who have been deprived of their means of subsistence and development are entitled to just and fair compensation.

ARTICLE 22

Indigenous peoples have the right to special measures for the immediate, effective and continuing improvement of their economic and social conditions, including in the areas of employment, vocational training and retraining, housing, sanitation, health and social security. Particular attention shall be paid to the rights and special needs of indigenous elders, women, youth, children and disabled persons.

ARTICLE 23

Indigenous peoples have the right to détermine and develop priorities and strategies for exercising their right to development. In particular, indigenous peoples have the right to determine and develop all health, housing and other economic and social programmes affecting them and, as far as possible, to administer such programmes through their own institutions.

ARTICLE 24

Indigenous peoples have the right to their traditional medicines and health practices, including the right to the protection of vital medicinal plants, animals and minerals.

They also have the right to access, without any discrimination, to all medical institutions, health services and medical care.

PART VI

ARTICLE 25

Indigenous peoples have the right to maintain and strengthen their distinctive spiritual and material relationship with the lands, territories, waters and coastal seas and other resources which they have traditionally owned or otherwise occupied or used, and to uphold their responsibilities to future generations in this regard.

ARTICLE 26

Indigenous peoples have the right to own, develop, control and use the lands and territories, including the total environment of the lands, air, waters, coastal seas, sea-ice, flora and fauna and other resources which they have traditionally owned or otherwise occupied or used. This includes the right to the full recognition of their laws, traditions, and customs, land-tenure systems and institutions for the development and management of resources, and the right to effective measures by States to prevent any interference with, alienation of or encroachment upon these rights.

ARTICLE 27

Indigenous peoples have the right to the restitution of the lands, territories and resources which they have traditionally owned or otherwise occupied or used, and which have been confiscated, occupied, used or damaged without their free and informed consent. Where this is not possible, they have the right to just and fair compensation. Unless otherwise freely agreed upon by the peoples concerned, compensation shall take the form of lands, territories and resources equal in quality, size and legal status.

ARTICLE 28

Indigenous peoples have the right to the conservation, restoration, and protection of the total environment and the productive capacity of their lands, territories and resources, as well as to assistance for this purpose from States and through international cooperation. Military activities shall not take place in the lands and territories of indigenous peoples, unless otherwise freely agreed upon by the peoples concerned.

States shall take effective measures to ensure that no storage or disposal of hazardous materials shall take place in the lands and territories of indigenous peoples.

States shall also take effective measures to ensure, as needed, that programmes for monitoring, maintaining and restoring the health of indigenous peoples, as developed and implemented by the peoples affected by such materials, are duly implemented.

ARTICLE 29

Indigenous peoples are entitled to the recognition of the full ownership, control and protection of their cultural and intellectual property.

They have the right to special measures to control, develop and protect their sciences, technologies and cultural manifestations, including human and other genetic resources, seeds, medicines, knowledge of the properties of fauna and flora, oral traditions, literatures, designs and visual and performing arts.

ARTICLE 30

Indigenous peoples have the right to determine and develop priorities and strategies for the development or use of their lands, territories and other resources, including the right to require that States obtain their free and informed consent prior to the approval of any project affecting their lands, territories and other resources, particularly in connection with the development, utilization or exploitation of mineral, water or other resources.

Pursuant to agreement with the indigenous peoples concerned, just and fair compensation shall be provided for any such activities and measures taken to mitigate adverse environmental, economic, social, cultural or spiritual impact.

PART VII

ARTICLE 31

Indigenous peoples, as a specific form of exercising their right to self-determination, have the right to autonomy or self-government in matters relating to their internal and local affairs, including culture, religion, education, information, media, health, housing, employment, social welfare, economic activities, land and resources management, environment and entry by non-members, as well as ways and means for financing these autonomous functions.

ARTICLE 32

Indigenous peoples have the collective right to determine their own citizenship in accordance with their customs and traditions. Indigenous citizenship does not impair the right of indigenous individuals to obtain citizenship of the States in which they live.

Indigenous peoples have the right to determine the structures and to select the membership of their institutions in accordance with their own procedures.

ARTICLE 33

Indigenous peoples have the right to promote, develop and maintain their institutional structures and their distinctive juridical customs, traditions, procedures and practices, in accordance with internationally recognized human rights standards.

ARTICLE 34

Indigenous peoples have the collective right to determine the responsibilities of individuals to their communities.

ARTICLE 35

Indigenous peoples, in particular those divided by international borders, have the right to maintain and develop contacts, relations and cooperation, including activities for spiritual, cultural, political, economic and social purposes, with other peoples across borders.

States shall take effective measures to ensure the exercise and implementation of this right.

ARTICLE 36

Indigenous peoples have the right to the recognition, observance and enforcement of treaties, agreements and other constructive arrangements concluded with States or their successors, according to their original spirit and intent, and to have States honour and respect such treaties, agreements and other constructive arrangements.

Conflicts and disputes which cannot otherwise be settled should be submitted to competent international bodies agreed to by all parties concerned.

PART VIII

ARTICLE 37

States shall take effective and appropriate measures, in consultation with the indigenous peoples concerned, to give full effect to the provisions of this Declaration. The rights recognized herein shall be adopted and included in national legislation in such a manner that indigenous peoples can avail themselves of such rights in practice.

ARTICLE 38

Indigenous peoples have the right to have access to adequate financial and technical assistance, from States and through international cooperation, to pursue freely their political, economic, social, cultural and spiritual development and for the enjoyment of the rights and freedoms recognized in this Declaration.

ARTICLE 39

Indigenous peoples have the right to have access to and prompt decision through mutually acceptable and fair procedures for the resolution of conflicts and disputes with States, as well as to effective remedies for all infringements of their individual and collective rights. Such a decision shall take into consideration the customs, traditions, rules and legal systems of the indigenous peoples concerned.

ARTICLE 40

The organs and specialized agencies of the United Nations system and other intergovernmental organizations shall contribute to the full realization of the provisions of this Declaration through the mobilization, inter alia, of financial cooperation and technical assistance. Ways and means of ensuring participation of indigenous peoples on issues affecting them shall be established.

ARTICLE 41

The United Nations shall take the necessary steps to ensure the implementation of this Declaration including the creation of a body at the highest level with special competence in this field and with the direct participation of indigenous peoples. All United Nations bodies shall promote respect for and full application of the provisions of this Declaration.

PART IX

ARTICLE 42

The rights recognized herein constitute the minimum standards for the survival, dignity and well-being of the indigenous peoples of the world.

ARTICLE 43

All the rights and freedoms recognized herein are equally guaranteed to male and female indigenous individuals.

ARTICLE 44

Nothing in this Declaration may be construed as diminishing or extinguishing existing or future rights indigenous peoples may have or acquire.

ARTICLE 45

Nothing in this Declaration may be interpreted as implying for any State, group or person any right to engage in any activity or to perform any act contrary to the Charter of the United Nations.

http://www.hookele.com/netwarriors/dec-En.htm
29 May 2001

References

Arctic Research Consortium of the United States. 1998. "Traditional Knowledge is Focus of Radionuclides Project." *Witness the Arctic: Chronicles of the Arctic System Science Research Program* 6, no. 2:20.

Banks, James A. 1998. "The Lives and Values of Researchers: Implications for Educating Citizens in a Multicultural Society." *Educational Researcher* 27, no. 7: 4–17.

Barnes, Helen Moewaka. 2000. "Collaboration in Community Action: A Successful Partnership between Indigenous Communities and Researchers." *Health Promotion International* 15, no. 1: 17–25.

Barnhardt, Ray. 1977. *Cross-Cultural Issues in Alaskan Education.* Fairbanks: Center for Northern Educational Research, University of Alaska.

Barnhardt, Ray, Howard Van Ness, Joe Bacon, Tom Cochran, Leslie Dolan, Barbara Harrison, Bob Juettner, Eric Madsen, Kathe Rank Nabielski, Molli Sipe, and Tom Wagner. 1979. *Small High School Programs for Rural Alaska.* Fairbanks: Center for Cross-Cultural Studies, University of Alaska.

Bartunek, Jean M., and Meryl Reis Louis. 1996. *Insider/Outsider Team Research.* Qualitative Research Methods Series, 40. Thousand Oaks, Calif.: Sage.

Berger, Thomas R. 1991. *A Long and Terrible Shadow: White Values, Native Rights in the Americas 1492–1992.* Vancouver: Douglas and McIntyre.

Bishop, Russell. 1996. *Collaborative Research Stories: Whakawhanaungatanga.* Palmerston North, New Zealand: The Dunmore Press.

Borman, L. D. 1979. "Action Anthropology and the Self-Help/Mutual-Aid Movement." In *Currents in Anthropology: Essays in Honor of Sol Tax*, ed. R. Hinshaw, 487–511. The Hague: Mouton.

Bourke, Colin, Eleanor Bourke, and Bill Edwards, eds. 1994. *Aboriginal Australia: An Introductory Reader in Aboriginal Studies.* St. Lucia, Queensland: University of South Australia Press.

Bourke, Colin, and Helen Cox. 1994. "Two Laws: One Land." In *Aboriginal Australia: An Introductory Reader in Aboriginal Studies*, ed. Colin Bourke, Eleanor Bourke, and Bill Edwards, 49–64. St. Lucia, Queensland: University of South Australia Press.

Bourke, Colin, and Bill Edwards. 1994. "Family and Kin." In *Aboriginal Australia: An Introductory Reader in Aboriginal Studies*, ed. Colin Bourke, Eleanor Bourke, and Bill Edwards, 85–101. St. Lucia, Queensland: University of South Australia Press.

Bourke, Eleanor. 1994. "Australia's First Peoples: Identity and Population." In *Aboriginal Australia: An Introductory Reader in Aboriginal Studies*, ed. Colin Bourke, Eleanor Bourke, and Bill Edwards, 35–48. St. Lucia, Queensland: University of South Australia Press.

Bowen, Elenore Smith [Laura Bohannan]. 1964. *Return to Laughter: An Anthropological Novel*. New York: Anchor Books.

Briggs, Jean. 1970. *Never in Anger: Portrait of an Eskimo Family*. Cambridge, Mass.: Harvard University Press.

———. 1974. "Eskimo Women: Makers of Men." In *Many Sisters*, ed. Carolyn J. Matthiasson, 261–304. New York: The Free Press.

Bunker, Robert, and John Adair. 1959. *The First Look at Strangers*. New Brunswick, N.J.: Rutgers University Press.

Burger, Julian. 1987. *Report from the Frontier: The State of the World's Indigenous Peoples*. London: Zed Books.

Busier, Holly-Lynn, Kelly A. Clark, Rebecca A. Esch, Corrine Glesne, Yvette Pigeon, and Jill M. Tarule. 1997. "Intimacy in Research." *Qualitative Studies in Education* 10, no. 2: 165–70.

Centre for Maaori Studies and Research. 1994. *Annual Report*. Hamilton, New Zealand: Centre for Maaori Studies and Research, University of Waikato.

Chang, Heewon. 1999. "Re-examining the Rhetoric of the 'Cultural Border.'" *Electronic Magazine of Multicultural Education* 1, no. 1, available at http://www.eastern.edu/publications/emme/1999winter/chang.html.

Chartrand, Paul. 1999. "Aboriginal Peoples in Canada: Aspirations for Distributive Justice as Distinct Peoples." In *Indigenous Peoples' Rights in Australia, Canada, and New Zealand*, ed. Paul Havemann, 88–107. Auckland, New Zealand: Oxford University Press.

Chinas, Beverly L. 1973. *The Isthmus Zapotecs: Women's Roles in Cultural Context*. New York: Holt, Rinehart and Winston.

Chiste, Katherine Beaty. 1999. "Aboriginal Women and Self-Government: Challenging Leviathan." In *Contemporary Native American Cultural Issues*, ed. Duane Champagne, 71–90. Walnut Creek, Calif.: AltaMira Press.

Chrisman, Noel J., C. June Strickland, KoLynn Powell, Marion Dick Squeoch, and Martha Yallup. 1999. "Community Partnership Research with the Yakama Indian Nation." *Human Organization* 58, no. 2: 134–41.

Cleveland, Harlan, Gerard J. Mangone, and John Clarke Adams. 1960. *The Overseas Americans*. New York: McGraw-Hill Book Co.

Craig, Gary, and Marjorie Mayo, eds. 1995. *Community Empowerment: A Reader in Participation and Development*. London: Zed Books.

Delgado-Gaitan, Concha. 1990. *Literacy for Empowerment: The Role of Parents in Children's Education*. New York: The Falmer Press.

Deloria, Vine Jr., and Clifford Lytle. 1984. *The Nations Within: The Past and Future of American Indian Sovereignty*. New York: Pantheon Books.

Deyhle, Donna L., G. Alfred Hess Jr., and Margaret D. LeCompte. 1992. "Approaching Ethical Issues for Qualitative Researchers in Education." In *The Handbook of Qualitative Research in Education*, ed. Margaret D. LeCompte, Wendy L. Millroy, and Judith Preissle, 597–641. San Diego: Academic Press.

Doughty, Paul L. 1987. "Against the Odds: Collaboration and Development at Vicos." In *Collaborative Research and Social Change: Applied Anthropology in Action*, ed. Donald D. Stull and Jean Schensul, 129–57. Boulder: Westview Press.

Efrat, B., and M. Mitchell. 1974. "The Indian and the Social Scientist: Contemporary Contractual Arrangements on the Pacific Northwest Coast." *Human Organization* 33: 405–07.

Egan, K., and Robert Mahuta. 1983. *The Tainui Report*. Revised ed. Occasional Paper no. 19. Hamilton, New Zealand: Centre for Maaori Studies and Research, University of Waikato.

Engelstad, Diane, and John Bird, eds. 1992. *Nation to Nation: Aboriginal Sovereignty and the Future of Canada*. Concord, Ontario: House of Anansi Press.

Erasmus, Georges, and Joe Sanders. 1992. "Canadian History: An Aboriginal Perspective." In *Nation to Nation: Aboriginal Sovereignty and the Future of Canada*, ed. Diane Engelstad and John Bird, 3–11. Concord, Ontario: House of Anansi Press.

Fleras, Augie, and Jean Leonard Elliott. 1992. *The "Nations Within": Aboriginal–State Relations in Canada, the United States, and New Zealand*. Toronto: Oxford University Press.

Freire, Paolo. 1970. *Pedagogy of the Oppressed*. New York: Continuum.

French, Marilyn. 1977. *The Women's Room*. New York: Summit Books.

Gibson, Margaret A. 1985. "Collaborative Educational Ethnography: Problems and Profits." *Anthropology and Education Quarterly* 16: 124–48.

Goodenough, Ward Hunt. 1963. *Cooperation in Change*. New York: Russell Sage Foundation.

——. 1971. *Culture, Language, and Society*. McCaleb Module in Anthropology. Reading, Mass.: Addison-Wesley.

——. 1976. "Multiculturalism as the Normal Human Experience." *Anthropology and Education Quarterly* 7, no. 4: 4–6.

——. 1981. *Culture, Language, and Society*. 2nd ed. Menlo Park, Calif.: Benjamin/Cummings.

Greaves, Tom, ed. 1994. *Intellectual Property Rights for Indigenous Peoples: A Sourcebook*. Oklahoma City: Society for Applied Anthropology.

Groome, Howard. 1994. "Education: The Search for Relevance." In *Aboriginal Australia: An Introductory Reader in Aboriginal Studies*, ed. Colin Bourke, Eleanor Bourke, and Bill Edwards, 140–56. St. Lucia, Queensland: University of South Australia Press.

Guyette, Susan. 1983. *Community-Based Research: A Handbook for Native Americans*. Los Angeles: American Indian Studies Center, University of California at Los Angeles.

——. 1996. *Planning for Balanced Development: A Guide for Native American and Rural Communities*. Santa Fe: Clear Light Publishers.

Harrison, Barbara. 1981. "Informal Learning among Yup'ik Eskimos: An Ethnographic Study of One Alaskan Village." Ph.D. dissertation, University of Oregon.

——. 1982. "Yup'ik Eskimo Women and Postsecondary Education." In *Cross-Cultural Issues in Alaskan Education*, vol. 2, ed. Ray Barnhardt, 192–206. Fairbanks: University of Alaska.

——. 1984. "New Teachers in the Alaskan Village." *Integrateducation* 11: 132–36.

——. 1986a. "Manokotak: A Study of School Adaptation." *Anthropology and Education Quarterly* 17, no. 2: 100–10.

——. 1986b. "Preparing Teachers for Bicultural Classrooms: Alaskan Parallels." *Delta* 38: 37–44.

———. 1987. *Rakaumanga School: A Study of Issues in Bilingual Education*. Hamilton, New Zealand: Centre for Maaori Studies and Research, University of Waikato.

———. 1988. "Bicultural Societies: Alaskan Parallels." *National Education* 70, no. 1: 38–44.

———. 1993. "Building Our House from the Rubbish Tree: Minority Directed Education." In *Minority Education: Anthropological Perspectives*, ed. Evelyn Jacob and Cathie Jordan, 147–64. New York: Ablex.

———. 1994. "The Politics of Community Based Vocational Training Programs for Maori in New Zealand." *Asia-Pacific Exchange (Electronic) Journal* 1, no. 2, available at gopher:// leahi.kcc.hawaii.edu:70/00/Kapi%27olani%20Info/APEX-J/Vol%201%2C%20No.%202/ Barbar%20Harrison.

———. 1998. "Te Wharekura o Rakaumangamanga: The Development of an Indigenous Language Immersion School." *Bilingual Research Journal* 22: 297–316.

Harrison, Barbara, with Patricia Billingsley, Marilyn Crace, Anecia Lomack, Mary Ann Mochin, and Molly Pauk. 1985. *Manokotak: A Case Study of Rural School Development in Alaska*. Fairbanks: Center for Cross-Cultural Studies, University of Alaska.

Havemann, Paul, ed. 1999. *Indigenous Peoples' Rights in Australia, Canada, and New Zealand*. Auckland, New Zealand: Oxford University Press.

Hazlehurst, Kayleen M., ed. 1995. *Popular Justice and Community Regeneration: Pathways of Indigenous Reform*. Westport, Conn.: Praeger.

Hemming, Steve. 1994. "Changing History: New Images of Aboriginal History." In *Aboriginal Australia: An Introductory Reader in Aboriginal Studies*, ed. Colin Bourke, Eleanor Bourke, and Bill Edwards, 17–34. St. Lucia, Queensland: University of South Australia Press.

Ilutsik, Esther. 1998. "The Founding of Ciulistet." In *Transforming the Culture of Schools: Yup'ik Eskimo Examples*, Jerry Lipka with Gerald V. Mohatt and the Ciulistet Group, 10–15. Mahwah, N.J.: Lawrence Erlbaum Associates.

Kaplan, Allan. 1996. *The Development Practitioners' Handbook*. Chicago: Pluto Press.

Kawagley, A. Oscar. 1995. *A Yupiaq Worldview: A Pathway to Ecology and Spirit*. Prospect Heights, Ill.: Waveland Press.

Kincheloe, Joe. 1995. "Meet Me behind the Curtain: The Struggle for a Critical Postmodern Action Research." In *Critical Theory and Educational Research*, ed. Peter L. McLaren and James M. Giarelli, 71–89. Albany: State University of New York Press.

Kukutai, Mite. N.d. *Life History of Mite Kukutai*. Hamilton, New Zealand: Centre for Maaori Studies and Research, University of Waikato.

LeCompte, Margaret D. 1995. "Some Notes on Power, Agenda, and Voice: A Researcher's Personal Evolution toward Critical Collaborative Research." In *Critical Theory and Educational Research*, ed. Peter L. McLaren and James M. Giarelli, 91–112. Albany: State University of New York Press.

LeCompte, Margaret D., Jean J. Schensul, Margaret R. Weeks, and Merrill Singer. 1999. *Researcher Roles and Research Partnerships*. Ethnographer's Toolkit, 6. Walnut Creek, Calif.: AltaMira Press.

Lipka, Jerry, with Gerald V. Mohatt and the Ciulistet Group. 1998. *Transforming the Culture of Schools: Yup'ik Eskimo Examples*. Mahwah, N.J.: Lawrence Erlbaum Associates.

Loomis, Terrence. 1999. *The Political Economy of Indigenous Peoples*. Working Paper, 4/99. Hamilton, New Zealand: Department of Development Studies, University of Waikato.

MacLean, Bryan. 1998. "Establishing a Community Psychology Approach for Indigenous Development: A Case Study of an Alaska Native Development Initiative." Ph.D. dissertation, University of Waikato, Hamilton, New Zealand.

Matthiasson, Carolyn J., ed. 1974. *Many Sisters*. New York: The Free Press.

May, W. F. 1980. "Doing Ethics: The Bearing of Ethical Theories on Fieldwork." *Social Problems* 27, no. 3: 358–70.

McLaren, Peter L., and James M. Giarelli, eds. 1995. *Critical Theory and Educational Research*. Albany: State University of New York Press.

Mead, Linda Tuhiwai Te Rina. 1996. *Nga Aho O Te Kakahu Matauranga: The Multiple Layers of Struggle by Maori in Education*. Auckland, New Zealand: Research Unit for Maori Education, University of Auckland.

Mead, Margaret. 1978. "The Evolving Ethics of Applied Anthropology." In *Applied Anthropology in America*, ed. Elizabeth M. Eddy and William L. Partridge, 425–37. New York: Columbia University Press.

Medicine, Beatrice. 1978. "Learning to Be an Anthropologist and Remaining 'Native.'" In *Applied Anthropology in America*, ed. Elizabeth M. Eddy and William L. Partridge, 182–96. New York: Columbia University Press.

Meijl, Toon van. 1988. *Waahi Whaanui Community Training Centre: An Overview of Its Operation under ACCESS Training Schemes 11 January–30 April 1988*. Unpublished MS.

Merton, Robert K. 1972. "Insiders and Outsiders: A Chapter in the Sociology of Knowledge." *American Journal of Sociology* 78: 9–47.

Michener, James A. 1960. *Hawaii*. London: Secker and Warburg.

Mishler, Elliot G. 1986. *Research Interviewing: Context and Narrative*. Cambridge, Mass.: Harvard University Press.

Napoleon, Harold. 1991. *Yuuyaraq: The Way of the Human Being*. Fairbanks: Center for Cross-Cultural Studies, University of Alaska.

Nelson, Nici, and Susan Wright, eds. 1995. *Power and Participatory Development: Theory and Practice*. London: Intermediate Technology Publications.

Ogbu, John U. 1978. *Minority Education and Caste: The American System in Cross-Cultural Perspective*. New York: Academic Press.

Parades, J. A. 1976. "New Uses for Old Ethnography: A Brief Social History of a Research Project with the Eastern Creek Indians, or How to Be an Applied Anthropologist without Really Trying." *Human Organization* 35: 315–20.

Perry, Richard J. 1996. *From Time Immemorial: Indigenous Peoples and State Systems*. Austin: University of Texas Press.

Rahman, Muhammad Anisur. 1995. "Participatory Development: Toward Liberation or Co-optation?" In *Community Empowerment: A Reader in Participation and Development*, ed. Gary Craig and Marjorie Mayo, 24–32. London: Zed Books.

Rivera, Felix G., and John Erlich. 1998. *Community Organizing in a Diverse Society*. Boston: Allyn and Bacon.

Schensul, Jean J., and Stephen L. Schensul. 1992. "Collaborative Research: Methods of Inquiry for Social Change." In *The Handbook of Qualitative Research in Education*, ed. Margaret D. LeCompte, Wendy L. Millroy, and Judith Preissle, 161–200. San Diego: Academic Press.

Schensul, Stephen L., and Jean J. Schensul. 1978. "Advocacy and Applied Anthropology." In *Social Scientists as Advocates: Views from the Applied Disciplines*, ed. G. Weber and G. McCall, 121–65. Beverly Hills: Sage.

Schlesier, K. H. 1974. "Action Anthropology and the Southern Cheyenne." *Current Anthropology* 15: 277–83.

Schon, Donald A. 1983. *The Reflective Practitioner: How Professionals Think in Action.* New York: Basic Books.

Skinner, B. F. 1948. *Walden Two.* New York: Macmillan.

Smith, Linda Tuhiwai. 1999. *Decolonizing Methodologies: Research and Indigenous Peoples.* London: Zed Books.

Spilde, Katherine A. 1999. "Indian Gaming Study." *Anthropology Newsletter* 40, no. 4: 11.

Stull, Donald D., Jerry A. Schultz, and Ken Cadue Sr. 1987. "In the People's Service: The Kansas Kickapoo Technical Assistance Project." In *Collaborative Research and Social Change: Applied Anthropology in Action*, ed. Donald D. Stull and Jean Schensul, 33–54. Boulder: Westview Press.

Swisher, Karen. 1986. "Authentic Research: An Interview on the Way to the Ponderosa." *Anthropology and Education Quarterly* 17, no. 3: 185–88.

Tainui Maaori Trust Board. 1990. *The Tainui Health Plan.* Ngaruawahia, New Zealand: Tainui Maaori Trust Board.

———. 1991. *The Tainui Education Strategy, Second Report, 1992–1997.* Ngaruawahia, New Zealand: Tainui Maaori Trust Board.

Tax, Sol. 1958. "The Fox Project." *Human Organization* 17: 17–19.

Te Puni Kokiri. 1994. *Mana Tangata: Draft Declaration on the Rights of Indigenous Peoples 1993, Background and Discussion on Key Issues.* Wellington, New Zealand: Ministry of Maori Development.

Torres, Carlos Alberto. 1995. "Participatory Action Research and Popular Education in Latin America." In *Critical Theory and Educational Research*, ed. Peter L. McLaren and James M. Giarelli, 237–55. Albany: State University of New York Press.

Turner, Iti Rangihinemutu. 1995. *He Kuia no Tainui, Te Wharekura 47.* Wellington, New Zealand: Learning Media.

———. 1996. *Life History of Iti Rangihinemutu Turner.* Hamilton, New Zealand: Centre for Maaori Studies and Research, University of Waikato.

Walker, Ranginui. 1990. *Ka Whawhai Tonu Matou: Struggle without End.* Auckland, New Zealand: Penguin Books.

Wallace, A. F. C. 1970. *Culture and Personality.* 2nd ed. New York: Random House.

Watahomigie, Lucille J., and Akira Y. Yamamoto. 1987. "Linguistics in Action: The Hualapai Bilingual/Bicultural Education Program." In *Collaborative Research and Social Change: Applied Anthropology in Action*, ed. Donald D. Stull and Jean Schensul, 77–98. Boulder: Westview Press.

Wigginton, Eliot. 1985. *Sometimes a Shining Moment: The Foxfire Experience.* Garden City, N.Y.: Anchor Press/Doubleday.

Willard, W. 1977. "The Agency Camp Project." *Human Organization* 36: 352–62.

Wolcott, Harry F. 1977. *Teachers versus Technocrats: An Educational Innovation in Anthropological Perspective.* Eugene, Oreg.: Center for Educational Policy and Management.

———. 1991. "Propriospect and the Acquisition of Culture." *Anthropology and Education Quarterly* 22, no. 3: 251–73.

———. 1995. *The Art of Fieldwork.* Walnut Creek, Calif.: AltaMira Press.

———. 1999. *Ethnography: A Way of Seeing.* Walnut Creek, Calif.: AltaMira Press.

Young, Elspeth. 1995. *Third World in the First: Development and Indigenous Peoples.* London: Routledge.

Author Index

Adair, John, 38
Adams, John Clarke, 55
Antonnen, John, 42

Banks, James A., 37, 47–49, 52–53
Barnes, Helen Moewaka, 36
Barnhardt, Ray, 59, 120, 129
Bartunek, Jean M., 36
Berger, Thomas R., 9, 10, 11–14,
    26–27
Bird, John, 23
Bishop, Russell, 36, 51–52
Boas, Franz, 65
Bohannan, Laura, 32. *See also* Bowen,
    Elenore Smith
Borman, L. D., 36
Bourke, Colin, 10, 18–19, 20, 21
Bourke, Eleanor, 10, 18, 19–20, 21
Bowen, Elenore Smith, 32, 58.
    See also Bohannan, Laura
Briggs, Jean, 61, 62
Bunker, Robert, 38
Burger, Julian, 5–6, 7, 21–22, 27
Busier, Holly-Lynn, 152

Cadue, Ken Sr., 39–40, 45, 226
Chang, Heewon, 76–77
Chartrand, Paul, 23–24

Chinas, Beverly L., 62
Chiste, Katherine Beaty, 63
Chrisman, Noel J., 36, 40
Clark, Kenneth B., 47
Cleveland, Harlan, 55
Cox, Helen, 19–20
Craig, Gary, 36

Delgado-Gaitan, Concha, 41, 45, 91,
    225
Deloria, Vine Jr., 23, 27–28
Deyhle, Donna L., 65, 67–68
Doughty, Paul L., 37

Edwards, Bill, 10, 21
Efrat, B., 33, 38, 67, 225
Egan, K., 212
Elliott, Jean Leonard, 7, 23
Engelstad, Diane, 23
Erasmus, Georges, 15
Erlich, John, 39, 55–56, 102

Fleras, Augie, 7, 23
Florin, Paul, 213–14
Franklin, John Hope, 47
Freire, Paolo, 38, 123
French, Marilyn, 111–12

Giarelli, James M., 38
Gibson, Margaret A., 40–41, 45, 94, 225–26
Goodenough, Ward Hunt, 35, 54, 55, 62, 75, 76–77, 80, 88
Greaves, Tom, 32, 70–72
Groome, Howard, 10
Grubis, Steve, 59
Guyette, Susan, 34, 80–82, 83, 85, 86, 90, 91, 98, 101

Harrison, Barbara, 62, 86, 146, 162, 176, 177, 180, 203, 226
Havemann, Paul, 6, 7, 10, 23
Hazlehurst, Kayleen M., 7
Hemming, Steve, 18, 21
Herskovits, Melville, 75
Hess, G. Alfred Jr., 65, 67–68

Ilutsik, Esther, 42–43

Kaplan, Allan, 55
Kawagley, A. Oscar, 50
Kincheloe, Joe, 37
Kukutai, Mite, 220

LeCompte, Margaret D., 36, 41–42, 45, 54, 65, 66, 67–68, 226
Levy, Robert, 60
Lipka, Jerry, 42–43
Loomis, Terrence, 7
Louis, Meryl Reis, 36
Lytle, Clifford, 23, 27–28

MacLean, Bryan, 43–44
Mahuta, Robert, 169, 170, 171, 175, 187n1, 200, 212
Maipi, Taitimu, 172, 179, 184, 212, 214
Mangone, Gerard J., 55
Matthiasson, Carolyn J., 62
May, W. F., 68
Mayo, Marjorie, 36
McLaren, Peter L., 38

Mead, Linda Tuhiwai Te Rina, 49–50, 52, 78n1. *See also* Smith, Linda Tuhiwai
Mead, Margaret, 31, 66, 70
Medicine, Beatrice, 49, 63, 69
Meijl, Toon van, 193
Merton, Robert K., 48
Michener, James A., 58
Mishler, Elliot G., 41
Mitchell, M., 33, 38, 67, 225
Mohatt, Gerald, 42
Myrdal, G., 37

Napoleon, Harold, 9
Nelson, Nici, 36
Nelson-Barber, Sharon, 42

Ogbu, John U., 7, 169

Parades, J. A., 39
Perry, Richard J., 7

Rahman, Muhammad Anisur, 36, 101–2
Rivera, Felix G., 39, 55–56, 102

Sanders, Joe, 15
Schensul, Jean J., 34, 36
Schensul, Stephen L., 34, 36
Schlesier, K. H., 36, 38
Schön, Donald A., 2–3
Schultz, Jerry A., 39–40, 45, 226
Shear-Wood, Corrine, 213
Skinner, B. F., 59
Smith, Linda Tuhiwai, 6, 9, 24, 32, 50, 52, 62–63, 78. *See also* Mead, Linda Tuhiwai Te Rina
Spilde, Katherine A., 28–29
Stull, Donald D., 39–40, 45, 226
Swisher, Karen, 50

Tax, Sol, 37
Torres, Carlos Alberto, 36, 38
Turner, Iti Rangihinemutu, 220

Walker, Ranginui, 8, 10, 15–17
Wallace, A. F. C., 75
Watahomigie, Lucille J., 39, 45, 225
Wigginton, Eliot, 118
Willard, W., 39

Wolcott, Harry F., 34, 47, 56, 59, 75–77, 86, 123, 141, 197
Wright, Susan, 36

Yamamoto, Akira Y., 39, 45, 225
Young, Elspeth, 7

Subject Index

Aboriginal and Torres Strait Islander
Commission, 235–36
action research, 36, 37, 39, 40
Alaska: Alaska Federation of Natives,
43, 129; Alaska Rural Systemic
Initiative, 43, 129; fieldwork in,
107–31, 133–59, 161–68; history of
contact, 14, 107–8, 112; land claims,
13–14, 107, 108; long-term programs
in, 42–44
alcohol use, potential problems with, 62,
116, 117, 122, 136, 137
Annenberg Rural Challenger, 43, 129
anthropology/anthropological:
anthropology and education, 129,
141–42, 162, 167, 186; applied
anthropology 36, 37–40, 72; ethics
in, 65–66, 69–70, 97, 151;
perspectives, 31–32, 47, 54, 60, 61,
62, 66, 73, 75–77
applied research, 45, 225. *See also*
applied anthropology
assimilation, 11, 13, 17, 19, 27, 48

Center for Cross-Cultural Studies, 142,
146, 161, 162, 167
Centre for Maaori Studies and Research,
169, 175, 179, 184, 185, 187n2, 200,
211–21

Ciulistet Group, 42–43
Coal Corporation, New Zealand, 178,
186, 190
collaborative research, 3, 35–45, 51–52,
69, 121, 164–68
colonization, 5, 7–9, 21, 24, 57–58, 63,
77, 112, 117
comparative studies, 5, 6–11
context: cultural 6, 70, 147; political, 7,
24, 51, 58, 101–2, 211, 231–34, 236;
specific cases in Alaska, 131, 159,
168; specific cases in New Zealand,
184, 186, 187, 208–9, 215, 223, 227
Cornell University, 37–38
coronation. *See* King Movement
critical theory, 31–32, 41–42, 51–52, 68
cross-cultural education, 40–42
Cross-Cultural Education Development
Program (XCED): advocacy in, 114,
127; collaboration in, 121, 123–24,
125–26; model for pilot project, 133,
153, 155, 159; program structure,
109, 128, 129, 130, 131, 161
culture, defined and discussed, 72–78

economic development, 26, 28–29, 37,
39–40, 45, 54–55, 80–82. *See also*
socioeconomic position of
indigenous peoples

empowerment, 24, 38, 39, 41, 45, 56, 124, 225
ethics, 31, 54, 57, 65–72, 97, 104, 226; becoming a subject, 190–91, 199–200; in specific cases, 124–25, 151–52, 165, 183, 204, 227–28
ethnographer/ethnographic research, 36, 54, 66
evaluation, 39, 87, 96, 140, 156

fieldworker: becoming a, 53–54; characteristics of, 54–57; definition of, 34; guidelines, discussion of, 57–78; guidelines applied to field settings, 122–25, 148–53, 164–65, 180–84, 203–5; guidelines listed, 103–4; guidelines summarized, 226–28; personal position of, 45
funding: administration of, 40–41, 45, 100–101, 192, 194, 200–201, 206, 226, 230; agency requirements, 58, 67, 68, 90, 91, 96, 193, 194–98; from college/university, 141, 143, 146, 149, 152, 161, 233; from government/Canada, 14–15; from government/US, 39–40, 81, 101–2, 109, 113, 131, 159; from government/New Zealand, 176–77, 108–209, 213, 214, 215, 223; from governments in four countries, 232; guidelines, 85–87, 93–94, 104, 126–27, 154, 166, 185, 205, 229; underfunding, 92, 96, 202, 217–18, 220, 221–22

gender roles, 54, 62–64, 130, 216
governance structures, 27–28

health: of fieldworker, 60, 111, 146; of indigenous peoples, 22, 235; programs, 100, 171. *See also* Tainui Health Plan
history of contact: Alaska, 14, 107–8, 112; Australia, 18–21; European and indigenous peoples, 9–11; New Zealand, 15–18; United States and Canada, 11–15
Huntly, New Zealand, 170, 178, 183, 189, 195, 197, 208

indigenous research, 31, 32, 33, 45, 49–53, 226
indigenous rights. *See* rights of indigenous peoples
insider/outsider research, perspectives, 33, 36, 47–49, 53, 162, 226. *See also* indigenous research
intellectual property, 26, 32, 33, 51, 70–72, 97, 104, 129, 157, 167, 186

kaupapa Maori research. *See* indigenous research
King Movement, 16–17, 172, 174–75, 181, 183–84, 200

land: beliefs about, 8, 148; indigenous rights regarding, 26; land claims, 26–27; land claims, Alaska, 13–14, 107, 108; land claims, Australia, 20–21; land claims, Canada, 14, 24; land claims, New Zealand, 181, 182, 223
language: indigenous rights regarding, 25; Maori, 17, 18, 49, 176, 187, 190; Yup'ik, 134, 137, 142, 143, 148, 149, 153, 158, 162
library in the village, 141, 144, 147, 149, 152, 154

Maori Queen. *See* King Movement
Maori Student Academic Advisory Centre, 215–18
Ministry of Education, New Zealand, 175, 221–23

National Science Foundation, 43, 129
New Zealand: fieldwork in, 169–87, 189–209, 211–23; history of contact, 15–18; land claims, 181, 182, 223

oral history project, 218–21
outsider. *See* insider/outsider research, perspectives

participatory research, 36, 39, 40, 56, 65, 101–2
program: failure, 79; guidelines, discussion of, 82–102; guidelines applied to field settings, 125–31, 153–59, 165–68, 184–87, 205–9; guidelines listed, 104–5; guidelines summarized, 228–32; planning for balanced development, 80–82

reflective practice in fieldwork, 2–3, 55, 78, 103, 105, 122
reports of projects: by local communities, 34; collaboration in, 34–35, 41, 162, 163, 185, 221; preparation of, 120, 146–47, 179–80, 213, 214, 216–17, 223; review by participants, 67, 72, 129, 151, 157, 184
reservation/reserve, 13, 14, 22, 27, 28–29, 50, 68, 69, 90, 91
rights of indigenous peoples, draft declaration on the, 24–26, 239–50

schooling for indigenous peoples: adult basic education, 143, 144, 149, 151; boarding schools, 9, 13, 136; community colleges, 133–59; elementary and secondary schools, 18, 161–68, 169–87; missionary education, 11, 17, 19; small high schools, 107–31; vocational training, 189–209
self-determination, 5, 11, 12, 14–15, 21, 22, 23–28, 31, 51, 103, 232–34, 236–37
sex outside of marriage, potential problems with, 61–62, 145–46, 152
socioeconomic position of indigenous peoples, 8, 21–23, 38
State Coal, New Zealand. *See* Coal Corporation
state owned enterprise, 177–78, 190

Tainui (Maaori) Trust Board, 174, 178, 182, 189, 192, 211, 224n1; Tainui Education Strategy, 221–23, 226; Tainui Health Plan, 213–15, 223, 226, 229, 230, 232
Te Puni Kokiri, 71–72
training for: board members, 91; economic development, 28, 37–38, 54–55, 74–75; education/teaching, 42–43, 133–34, 158, 180; employment, 189–209; fieldworker(s), 1, 141–42, 221, 234, 236; health/human services, 43–44; program staff, 93, 95, 100, 194, 207–8, 230, 231; research, 34, 53, 130, 161–62, 163, 230. *See also* Cross-Cultural Education Development Program
treaties, 12, 13, 14, 15–16, 51, 211

University of Alaska Fairbanks (UAF): collaborative programs, 42–44, 107–31, 161–68; Rural Student Services, 215; rural teachers, 59. *See also* Cross-Cultural Education Development Program *and* Center for Cross-Cultural Studies
University of Waikato: collaborative programs, 211–24; indigenous staff exchanges, 49; Management Studies, 174; research reporting policies, 232–33. *See also* Centre for Maaori Studies and Research

Vicos Project. *See* Cornell University

Waahi Marae, 170–75, 178–79, 183–84, 185, 189, 191, 198, 213, 221, 225
Waikato region, 172, 174, 178, 180, 181, 189, 190, 212, 214

XCED. *See* Cross-Cultural Education Development Program

About the Author

Barbara Harrison completed a B.A. in sociology and anthropology at the University of Illinois at Chicago Circle. In 1975, she traveled to Alaska for a summer job in Barrow, the northernmost community in the United States. Her real life introduction to indigenous cultures occurred there, in the center of the Inupiaq-speaking population of Alaska's North Slope. She completed a field-based master's degree program in cross-cultural education at the University of Alaska Fairbanks and a Ph.D. in anthropology and education at the University of Oregon. After teaching at the University of Alaska Fairbanks, she relocated to New Zealand, working first as the coordinator of a Maori community-based vocational training center and then, for eleven years, as senior research fellow at the Centre for Maaori Studies and Research at the University of Waikato in Hamilton, New Zealand.